"MY DEAR VICTORIOUS STOD"

Other books by David Frith:

Runs in the Family (with John Edrich)
The Archie Jackson Story
The Oxford Companion to Sports and Games (contributor)
Cricket: More Than a Game (contributor)
The Fast Men
Cricket Gallery (editor)
England versus Australia : A Pictorial History
of the Test Matches Since 1877
The '77 Australians (with Greg Chappell)
(in preparation)

"'My Dear Victorious Stod'"

a biography of A. E. STODDART

DAVID FRITH

LUTTERWORTH PRESS
Richard Smart Publishing

Published 1977

This edition published by
Lutterworth Press, Luke House,
Farnham Road, Guildford, Surrey
and Richard Smart Publishing

ISBN   0 7188 7017 4

Printed by John G. Eccles
Printers Ltd, Inverness

First published 1970 by the
author in a 400-copy limited edition

To Debbie,
who endured this visitor
from the past with such
understanding

CONTENTS

ILLUSTRATIONS

PREFACE

Why a biography of A.E. Stoddart? The question was often asked during the research which culminated seven years ago in a privately-published book in a strictly-limited edition of 400 copies. The short answer then was: "Because here was a wonderful cricketer who has been piteously neglected by historians."

Though it may be that my imagination is running wild, it seems to me that "Stoddy", that most romantic of sporting figures of the 1890s, has latterly been given some of that overdue recognition. The tale which follows through these pages will, perhaps, justify the suggestion that he ought always to be remembered in company with Grace, MacLaren, Jackson, Jessop *et hoc genus omne.*

The investigation was absorbing to the point of obsession. Days and nights spent delving through old and out-of-the-way records, and interviews with the precious few who could remember, often produced fresh gems for documentation, though at times points remained stubbornly unclear. There are still small gaps in this life story tantalisingly unlikely, I believe — after an initial three-year search and subsequent enquiry — ever to be coloured in.

When the bulky first draft was ready, and my questions had had their replies from Brentwood, Melbourne, South Shields, Hampstead, Coventry, Sydney, and places between, by the ghost of "Stoddy"! — one last crucial response drifted in, leading to the discovery of the man's own scrapbooks. Further data was gratefully blended into the narrative.

Here and there in his albums of cuttings, unaccountably, he had written "For the book". No memoirs ever did materialise, though he had time to spare in his embittered middle-age to chronicle the contests, the men (and women), and his travels during the 1880s and 1890s.

Since the first, limited edition, further snippets have come to light, and these have been added as footnotes throughout the volume. There is a slight variation too in the selection of illustrations, and I am glad of the addition of John Arlott's foreword, warm as the man himself.

"I must do something handsome for my dear victorious Stod," *Melbourne Punch* imagined Queen Victoria to have said. No knighthood. No CBE. But, three-quarters of a century later: this tributary reconstruction of a great sporting life.

DAVID FRITH

Guildford, 1977

FOREWORD

The shelf of cricket biography and autobiography is long. During the recent age of the live "ghost", probably over-long. The only substantial gap in it was the one David Frith has filled with the study of Andrew Stoddart. Lives of all the other great players of what might be called the modern age had already been published; and now the wonder must be that this one was for so long ignored.

Perhaps for lack of such a study, Stoddart, of heroic stature, widely acclaimed and well liked in his own time, had become a shadowy figure to cricket enthusiasts of today. Mr Frith has not only recalled the statistics, facts and events of his career, but has put flesh on their skeleton in a fashion possible only to a faithful researcher who also feels his subject.

Stoddart emerges not only as an outstanding sporting performer — rugby player, cricketer and captain who achieved marked success — but as a period character. Here is the typical amateur games-player of the latter part of the nineteenth century, wealthy, accomplished, relishing top-level sport as an aspect of leisure. Once, too, he afforded a glimpse of the attitude of mind, not uncommon in the earlier days of representative cricket, which could regard the advent of a touring team and even of Test matches as an interruption of the Championship programme. Both he and F.S. Jackson on occasion withdrew from a Test to play in a crucial county fixture.

There is more than a hint, too, that Stoddart might have provided the material for a novel. The Victorian public was not inquisitive about the private lives of its idols; or, if it was, it went unsatisfied. This story, though, of a life of privilege, splendid sporting achievements, the strange late marriage, and the tragic end, give this biography greater profundity than the average "sporting life".

The first, limited edition of "*My Dear Victorious Stod*" established David Frith as a knowledgeable and perceptive cricket historian who diligently followed every avenue of enquiry, but never allowed enthusiasm to cloud his judgment. The continuing demand for that long-sold-out edition has promoted this re-issue with the addition of fresh information and lately-discovered illustration.

JOHN ARLOTT

Alresford, 1977

There went a tale to England,
  'Twas of the Test Match won,
And nobly had her cricketers
  That day their duty done.
They didn't fail like funkers,
  They kept up England's tail,
They kept their pro's from off the booze
  And knew they could not fail.

Then wrote the Queen of England,
  Whose hand is blessed by God,
"I must do something handsome
  For my dear victorious Stod.
Let him return without delay
  And we will dub him pat—
A baronet that he may be
  Sir Andrew Stoddart, bat''.

(Melbourne Punch)

CHAPTER 1

A CHILD OF TYNESIDE

A. E. Stoddart's name has been wreathed in mystery over the past half century. So little is known of him; yet so much did he accomplish, and so much is there to tell.

He was a sportsman of eminent style on cricket and rugby fields, and his fame ought to have been assured in perpetuity. He stood in rare esteem in Australia after four cricket tours and a rugby tour. But of his sixteen Test matches only five were at home in England, where more pens scratch, and where fickle pundits construct idols according to the public mood. Test centuries made abroad usually and, perhaps, unfairly receive less acclaim.

For much of his career Stoddart performed in the sizeable shadow of W. G. Grace. And, as Captain Philip Trevor pointed out in 1901 to his readers of the future, aggregates and averages interested Stoddart appreciably less than they did the recorders: "One's difficulty is that Mr Stoddart became great in what may be called the transition stage of batsmanship. He led a host of followers as far as the very banks of Jordan, and then declined himself to enter the promised land.

"Mr Stoddart was wont to strike the bowler hard when the latter was fierce. What would he do with him, one may well ask, now that he has become tame?

"Years hence, when cricket literature, historical or otherwise, takes the form of mere statistical reports, the name of Andrew Ernest Stoddart may not perchance appear in big print, but such of us who insist on inquiring not only what a man did, but also how he did it, will refuse to regard the size of the type used as our means of measurement. Mr Stoddart was not in the habit of getting two thousand runs per cricket season, but he was very much in the habit of taking the bowler by the scruff of the neck when he had become troublesome; and it is as a winner of matches chiefly that his fame will live."

But his fame evaporated swiftly after his dramatic withdrawal from the first-class game at the end of 1898. The most renowned of cricket's Golden Ages was unfolding itself, with such magic figures as Jessop, Foster, MacLaren, Jackson, Tyldesley, Fry, Ranjitsinhji, Hirst and Rhodes becoming legendary names. The advent of the new century and the death of Queen Victoria shut tight a period of history, and cricket's evolution carried relentlessly on.

Stoddart became secretary of Queen's Club, West London, in 1906 and faced the hardest phase in any athlete's life—the decline into inactivity. He and his new bride maintained social contact with the cricket world, entertaining at their home in St John's Wood, in sight of the ground he had graced most of his cricket life.

A good deal heavier, greying, but still radiating an unmistakable presence, he whiled away his time at the club, enjoying whisky and conversation with the members, his life-long modesty cramping any temptation to plunge into reminiscence. His Stock Exchange activities hardly provided a relief from the boredom.

The years shuffled by, and some months after the world had lowered itself into the mire of the Kaiser's War, his finances in jeopardy, suffering the wicked depression of incipient pneumonia and generally unable to face up to his existence any further, this lonely man who once had the sporting world at his feet set about ending it all. He was just 52.

Long before the gunshot, A. E. Stoddart, genuine double International, had been shut away incomprehensibly in the dimly-lit gallery of England's half-forgotten heroes.

On March 10th, 1863, the United Kingdom was lit up in celebration of the marriage of the Prince of Wales (later King Edward VII) to Princess Alexandra. Jenny Lind's sweet voice added lustre to the ceremony at Windsor, and W. P. Frith, then in his heyday as an artist, sketched frantically into his drawing pad for the benefit of future generations.

North across many miles of bonfires and illuminations Mrs. Elizabeth Stoddart awaited the gentle son she was to bear the following day.

The family lived at 10 Wellington Terrace, which now forms part of Beach Road, Westoe, South Shields. It is, though terraced, a very large house, in a higher, select part of the town, and the street runs down to a stretch of sands which holds back the North Sea (known in Stoddart's youth as "the German Ocean").

His birthplace is now occupied by the Bader Boys' Club.

At number 6 lived Ernest Thompson Seton, the author, artist, naturalist and pioneer of scouting in Canada, who was two years old when Stoddart was born. It is probable they played together as youngsters.

Stoddart's father, George Best Stoddart, was a King Street wine, spirit and porter merchant, bonded store dealer, land agent, and one-time owner of Bedlington Colliery. He was one of the founders in 1850 of The Borough of South Shields Cricket Club, and the son of Andrew Stoddart, who was forty years agent to the Dean and Chapter of Durham early in the 19th Century. This Andrew Stoddart was to die 46 years to the actual day before his sporting grandson.

Stoddart Street, in Tyne Dock, should keep the family name forever part of the town.

When little Drewy (as the family referred to him) was nine, and, perhaps coincidentally, the coalmining industry was in the throes of major reform, the

Stoddarts and their five children moved from County Durham to London. They took up residence in Ormonde Terrace, by Primrose Hill, with its enchanting setting—facing Regents Park Zoo. It was, for any boy with time on his hands, irresistibly close to Lord's Cricket Ground, where great matches were far fewer than today. Drewy had already played cricket at Wood Terrace, South Shields, and was to retain membership of that club all his career.

He was enrolled at St. John's Wood School, popularly known as "Olivers'", in Acacia Road. It was an establishment modest in size, serving as a prep school or, if the boys were not to have a public school education, where they could continue till 18 or 19. Stoddart was one of these.

There is record of his playing cricket for the school in 1876, when he was 13. The solemn little chap went in low in the order and was bowled for 2 by his future Hampstead club colleague "Skipper" Pawling.

At the age of 16 he fell in love with a girl who knew a boy at the junior school adjoining Olivers'. Drewy would pass love letters through a gap in the fence to the boy, Francis Cooke, who duly had them delivered to Stoddart's fancy. One imagines that the starry-eyed youth from South Shields hit the ball even harder after receiving her replies via little Francis behind the tool-shed at the end of the garden playground.

Carrying his 95 years lightly, Mr Cooke recounted his duties with wistful joy not far short of a century later; and another nonagenarian, Mr Cecil Turner, recalled the immense pride in *his* household when a brother bowled the adolescent Stoddart in a playground game. I sensed it was something of an agony for both these fine old gentlemen not to be able to open memory doors which, in their tenth decade, seemed closed forever.

Stoddart's cricket was developing significantly in parallel with his rugby prowess. At 14 he had joined the Harlequin R.F.C. A photograph of the 1880-1 team shows him, chest out, upper lip hairless, standing behind darker, heavier brother Harry, who bore the same Stoddart handsomeness.

They were both making lots of runs for the Blenheim Cricket Club about this time, and Drewy's first recorded century was in 1880, for Blenheim against Eton Park. In school and neighbourhood circles he had become the object of idolatry on a local scale that was soon to swell to national hero-worship.

His father died in the Spring of 1882 after long suffering from the dreaded consumption, and about this time he lost an uncle, John Broughton, formerly mayor of South Shields. It was the momentous year in cricket history when the Australian "colonials", with Spofforth the bushranger-in-chief, rocked England with their 7-run win at the Oval which led to the body of English cricket being tearfully cremated.

The young man living in St John's Wood was now approaching 6 feet in height, with strong limbs and torso indefinably but unmistakably marking an athlete. In the years ahead many pounds of his energy were to be expended in battles for these newly-burnt Ashes.

FOOTNOTES: *1. F.R.D'O. Monro stated in a letter to* The Cricketer *in 1950 that the Stoddart family moved in 1873 to a village near Coventry (Radford?) and on to London two years later.*
2. Francis Cooke died on November 3, 1974, aged 102.

After leaving Olivers', where the Rev. Mr Oliver and Mr Bird had given him his grooming, Stoddart became articled to a firm of architects in London and entered the Royal Academy School, though judging from the absence of records, it seems he failed to survive the probation term.

Blenheim C.C. used the Eton & Middlesex ground, and here, week after week, Stoddart played with brother Harry and others who were to become close friends over the years: Jack Trotman and George Jeffery, fine footballers both, and the Whinneys, related to the Stoddarts by marriage.

In 1882 a man named Cooke took seven Blenheim wickets for o, leaving Stoddart and his companions gasping at 13 for seven wickets; but 1883 was a good year. He took a stack of wickets for Blenheim and recorded two centuries —one against his old school (raising his image to further dizzy heights) and 123 against Willesden, when Harry hit 90 and the Stoddart boys between them reduced the field to chaos.

Net practice was keen and amusing, and often young Cooke would hurry along in time to bowl to his idol, who sometimes set a piece of paper on a length and challenged him to pitch the ball on it. The sessions were usually concluded with a full-blooded drive across the ground, and by the time Francis Cooke had retrieved the ball the net would be empty and he would have no alternative but to return home and face up to his homework.

That autumn Stoddart, controversially and to the chagrin of 'Quins, joined Blackheath Rugby Football Club, commencing an association that was to last throughout his career at the top in rugby. Billy Williams, full-back, Middlesex wicketkeeper, and later responsible for siting Twickenham rugby ground, brought him down to Blackheath and that winter he swept and swerved his way to nine tries (three in his first match), second to the immortal W. N. Bolton, who recorded 28.

In 1884 his path crossed once more with that of Francis Cooke, who was on holiday at Bournemouth, fishing from the pier, pulling in smelts as fast as he could drop his line back in the water.

"Hullo, young Cooke."

It was a soft voice, faintly North-east. Cooke turned to see Drewy Stoddart, who joined string to his fashionable cane and assisted in the catch. At the end of an absorbing hour they walked off the pier, Cooke with almost sufficient provision for the rest of his holiday and Stoddart with unexpected bounty for his landlady.

He scored two centuries for Bournemouth that August, but the following year was to be the important year, for in 1885 he joined Hampstead Cricket Club, for whom his performances entitle him to rank as the greatest club cricketer of them all.

CHAPTER 2

A WORLD RECORD

"Football is my game," he once said. And it seemed his game in the winter of 1884-5. He touched down sixteen times for Blackheath to be top try-scorer for the season, gained representative honours for South v North, and seemed to play better the higher the company he kept.

Five other Blackheathens lined up with him for the South on his home ground, the Rectory Field, five days before Christmas. No pains had been spared in gathering the finest players in England, and Stoddart acquitted himself well in the boisterous conditions.

With the Australian, Wade, he continually menaced the North line, and his kicking was especially penetrative. The South managed to cling to a one try to nil advantage, and even if as the crowd broke up there was a feeling that the South had had all the luck, for A. E. Stoddart it had been a competent introduction into big football.

Then on January 3rd came the greatest honour of them all: he was awarded his first England cap for the Wales game at Swansea—an extremely fast match won by England after misgivings by one goal, four tries to one goal, one try. The 5000 spectators witnessed an interesting contest, with the Welsh forwards putting up stout opposition.

A month later Stoddart again took up his wing threequarter position for his country against Ireland at the Whalley Range ground at Manchester, and his brilliancy coupled with that of club-mate Bolton and J. J. Hawcridge along the back-line, and Alan Rotherham at half-back, more than evened the balance in a match in which the English forwards were "palpably worsted by the Irishmen in the scrimmage" (despite the fact that most of the visitors were still suffering from seasickness).

His black and red jersey, copious knickerbockers and International jumper lovingly placed away in a drawer and a fresh set of white cricket gear out of mothballs, he commenced his career with Hampstead. Harry by now had left England for good after a disastrous romance; thus, with the elder Stoddart setting himself up as a rancher in the Wild West of Colorado, the mighty fraternal batting partnership was dissolved for ever. Drewy was never again to be overshadowed by big Harry.

He made his mark with Hampstead immediately by opening and top-scoring with 16 out of 58 and taking seven wickets against Blackheath Morden. Three days later at Kensington Park's pleasant ground at Wormwood Scrubs he topped the innings again with 65, and repeated his dominance at the end of June with 26 against Crystal Palace. Yet far more substantial things lay

FOOTNOTE: *Alan Rotherham committed suicide on August 30, 1898.*

ahead.

Against Granville he carried his bat for 185; a fortnight later there was another century off Hendon, then 100 for Hampstead against an M.C.C. side. Next week it was seven Richmond wickets, and in the return with Blackheath Morden he battered 108 runs and took six wickets. On the following Saturday he powered his way to 126, and *Cricket,* the twopenny weekly journal of the times, had to step in:

"Mr Stoddart, whom I take to be the well-known Rugby International footballer, has completed as many as four centuries for the Hampstead Club. As, in addition, Mr Stoddart is a particularly good bowler as well as a brilliant field, I should fancy the executive of the Middlesex County Cricket Club, for which I believe he is qualified, would do well to seriously entertain the advisability of giving him a good trial."

How proud he must have been to show this to his mother.

The attention of Bob Thoms, the kindly umpire and talent scout, had already been drawn towards the high-scoring youngster by Smith-Turberville of Hampstead, and Thoms' recommendation carried weight in gaining the County Club's interest. In later years he often greeted Smith-Turberville with a hopeful "Got any more Stoddarts knocking about Hampstead way?"

The invitation to play for the County XI duly arrived. He was staying with a brother-in-law at Coventry when a wire was forwarded from home asking him to play against Yorkshire.

"Here's a how-d'ye-do!" he exclaimed, for it had never occurred to him that he was good enough to join the swells he had seen emerge from the pavilion at Lord's. And there was the added difficulty that his cricket gear was in London, and the match was to start in Bradford the next day.

His brother-in-law lent some flannels, which were rather too large; and the coachman lent an old green carpet-bag, prehistoric pads and mediaeval bat; some tennis shoes completed his equipment and off went "Stoddy" to Bradford, longing all the while for his own carefully-selected bat and neat clothes.

As the bags came out of the van the green carpet article appeared among the smart leather ones, and a dandy Middlesex cricketer, spotting it, remarked to the porter: "All except that one!" But Stoddart, unashamed, boldly claimed it.

On August 17th, 1885, opening with E. H. Buckland, he was yorked by "Shoey" Harrison for 3 (perhaps the bat and the clothes did it) and in due course took none for 7 and caught Bobby Peel, whose 71 kept Yorkshire at the throat of Middlesex.

Stoddart made 21 at the second attempt, caught driving Peate but looking a batsman who could be of great value to this county still smarting from the indignity of a 25 all out against Surrey. Certainly A. J. Webbe was satisfied with his new recruit as Middlesex gained a cheering victory.

Immediately afterwards Middlesex opposed one of the greatest selections of cricketing strength ever marshalled into one field: Nottinghamshire, then enjoying the fourth of its five consecutive County Championships.

There was the supreme Arthur Shrewsbury; brooding, plodding Scotton; the massive exhibitionist Sherwin behind the stumps; Billy Barnes, the all-rounder with the Mephistopheles smile; Wilfrid Flowers, also obviously well-fed on Nottingham nourishment; "Dick" Attewell, penetrative or tight, as conditions demanded; and the towering eagle-nosed William Gunn, finest cutter and driver when caution made way; all of them current or coming Test players.

Stoddart opened with Buckland and had 102 up for Middlesex in just over an hour and a half against this menacing attack. Stoddart went on to 79, "the feature of the match", hitting grandly all round the Trent Bridge Ground, sounding a fanfare to the cricket universe with each boundary hit.

In the twilight of his career he averred that what with the old cricket bag and the crummy pads, had he not made this fair score he would never have been heard of again outside Hampstead, which, as C. B. Fry once wrote, you may or may not believe.

During the interval Stoddart went for a stroll round the ground with Webbe, and they were gently accosted by a London boy who had taken time out of his Derbyshire holiday to visit the county match. His name: Francis Cooke. Stoddart, the young county batsman, seemed pleased to find him there.

Cooke walked with the two cricketers and when, without any trace of "side", they invited him into the rarified atmosphere of the pavilion, his cup of joy was full.

Notts went on to squeeze a first-innings lead and dispatch their visitors for a mere 144 second innings (Stoddart 15) ; but time finally ran out.

The next stop was Clifton; the opposition was Gloucestershire. For the tyro Andrew Ernest Stoddart it was an occasion of some moment—a confrontation with the illustrious Doctor William Gilbert Grace, who was due for a score.

And the Doctor, after having attended a patient all the previous night, gave a generous sample of the sort of cricket which had elevated him to such unprecedented levels of cricket glory. He won the toss and opened the innings, and just over a day later, when the innings wound up for 348, he was 221 not out, his highest for eight years.

By close of play Tuesday the Doctor and Woof had dispensed with Middlesex once and half again—bowling unchanged through the first innings of 110 (W.G. 6-45) and finally bringing others in on the act as Middlesex slipped to a peaceful innings defeat. W.G. snared five more wickets in the last innings, and young "Stoddy", having made 2 in the first, was bowled by him for a duck in the second.

It had been quite an experience.

There was one more county match this year, against Kent at Maidstone, and Stoddart made 21 out of 187 on a moist wicket. Again Stoddart the bowler was ignored, and when Middlesex batted again his final important innings of the season amounted to a paltry eight, though all around him was ruin.

It seems doubtful that Stoddart was finding complete bliss as a county cricketer. Cliques existed among the amateurs, many of whom had distinguished family and educational backgrounds, leaving the Durham boy at this stage a "loner". A. J. Webbe was kind to him, saw his potential, helped and advised him. But confusion clouded his mind as he contemplated the future.

For the first time his name appeared in Wisden's Cricketers' Almanack, listing him as an all-rounder "likely to be of great service to the county".

In the rugby world he was worshipped and unanimously regarded as the finest wing-threequarter there had ever been. What a spectacle it must have been as the ball was tossed out to him and he set sail for the line, sweeping past the opposition until only the full-back blocked his way: here he often waited till the last second, leapt high over the lunging defender and sprinted in to score.

The high-jump tactics more than once landed him in trouble, and one head injury when a desperate opponent grabbed his boot meant a long spell in hospital. Twice in his career he suffered concussion of the brain.

He could drop-kick beautifully with either foot, and it was a memorable kick into a howling gale for Middlesex against Yorkshire that gave his county victory by one all-important goal to 4 then-insignificant tries; and the scoring system, as a result, was reviewed and altered.

The pattern of the rugby game then was quite different to that of today. Scrimmages went on almost endlessly with forwards kicking and thrashing out the issue whilst the threequarters waited patiently. When their turn came they had the opportunity of disporting themselves in sparkling syle, as when Stoddart once at Manchester zig-zagged through the opposing backs from within his own half on a very wet ground to score the *three* tries of the match.

One of his most interesting and unusual exploits was passed on by A. A. Thomson: "Once, playing for Harlequins against West Kent on Chislehurst Common, Stoddart dashed towards the enemy line in his usual steam-engine fashion, only to find that the area behind goal was deep—not inches but feet—in water. Without an instant's hesitation he dived in, head first, like a tufted duck, and was an unconscionable time in coming up again. The referee had almost decided to have the pond dragged, when Stoddart reappeared, smiling, having scored what was probably the first submarine try in rugger history".

He was again Blackheath's top try-scorer in 1885-6, with eleven touch-downs, and played in all three Internationals. At the Rectory Field, Wales showed improved form, and perceptive judges at the time were reading sagely into their display; they went down by a try to 2 tries and a goal despite superiority in the scrimmages and determined tackling.

Stoddart, playing with his friend George Jeffery under the famous C. J. B.
Marriott, Blackheath's captain, landed a place-kick after the English forward,
Elliot, had astonished everyone by calling for a mark after catching a Welsh
miskick and disregarding what amounted to a clear run in for a try. Elliot's
mark, it was said, might have won applause in Durham (his county of origin)
"but it met with emphatic and forcible expressions of disapproval from the
English captain and the 'finished' players of the South." Stoddart's kick ensured
that "the laugh at the finish was on Elliot's side".

At Lansdowne Road, Dublin, before a very large crowd, Marriott kicked off
and the Stoddart-Rotherham magic was soon evident, the ball swinging its way
along the back-line and Stoddart bringing off several bewitching runs. He took
the penalties, though not to any real advantage, and the match developed into
a grim tussle, with the lighter Irishmen slowly giving ground.

Wilkinson went over for England, but Stoddart's place-kick failed. Nevertheless the Englishmen took the result and felt justifiably pleased with
themselves as they splashed in the bath afterwards.

Foul weather postponed the Scotland match at Raeburn Place, Edinburgh,
from March 6th to 13th, and a tough, determined game ended without score.
Stoddart was described as being "indisposed". For one reason or another it was
to be his last Home International for four years.

He enjoyed most sports, and, according to Herbert Chipp, he could have
attained a very high standard at lawn tennis. "It was truly refreshing to hear a
cricketer of Stoddart's rank and achievements speak with admiration of a game
for which in those days most followers of cricket had no epithet contemptuous
enough."

He had embarked upon tennis with tremendous zeal, receiving his first
lessons from André, who had him mystified in the beginning: "I don't understand *this* game," Stoddart exclaimed to a friend, "the fellow kept on saying
'Keep the head up, sir, keep the head up', till I was looking at the skylight and
couldn't see the blessed ball at all. All I've got out of my first lesson is a crick in
the back of the neck".

André of course, had meant that the head of the racquet, not the player,
should be kept up, as recommended by the great Peter Latham.

Tennis elbow ultimately contributed to his withdrawal from active sport
around 1907. He had refused to rest the injured arm and it had become really
bad, forcing him to give up golf just as he had developed a strong taste for it.
The jar of cricket ball on bat also became unbearable, and so a man who had
lived for sport and prided himself in his physical condition actually grew ill
from lack of that same exercise.

At least, in his prime, whilst the chance was there, he had ridden horse and excelled at real tennis and hockey (playing skilfully as wing forward for Hampstead). He was observed to be a first-class billiards player, and without being a Charlie Mitchell, he was a force to be reckoned with in the boxing ring —truly a sporting man of leisure born into an appropriate era.

The year 1886 saw his establishment as a Middlesex opening batsman, under the captaincy of G. F. Vernon, with J. G. Walker occupying the other opening berth till later in the summer. Then Alexander Josiah Webbe, Harrovian, Oxonian, gentleman, reliable, experienced, 31 years of age, came back after the death of his brother to form with Stoddart one of the great opening duets.

It was a year of destiny for Drewy Stoddart. In July *Cricket* featured him as its front-page celebrity, and then later in the month announced that he intended to settle in Colorado in the autumn. Perhaps Harry's letters had excited him.

"I should fancy," opined the editor, " so keen an athlete will find it very difficult to tear himself away from cricket and football, in both of which he has made his mark, and I should not be surprised after all to hear that at least he has deferred the parting, which is said to be such sweet sorrow.

"Personally I hope to see him yet in the attainment of the highest honours of amateur cricket."

The writer's hopes were fulfilled beyond expectation in the exciting years to come, but at the time of writing "Stoddy" was experiencing grievous disappointment with Middlesex, averaging 19 in sixteen innings and finding the Lohmanns, Peates and Emmetts on rain-affected wickets a degree more difficult than the average club bowler.

George Lohmann, the blond and charming ladies' man, was to prove a regular problem. Stoddart liked to hit the medium and fast bowlers hard and it spelt his doom frequently against England's greatest—Richardson, Lockwood and later Hirst, with his left-arm swingers. But if these were to become his bêtes noires there were four who were more noire than the others: Attewell, Arthur Mold, Bobby Peel and the Australian, C. T. B. Turner.

Attewell, the admirable and kindly professional, took his wicket more often than anyone else did, and in so sensitive a man one wonders to what extent he worried himself out as the Attewell dismissals piled up. The bowler, for his part, played down his own powers, and paid tribute many years later by saying that on a good wicket you could not bowl a ball to Stoddart which he could not hit for four if he really desired.

Mold, of the dubious delivery, was deadly and destructive on wickets giving the slightest assistance—and there were enough of these around in the 'eighties and early 'nineties. Wilfred Rhodes in his 91st year patted his thigh tenderly and vividly recalled the knife that seemed to turn in his flesh after Mold had crashed through.

Charlie Turner, the terror with protruding ears, captured Stoddart's increasingly desirable wicket 19 times in all, nine times in Tests. But then "the Terror", only five feet eight and with the head of a Claudius, caused more than just one England batsman troubled sleep.

Andrew Stoddart warmed up for this phenomenal club season of 1886 with several fine innings, including 127 against the long-suffering Granville side from whom he was to carve another "ton" in July.

The county campaign commenced with a 2-day innings defeat by Surrey —Stoddart 3 and 4—and on the Monday he made his way to Lord's for his first game on the historic strip.

He may have stroked his moustache pensively that evening after twice having been dismissed cheaply in one day's play. Rain had dampened the wicket, helping 22 batsmen back to the pavilion before sunset.

He spent practically the entire month of June at Lord's, witnessing at close quarters a five-hour 91 by the notorious plumb-bob from Yorkshire, Louis Hall, and a stirring innings by Ulyett. He had reason to be satisfied with a 29 against Yorkshire, and, given a bowl at last, pocketed his first victim, the Hon. M. B. Hawke, soon to be Lord Hawke.

He made 42 against Gloucestershire before W. G. got a round-armer through him, and a six-wicket victory was gratefully chalked up. Then, without any disgrace, Middlesex gave ground to Notts, now winning their fifth title in a row, and always to be acknowledged one of the strongest combinations ever to dominate a cricket field.

Stoddart next made 36 against Surrey on a firm wicket, when all four innings were in the mid-200 s—surely the finest balance for any spectator's consumption.

Now, on June 24th, he came face to face with Australian bowling for the first time. Scott's men had a disastrous time in 1886, losing the three Test matches and many of the other games, Here, at Lord's, they almost threw away victory over Middlesex. Stoddart made only 3 and 16, and the Australians needed a mere 123 to win. When 100 was posted with only three out it seemed all over, but Burton kept taking wickets, and soon, amazingly, Pope and wicketkeeper Blackham found themselves in the last ditch with 8 still required.

For the great 'keeper it was a strange pre-enactment of a similar situation in years to come, when a Test match at Sydney rested just as delicately on the determined shoulders of his bat. Now, at Lord's, he saw his team home, and the spectators congratulated themselves for being present at a cricket match worth the title.

At Chiswick Park a week later the Australians' 345 was enough for an innings win, Stoddart making 8 low in the order—before Garrett of the sinister beard trapped him—then seeing out the second innings on that hot afternoon with 27 not out.

That was all for a month—no more first class cricket, but, after concentrating as well as ·he could upon stocks and shares, there were two centuries for Hampstead, and a sensational seven wickets for 3 against Crystal Palace.

In the Hampstead pavilion on August 2nd, 1886, A. Russell Parker was presented with a gold watch to commemorate twenty years with the club. He expressed his thanks and his pride in "the best club, the best ground, and one of the best men in Middlesex", referring unmistakably to Stoddart.

A match against Stoics was programmed for that Wednesday upon the Hampstead ground so worthily praised by Russell Parker in his speech; and on Tuesday night Stoddart and some of his friends went dancing and afterwards got to playing poker "just for half an hour". It was after midnight when they commenced, and when the well-dressed young stockbroker (now sometimes called "The Masher" for his elegance) found himself winning an appreciable amount of money he played irresistibly on, mesmerised perhaps by the pattern of play, reluctant to leave the table with his friends' losses. He gave them generous time to recover: one round of jackpots followed another and his play grew wilder each hand, but he kept winning. As dawn broke they decided stumps ought to be drawn!

There was hardly any point in going to bed this fine summer morning, so it was warm baths all round then a cab to the swimming baths to freshen up. Stoddart usually did rise early (except on the day of a big match, when he often saved himself by rising almost when it was time to take the field) but this was bordering on absurdity. He always was slow and meticulous about his toilet, and he always ate a late breakfast; and this great day, after a hearty meal, it was a case of ambling straight down to the ground, where the wicket was pitched in the centre of the expanse.

"Stoddy" padded up and took Marshall with him to the wicket at 11.30. Marshall was soon bowled, and "Daddy" Besch walked out to join the erstwhile gambler. After an hour's murderous assault Hampstead were 150 for one wicket, and after Besch had gone two short of a century and Smith-Turberville had been bowled for five, Swift came in and helped thump the total to an incredible 370 at lunch after two and a half hours play.

Lunch took an hour, then Stoddart and Swift resumed their tempestuous fun and finally achieved 383 runs together. Russell Parker came in and, possibly mindful of the security of his gold watch, was caught for only four. Doyle and then Dollar supported Stoddart in his furious rampage. His "Magic" brand bat sent the ball singing to the edges of the ground with power-drives born of muscular forearms and a middleweight's shoulders. The afternoon sun blazed down as he hurtled through the 300's and, at about 5 o'clock, reached 400. Everyone was wide-eyed.

The highest score ever recorded, 419 not out made a year previously by J. S. Carrick at Chichester, was just a few strokes away. Heroically the Stoics bowlers kept to the task, but the Hampstead champion took the world record, and immediately gave the sole semblance of a chance: at 421 he drove screamingly to mid-on, who failed to hold it, and two runs were taken.

Past 450, and the umpire, probably amused as well as fatigued, urged him to make sure of his half-thousand.

At 485, when the stoical trundlers and fielders must have been looking desperately to their only salvation, the clock, Stoddart miscued a hit to leg off Rennie and sent the ball swirling high into the wind. It was said they ran almost three, "Stoddy" quoting 100-1 on the ball, before it plummeted into the hands of Kelly, the tall and inexhaustible fast bowler grazing at deep point.

Hampstead's final tally of 813 (not a wide bowled throughout) was the highest total ever in a one-day match, and one report stated academically that Stoics did not bat; there was no declaration law then, and though many may have wondered down the years why the Hampstead men did not throw their wickets away around, say, 400, the innings did at least make a fruity talking point, and, more pertinently, it gave a memorable fillip to the career and reputation of A. E. Stoddart.

It was once suggested that this must have left him feeling very anxious to get some sleep, to which he replied, "Well, perhaps I was, but we had a lawn tennis match, a four, on that evening, so I had to play that. Then I had another tub, and had to hurry too, because we had a box at the theatre and a supper party afterwards. But after that I got to bed all right, and it wasn't nearly three!"

His 64 hits for four (plus three over the top and an overthrow 8) had not drained his energy or enthusiasm one jot, for three days later he was entertaining the local Saturday crowd again. This time it was with an innings of 207 in even time off Blackheath. Again the visitors had no time to bat against the 459 for four, and the hospitality of the Hampstead cricketers could quite logically have been queried. (A 4¼ inch guage, incidentally, was kept in the pavilion to ensure that no bat exceeded the regulation width!)

Stoddart was in Gloucester by Monday, capitalising on his fine form with three hours at the wicket, putting on 90 with his captain and seeming certain to reach his first century for Middlesex. W.G., bowling monotonously on, sensed the youngster's eagerness and said, "I think you won't be long in getting your hundred." He served up his famous long-hop and Stoddart obligingly hit it to Woof and was out for 98.

Now to the Bat and Ball ground at Gravesend and fielding out to Kent while across at the Oval W.G. was busy making 170 in the Test match, his opening

FOOTNOTE: *F.F. Kelly, a left-arm bowler, is pictured on page 69 of* Cricket, *1911, and page 593 of* Cricket, *1912.*

partner, Scotton, scoreless for 67 minutes, contributing a phlegmatic 34 to their stand of 170 and driving Punch to pen the immortal "Wail of the Weary".

At the end of this day Webbe and Stoddart had posted an unbroken 106, carried on Friday the 13th to 205, when the captain left for 103. Stoddart soon reached his maiden first-class century, a chanceless effort of 116 eventually cut short by an agile throw from Alec Hearne.

In four innings over ten days he had compiled 906 runs! Well might F. B. Wilson have written that "he was probably one of the most tireless men who ever lived."

Middlesex were happily placed that evening, but their bowling lacked the penetration to win a game on such a perfect pitch. It lacked the ability to dismiss a team of solid batsmen on a soft wicket, too, as was proved in the next match.

They met Yorkshire at Bradford and the situation at lunch gave little indication of what was to come. It seldom does. On a slow wicket Stoddart and Webbe had put on 54 before Stoddart was bowled by Merritt Preston, whose bowling had killed a batsman in a Yorkshire club match. Yorkshire made 401, then Emmett pushed Middlesex out again for 82, conceivably enjoying a jocular commentary with his mid-off throughout.

At Trent Bridge Stoddart displayed an unexpected ability to stay and grind it out with the bowlers. The Notts trundlers sent down 165 four-ball overs and 92 of them were maiden, left virgin by Middlesex bats ambitious to show their equality with the champions. Stoddart's astonishingly gritty 32 against Shaw, Attewell, Flowers and Barnes was the highest innings of the match and actually lasted 200 minutes.

There was only one more game for him that season, a sensational match at Scarborough between the Gentlemen of England and I Zingari, when he topped the first innings with 23 against the unchanged attack of A. G. Steel, nostrils flaring, spinning his leg-breaks two feet, and H. W. Forster, later Governor-General of Australia.

The Gents batted again with a deficit of over 200 and at 133 for four C. I. Thornton strode in to play an innings that has excited statisticians and connoisseurs of big hitting ever since. His 107 not out in 29 scoring strokes quite naturally overshadowed Stoddart's 57, and his seven hits clean out of the ground included the immortal smack into Trafalgar Square (Scarborough).

Once at Scarborough, when the rain dripped down and the cricketers were confined to barracks, W.G. overheard Stoddart in song with H. V. Page. "Stoddy" had a pleasant singing voice and often sang at family gatherings: often too he used to knock out a melody on the banjo. On this occasion the Doctor, appreciating the harmony, implored: "Now, Stoddy, let's have another of those little dittoes!"

The Old Man was as capable of the malapropism as the cover drive.

Cricket now reassured its readers that "Mr Stoddart has found it difficult to tear himself from cricket and football here. I have it, in fact, on the best authority that he has decided after all to remain in England."

So keen was he that his Hampstead chum, A. S. Johnston, once found himself virtually commanded to join Blackheath Rugby club.

1886 had been for him a glittering cricket season: joint leader of his county's batting, with 506 runs at 28; and over 1600 for Hampstead at 83, with 72 wickets thrown in as flavouring. (E. H. D. Sewell once wrote that Stoddart had the massive aggregate of 3067 runs in all games this season.) A record of some oddness also came his way that autumn: he made the highest score ever recorded with a broomstick, 110 not out!

Now for the winter game, where a few drops of rain are not always unwelcome.

FOOTNOTE: *The* Baily's Magazine *interview (September 1893) states that Stoddart scored 3067 runs in 60 innings.*

CHAPTER 3

RUNS GALORE

Stoddart scored eleven tries for "the Club", Blackheath, in 1886-7, heading the honours list, but sustaining a sprained ankle in the South v North match. He took part in none of the Internationals, of which England drew two and lost to Ireland, but he did play for Middlesex against Lancashire in the Jubilee Festival match at the Oval before the Prince of Wales, Prince Christian and Prince Christian Victor.

As early as February of 1887 he had indicated his willingness to tour Australia in the autumn with the proposed English cricket team. It was the sort of promise to buoy him through the gloomiest passages, and as in 1886, he commenced this season with a marked absence of success after an opening 173 for the Football Club against the Cricket Club at Blackheath.

It was the briefest stroll from his home to Lord's cricket ground, where groundsman Percy Pearce and his staff adored him and addressed him uninhibitedly as "Stod"; yet for four matches running did he trace over those steps and only once could he smile with feeling—after a 42 that ensured victory over Yorkshire.

W.G. made 113 for Gloucestershire, following up with a load of wickets, including Stoddart, for whom he, as well, was developing a soft spot. (W.G. had obtained his FRCS from Durham). In the final innings Stoddart's early dismissal by the brothers Grace deprived his side instantly of much of its attacking function.

F. S. Ashley-Cooper was there and noted in his scholarly manner that Stoddart, "like all young 'uns, was induced to believe that there was more in it than met the eye. He began with the obvious intention of sticking to back-drill until he got one he could jump at. Whether the Old Man signalled to Teddy or not, I don't know. What happened was that he dropped one just short of a length on the leg-stump. It reared a bit, and Stoddart climbed up well on top of it, meaning to drop it at his feet. He played the stroke perfectly, but Teddy had crawled in under his nose; he caught the ball in his right hand, transferred it to his left, and handed it to Frizzy Bush, who was keeping wicket, without either of them moving a foot.

"I reminded Stoddart of the incident shortly before he died, and found that it still rankled, although he quite appreciated the humour of it."

There was a solitary Sunday between this duck and the next, and 1 and 3 in an innings defeat by Notts was hardly offset by the chance of studying Shrewsbury from mid-off for over four hours whilst he put together 119 runs. Yet within a week Stoddart was to join him in a famous first-wicket stand that would erase all the early disappointments of 1887.

> *When Stoddart makes her hum,*
> *Up at Lord's,*
> *Till the bowler bites his thumb,*
> *Up at Lord's,*
> *How the Middlesex supporters*
> *Turn vociferous exhorters*
> *As he jumps on Lockwood's snorters,*
> *Up at Lord's!*
>
> (*Norman Gale*)

At last the sun shone and batsmen everywhere flexed their shoulders and promised vengeance upon the trundlers who had had their own way since Spring had first flaunted her ankles. An illustrious collection of cricketers arrived at Lord's under a blue sky to partake of the M.C.C. Centenary Match, and after the Marylebone side had made 175, Shrewsbury and Stoddart, so unalike yet frequently identified together by later generations, commenced the reply for "England"; if the sun had not dazzled one of the fieldsmen when Stoddart was 13 the bowlers would have been spared a good deal of bother over the next few hours.

The Notts pro and the Middlesex amateur faced them all and sent the ball scudding across the St John's Wood turf till the M.C.C. total seemed meaningless. They had passed it that night, when Stoddart, 111 not out, must have slept sweetly as any cricketer after his first century at Lord's. Shrewsbury, who had been through it all before, was 70.

They resumed, with Barnes, Rawlin and Flowers, all with flesh to spare, bearing the brunt of the hard labour. Stoddart, full of joy and confidence, showed the crowd his strength in front of the wicket and his hooking power. He may even have indulged his dog-stroke occasionally, left leg raised à la Murdoch, the ball flying fine or square to leg. It was his only departure from elegance in an imposing array of explosive but graceful attacking strokes radiating from a sure defence which matured annually. He stood with his chest square to point; not for him the "pernicious two-eyed stance".

Sensitive Shrewsbury went meticulously on his way, knowing that his own bed was far away and he would, as usual, have to put up with a strange mattress and something less than a full night's sleep.

The opening stand threatened the record 283 of W. G. Grace and B. B. Cooper, but when the partnership had realised 266, Stoddart fell; he had hit 19 fours in his 151 and the crowd with whom he was now so popular paid him a thunderous tribute.

Briggs again did the damage when M.C.C. batted, in league this time with Billy Bates, whose time was fast running out. The match would have been something of a travesty if W.G. had not made *some* runs, and he obliged in a minor key with 45 as his team slid to an innings defeat before the little schoolboy, Pelham Warner, sitting engrossed by the sight-screen.

Or, in a shiny hansom cab,
With bells that clinked a careless life,
Cutting the corners like a knife,
We'd helter-skelter to the ground,
And eyes would glisten, pulses pound,
To read the posters as we galloped past:
'Stoddart Still Going Strong', or 'Shrewsbury Out at Last'.

(*Herbert Farjeon*)

The Hampstead people had another treat on the following Saturday as Stoddart took the Willesden attack apart with 238; the side's 399 for six suggested a programme of two-day matches in future— if even that would be sufficient.

At the Hampstead Sports there was further evidence annually of his amazing muscular co-ordination; one year he won eight events in an afternoon, and always he was a classic exponent at the egg-and-spoon race!

He made 78 against Kent, and the latter half of the week was spent at Chiswick suffering humiliation before the youth of Oxford University. Kingsmill Key made 281, Hylton Philipson, erudite and talented, 150. A. E. Stoddart's stunted performance amounted to 1 and 10.

It was only a momentary lapse. Surrey, after pardoning him before he had scored, felt the force of his bat as June burned itself out. It was not one of his showpiece innings but, as so often a partisan insists, the runs were on the board, 85 of them.

Now, in his first Gentlemen v Players engagement, he fielded out to another Shrewsbury century. W. G. captured five of the best wickets, then escorted Stoddart to the centre to chase 396. They made 38, and by lunch Billy Barnes had 6-7 off 16 overs, the Gents eventually folding up for 102. In the follow-on they made 171. Stoddart had made 15 and 13—a sober introduction indeed.

They tried again straight afterwards at the Oval, but it was almost a repeat enactment. The professionals once more topped 300 and the amateurs were bundled out ingloriously for 161 and 162, Stoddart heading the first innings with 40 and making a fast 25 in the second.

Now came a fantastic Cricket Week at Hampstead during which he scored 900 runs in six innings, half of them undefeated. He also found strength to take 17 wickets. He made 205 against Ne'er-do-Weels, carried his bat against London Scottish for 275, then 55 and a mini-century (114 not out) preceded the final flourish of 230 not out off the Old Finchleians' attack (or retreat?).

Three double-centuries in one week sent the mathematicians snatching for their record books.

A. J. Webbe caused a stir in August by carrying his bat twice: for 192 against Kent and 243 in a great recovery against Yorkshire. And at Huddersfield when the cricket was done they all had a game of football.

There was a fine batsman's wicket at Trent Bridge, too, where Shrewsbury kept the Middlesex men running about for over *10 hours* while he accumulated 267 runs. Barnes made a century and Scotton was there in all his molluscan glory for 51.

A thrilling win over Gloucestershire followed, with O'Brien, who usually batted *sans box* and sired ten children between cricket matches, making 83 excellent runs, and F. G. J. "Alphabet" Ford, the tall, slender forerunner of Woolley, 38.

Stoddart's figures had been unspectacular all this month. Perhaps with thoughts on the Australian trip and an understandable reaction from the orgy of run-making the previous month, his grey eyes were not always as intent on the swinging ball as they might have been.

Against I Zingari at Scarborough he did give the English public something to remember him by, scoring 116; then given a bowl he bowled the blue-blooded wicket of Prince Christian Victor, grandson of Queen Victoria, first ball.

He further demonstrated his usefulness with the ball on Scarborough's joyous and breezy ground with 6-33 for M.C.C. against Yorkshire, deflowering Louis Hall for 0 and dismissing Peel, one of his bogeys. These performances established him as something more than a specialist batsman. As a bowler he broke back nippily from the off, pitching a good length generally, his flight deceptive at times, though his virile attempts to spin the ball occasionally brought his action under scrutiny.

In the final match of the season, South v North, his 29 was next to Maurice Read's brilliant 84, but Hall caught up with his tormentors at last with 105. The game drifted away, and a week later Stoddart and his team-mates had packed and sailed out of Tilbury in "Iberia", bound for Australia.

CHAPTER 4

AUSTRALIA THE FIRST TIME

Hawke's side, under Melbourne sponsorship, consisted of 13 players including Andrew Stoddart; and the rival party was got together by Shaw, Shrewsbury and Lillywhite under the auspices of the Sydney Association, with C. Aubrey Smith as captain.

Hawke declared upon arrival in Australia: "We have come here just to enjoy ourselves and we mean to do it. But the great point is that it does not matter to us whether we win or lose, though, of course, we should like to win for the sake of England. I mean by this that our men are likely to hit out and play with dash and freedom."

Would he have shuddered at Jardine's or Hutton's policies more than they would have shuddered at his?

There was good cricket for Australians to watch during that sweltering summer despite the fact that W.G. had declined to tour and despite the cumbersome, profitless arrangement of rival touring parties. Stoddart's panache appealed to the people of this new land and to exiled fellow countrymen seeking a new life yet always susceptible to the gallant reminder of home. He found Australia's cricket pitches generally to his liking, and when the tour was over he stood at the head of the batting table with 1188 runs at 38—hot work in brown boots.

Altham & Swanton's History has marked this point in time: "Perhaps the most notable feature from an historical standpoint was the introduction to Australia of A. E. Stoddart, destined as a batsman to play a very great part in the international cricket of the future, and as a man to win the heart of every sportsman in Australia."

Both teams went about their travels through the sunburnt country, fêted wherever they went and enjoying an outdoor life such as England's tame green fields never afforded.

Stoddart found things to his liking from the start with a "dashing" 64 in Adelaide and reaching the nineties against Spofforth, Trumble and Boyle in Melbourne. He also caught Horan brilliantly running backwards in the outfield; and again a week later he just missed a hundred at the goldfield town of Ballarat, where the team had to down gallons of champagne at two civic receptions.

On the way he had taken 8-27 against Castlemaine, where the tourists had strawberries each morning, but up in Sydney they suffered their only reversal of the tour. Vernon, who had fallen down a companionway on the voyage out, played his first match here, his head injury now knitted up; but high scores from Percy McDonnell, Harry Moses and the handsome Sammy Jones, and a collapse by the English team gave N.S.W. a 9-wicket win.

The terrible pair, Turner and Ferris, opposed English batsmen for the first time, but during his 55 Stoddart played "all round the wicket in hard, clean and graceful style". Reminiscing years later, Lord Hawke referred to him as the British Victor Trumper.

There were drawn games against odds at historic Parramatta and Richmond (where news of the death of Hawke's father came through, and Vernon took over the leadership), and at Manly, the picturesque seafront suburb across a bridgeless Harbour. Stoddart used the coconut matting strip well enough to take 7-34.

Under the leadership of double-International Vernon, the Englishmen headed back into Victoria, adopting now the caps and sashes of their sponsors, the Melbourne Club. About this time, too, umpires were creating a stir with their white coats; hitherto the post had lent itself to dress of the most off-hand and informal nature. Now sophistication had arrived at the cricket ground and was starting to unpack its bag.

Against Eighteen Melbourne Juniors Stoddart batted over six hours on a matting wicket for 285, the highest made by a touring Englishman till R. E. Foster's wonderful 287 in 1903-4. Against fourteen bowlers and undeterred by six chances, he placed 24 fours through the thick maze of fieldsmen. The local lads, strong as they might have been physically and psychologically, wilted to 70 for fifteen wickets before a mere hundred people.

They drew with Maryborough, shot some game, and beat Sale by an innings, both games against Twenty-twos, a fair quota of the population in each case; and four days before Christmas whilst practising on the Melbourne ground, Billy Bates was struck the dreadful blow which literally finished his cricket life, a Yorkshire yeoman lost to the game, but with his Test hat-trick a gleaming mark in the voluminous records of Anglo-Australian encounters.

It had become a sad tour, and the sensation in the South Australia match did nothing to lessen the distraction. With the Englishmen 239 ahead, someone flooded the pitch and cut chunks of turf away during the night.

The omnipotent George Giffen was horrified and embarrassed and countered Vernon's suggestion to abandon the match by urging the rolling of a new wicket. In the end they resumed on the damaged strip, Giffen amazed everyone with an innings of 203, and South Australia salvaged an astonishing draw.

Stoddart had fallen in love with Australia by now, and the *Sydney Referee* published a report hereabouts that he had intentions of taking up residence in N.S.W. The restless soul was susceptible to the enticements: Shrewsbury's possible migration was also rumoured.

A side billed as Combined Australia now took on Vernon's team at Melbourne, and Harry Trott, in an opening spell of medium-paced leg-breaks, had Stoddart, Abel, Peel and O'Brien out with the total 16. But the last four wickets added 241 and at stumps the Combined XI were in trouble.

It was 1888 when the contest was resumed on Monday, and the new year brought success for the Englishmen. The opposition fell away for 136 and 78 after a thunderstorm, giving Vernon's side a victory of considerable prestige value.

Stoddart indulged himself excessively in the minor matches which followed: 8-36 at Yarra Bend, 91 off the bowling of Northern Tasmania, then six wickets and 40 runs at Latrobe. Then he caught cold and could not play against Cootamundra, when little Abel, who had recently lifted a loaded rifle for the first time and made a kill first shot, carried his bat for 92 to emphasise still further that physical appearance should not always count for everything.

At this point the greatest match ever between an English and an Australian team was arranged. Rivalries were forgotten as the two English camps pooled resources and selected what was thought to be the strongest team available. Unhappily many of Australia's front-rank players were not available, and the low-scoring match ended in hollow victory for England, captained by Walter Read.

The event is important, however, in that it was Stoddart's first Test match. The Sydney ground was sodden from recent rains, and when McDonnell put England in, the decision proved misguided even before the day was out.

Shrewsbury and Stoddart soon had the runs flowing, "Stoddy" hitting Ferris hard and often while little Arthur took care of Turner. Moses would have caught Stoddart on the boundary if a drain had not impeded him as he ran round the pickets; but soon a big hit did go to hand and Stoddart was out off Turner for 16.

Shrewsbury batted painstakingly on as wickets began to clatter before Turner, who probed skilfully for the softer spots in the wicket and exploited them with true greatness. The Nottingham master often frustrated him by padding out the sharply-breaking ball, but England managed only 113 in the end against the "terrible twins".

Yet by close of play England were on top: Australia had lost 8 wickets on a fearful pitch whilst scavenging 35 runs. Lohmann and Peel were unanswerable. The only wicket not attributable to the "sticky" was that of Burton, who lashed what seemed a certain five until Stoddart, running back very fast, took a great catch.

Players and spectators waited most of Saturday for the rain to cease, but play was impossible. A sunny Sunday would have made things interesting had not the skies opened again that evening. They remained open most of Monday. Two playing days had been lost when action was resumed on Tuesday. Australia mournfully folded up for 42, and it was left to Stoddart and Shrewsbury to start building upon the 71 runs in credit.

Again Stoddart treated Ferris mercilessly, although the left-hander bowled Shrewsbury for one and soon accounted for Ulyett. Once more it was Turner who claimed Stoddart's wicket, caught by Blackham for 17. Turner, often dropping them short, captured seven wickets this innings and Australia required 209—a seemingly hopeless target.

That evening they lay mortally wounded at 47 for five, Lohmann, Peel and Attewell having thrust deeply into the order.

The weather was dull as the last rites were performed, England winning by 126 runs. Mission accomplished, the two parties split up and went their separate ways, Vernon's to prepare for the return with N.S.W.

The ubiquitous Turner stood at the commencement of his run, ready to open the match. Stoddart awaited him. The first ball he hit for 4, but the next was through him and into the stumps.

The tourists did not falter, however, but reached 337 against which N.S.W. could muster only 445 in two innings. A peculiarity was Stoddart's dismissal of Turner in each innings, a reprisal action which had its sequel as the English team chased the 109 for victory. Turner yorked him for 0.

They hit off the runs and moved on to humiliation at Goulburn. Here, after dismissing the local XXII for 124 (Peel 13-43, Stoddart 5-40) they crashed for 31, the lowest ever by an English team in Australia. It was a struggle to stretch the follow-on innings to 157, by which time the clock-hands had circled to safety.

The final match against odds resulted in an innings win at Wagga Wagga. Then there was a match against the Australian XI bound for England that year, and in sunny conditions Vernon's men stole a 2-run lead on first innings. Turner chalked up Stoddart's wicket yet again as the second innings got under way; but then six other frustrated batsment fell victim to the Terror, lofting him, edging him, or missing him altogether as the wicket became stickier every minute.

The Australians' target was 120, but it was never on as long as Peel and Attewell made the ball fizz. The Notts pro, most dependable bowler on tour, finished with 7-15, and the Australians ruefully sailed for England knowing that such ignominy—32 all out—could scarcely be exceeded.

In the last of the big matches Attewell was at it again, sending Victoria spinning to abject defeat after Read had walloped 142 not out and "Stoddy" had sounded his own farewell with a chanceless, hard-hit 75 against, at times, an all-offside field placing.

At the conclusion the team was entertained at a farewell dinner under the grandstand, where compliments flew thick and fast, and it was remarked with no little feeling that "if the public did not come to see them play, the public were the sufferers by it." George Vernon thanked the club for its hospitality and for having provided Jim Phillips as touring umpire, little appreciating, perhaps, what mileage and headlines lay ahead for the red-haired Australian.

The next day, a match was played against the Melbourne Club in aid of the incapacitated Bates, but hardly 100 people attended, and the absent beneficiary failed to benefit.

The English party sailed for home in the Orient steamer "Austral" without, of the original party, Lord Hawke and Billy Bates, George Vernon (who followed later) and the batsman Australian crowds most enjoyed: A. E. Stoddart.

Whilst the cricket tour had been progressing, the shrewd promotional duo of Shaw and Shrewsbury were organising a football tour of Australasia.

As it happened, the tour was a financial failure, further melting the build-up of profit made by Lillywhite and the two Nottingham men over the previous years. It was, for them, the end of tour management.

The main party, comprising nearly all Northerners, set off from England in March 1888, to be met by Stoddart upon arrival. While England suffered an extremely wet summer, and Jack the Ripper was at the height of his bloody career, and the cricket Tests resulted in a 2-1 win for England with the ludicrous average of 11 runs for every wicket that fell, these football pioneers travelled Australia, winning the conventional matches with ease but finding the Australian Rules contests a bit too much for them.

Stoddart, seeing as much of the country as any swagman, bewitched the spectators with his powerful, weaving runs down the sidelines. He alone mastered the broader Victorian rules, receiving wide acclaim. They beat N.S.W. three times and Queensland twice, the former games being regarded locally as true Internationals; but a pall fell over the venture when the tour captain, R. L. Seddon, of Lancashire, drowned while sculling on the Hunter River near Maitland. Stoddart was immediately elected to take over the captaincy and management.

Early in September they crossed the Tasman Sea and opened an extremely tough final phase. Only Auckland and Taranaki beat them in the 19 games undertaken in New Zealand, but the play was often outrageously rugged.

The New Zealanders, isolated in their corner of the Pacific, learned a great deal from the tour. Stoddart's men demonstrated the feign pass, the side-step, and, in the face of heavy criticism, the advantages of heeling from the scrimmage. Systematic passing along the back line, with the glamour of Stoddart to climax it, also opened the Kiwis' eyes; the game was revolutionised in the little islands, thanks in many instances to Stoddart's patient explanations to umpires, players and spectators alike.

Against Hawkes Bay the Englishmen saw their tuition amply absorbed by Jack Taiaroa, the local captain. Stoddart was bundled into touch after a fine

FOOTNOTE: *Stoddart told Australian batsman J.E. Barrett (Cricket, 1891) that rugby was more enjoyable as it allowed each player a chance to distinguish himself in trying for goal.*

burst. He regained balance, bounced the ball in the field of play, caught it and dived over for a try. There was absolutely nothing in the laws to forbid this.

As the conversion kick was being lined up, Taiaroa said to Stoddart: "What trick is this, Englishman?"

The Englishman explained that this was general practice, and the Maori nodded gravely.

In the second half Taiaroa did exactly the same, and, grinning broadly, turned to Stoddart and said: "My word, that's the best trick I ever learned!"

"Stoddy's" reaction was almost certainly congratulatory.

He praised Otago, also, even though the brilliant half-back, Keogh, sat on the ball after scoring a try and put his thumb to his nose.

The English players finally walked up the gangway, perhaps a little stiffly, and eventually reached home on November 11th. Drewy Stoddart had been away from England for fourteen months.

CHAPTER 5

MAORIS AND BOBBY PEEL

Stoddart's friend George Jeffery, a Cambridge blue, captained Blackheath during the 1888-9 rugby season, which was a quiet one for Stoddart, apart from the International fixture at the Rectory Field against the touring Maori team.

These good-natured giants played 107 matches in New Zealand, Australia and Great Britain during the course of their travels, and went home a tired, battered band of men, wiser in many ways and having given a lot of pleasure to those who had watched with curiosity.

The deep-throated "Ake, Ake, Kia, Kaha!" had startled many an inoffensive Englishman looking on, and at times their vigorous methods had sparked off resentment on the touchlines and in the stands. The unpleasantness reached a pitch during the game with England, when some of the Maoris demonstrated against the referee, the eminent Rowland Hill, by walking off the field.

One of the New Zealanders, T. R. Ellison, later recorded the incident which finally shattered their patience: "Mr Stoddart made a fine, dodgy run and, after beating several of our men, I lured him into my arms by applying the feign dodge. By a quick wriggle, however, he escaped but left a portion of his knickers in my possession. He dashed along and the crowd roared; then suddenly discovering what was the matter he stopped, threw down the ball and, in an instant, we had the vulgar gaze shut off by forming the usual ring around him."

Evershed, an England forward, seized the ball while repairs were under way and went over for a try which the Maoris hotly disputed. Those who strode off the field were persuaded to go back, and the match continued, but the Rugby Union afterwards exacted an apology.

Stoddart scored a try for England, who won by one goal and 4 tries (then 7 points) to nil.

His imaginative play yet again was setting the rugby world a-chatter. In one game he caught the ball only two yards from an opponent. Instead of running on, he took a few steps backwards, nonplussing the opposition, who could only stand and gape as he dropped a perfect goal.

In February he starred in a match between The Rest of England and Yorkshire when the Champion County surprisingly went down by 3 goals to nil. Alderson in the centre and Stoddart on the wing for The Rest stole all the glory.

Then the daffodils began to raise their heads, and the winds of March whispered of the joys to come in the Spring.

Cricket took two steps closer to the game we know when the over was increased to 5 balls, and declarations were permitted on the third day of a match. The prolonged over apparently suited Stoddart, for one: his 30 wickets for Middlesex constituted his best annual tally.

He was due to play for South v North at the Oval in May, but withdrew "in consequence of business" on the day of the match. By now he was lodging at 2 Rothwell Street, a handsome avenue of terraced houses on the opposite side of Primrose Hill from Ormonde Terrace. (His mother had moved to Quarry Close, Coventry, to live with her daughter, Cissie, who had married Monty, son of Sir Samuel Wilks, physician to Queen Victoria).

During May he had scores for Hampstead of 77 and 97, then against Marlow, who had them seven down for 2, he salvaged the innings with 15 not out. The joys of club cricket!

His first county game had barely started before it was ended, Notts winning on a rain-affected wicket.

Good opening stands with Webbe helped towards a victory over Gloucestershire: a win against W.G. was always especially gratifying, although the Doctor, 40 years old, with many seasons left in him, reached 101 before Stoddart caught him at mid off. Stoddart steered Middlesex to victory with 78 not out, hitting in a style that was now repeatedly categorised as "brilliant", for want of better adjectives, and using some of the precious element—luck. This innings remained his highest in a drab first-class season.

At Manchester they had another win, again sparked by Stoddart's free and powerful 71. He added to his select list of dismissals those of the poetic pair, Hornby and Barlow.

Large crowds at Lord's saw Surrey win the local derby with Stoddart hitting 64 in his very best style, as usual making about two-thirds of the runs added whilst he batted.

Now came a historic match at Lord's against Yorkshire when the stars were several: Louis Hall carrying his bat for the *fifteenth* time for Yorkshire; fine hands from O'Brien and Vernon; and "Stoddy's" 46 in 40 minutes; then Peel with 158 played what was then said to have been the finest innings by a left-hander at Lord's.

This game which most of us would give a year's beer money to see played over on television (with edited highlights only of Louis Hall's effort) now moved to its white-hot conclusion.

Needing 280 to win in less than even time, Middlesex had a rapid 129 up when Timothy Carew O'Brien entered.

151 runs in 90 minutes off Yorkshire bowling posed no problem if he could get his bat swinging. And he did.

He slammed the ball high and ran sharp singles with Vernon and snicked and cut his way to the unlikely target. When the dust had subsided and the crowd, flushed and fidgety, raised its voice for the final hoarse chorus, Middlesex had won by 4 wickets and O'Brien was 100 not out. It followed a trifle of 92 in the first innings.

> *Father, dear father, DO take me to Lord's;*
> *The clock on the stairs has struck one:*
> *The tape says that Stoddart the smiter is in;*
> *'Tis a pity to miss all the fun.*
>   *Father, dear father, I'll ring for your boots;*
>   *The clock on the stairs has struck two:*
>   *The crowd will examine the pitch during lunch,*
>   *And leave a seat vacant for you.*
> *Father, dear father, don't write any more;*
> *The clock on the stairs has struck three,*
> *And Stoddart has just cut a ball to the ropes;*
> *'Tis a sight every girl ought to see.*
>   *Father, dear father, I've brought you your hat;*
>   *The clock on the stairs has struck four:*
>   *The bowlers are both of them well on the spot,*
>   *But Stoddart continues to score.*
> *Father, dear father, oh! why don't you start?*
> *The clock on the stairs has struck five:*
> *The tape says that Stoddart is still at the stumps,*
> *And has made a magnificent drive.*
>   *Father, dear father, 'tis really too bad,*
>   *The clock on the stairs has struck six:*
>   *The eager spectators are mad with delight,*
>   *For Stoddart is still at the sticks.*
> *Father, dear father, you need not go now,*
> *The clock stands at six fifty-four;*
> *And Stoddart the smiter has carried his bat*
> *For a grandly made three-figure score.*

(Douglas Moffat)

Those showpiece occasions, the Gentlemen v Players matches, came early in July. In the first, at the Oval, Stoddart and W.G. walked out to face the best paid bowlers in the land. The younger man found more profit in the bowling than the Champion, and at 81, made in little over an hour, he was caught for an excellent 59. O'Brien's hurricane 90 carried them to 347.

But Barnes made 90, and with the long-established firm of Shrewsbury and Gunn doing steady business the Players made 396. There was small resistance the following day. The Players needed only 177 and got them easily.

Stoddart returned some very useful performances for the Gents over the years, and in the next game he took 3-41. Rain then ruined the wicket and the amateurs collapsed before Briggs and Lohmann.

Now, on each of three Saturdays, Stoddart made a century at Hampstead, more or less as a reminder of his supremacy at this level of the game. The heartening progress of Middlesex was checked by innings defeats before Lancashire and Kent, then the Oval crowd saw their idol, Walter Read, make a century, supported by sizable innings from the cast-eyed Abel, portly Key, and George Lohmann, who looked even more god-like beside these other two.

Stoddart rolled his way through 30 overs as Surrey piled up 507, then he drove his way to a chanceless 72, an attractive innings, much overdue perhaps. But his side fell many runs short, and in the follow-on he was smartly stumped for 35 and might thankfully have adjourned that evening to one of his favourite pubs—The Winchester, in South Hampstead—for a quiet drink with Jack Trotman or George Jeffery, or to the Constitutional Club (artist Romney's old house) on Holly Hill, or perhaps up to the Hampstead ground where his presence was always a stimulus.

He enjoyed unobtrusively coaching the youngsters, and they usually doted on every word, just as kids have done at the knee of Billy Beldham, or gazing up into Cowdrey's kindly eyes.

The rest of the county programme was plainly woeful for Stoddart the batsman. Rollicking Bobby Peel's inexhaustible left arm cut him down for 2 and 1 at Halifax, and at Cheltenham "Father" Roberts, another left-hander, with 38-42-40 figure, had him caught for 0. Francis Ford led a fight back, and in the second innings Stoddart hit 45, the two together representing one of the most thrilling acts in late-Victorian cricket. In the end Gloucestershire were forced to defend for their lives.

Stoddart was at least taking wickets, opening against W G's men and claiming 5-97, and taking his form to Scarborough, with five I Z wickets. But the awful Peel had him twice in a 12-a-side match, and a man less gentle than "Stoddy" might have gazed meaningfully to the North Sea and pictured the fair Yorkshireman's head bobbing down for the third time.

He went about things more constructively. In the South v North fixture he bowled Peel for nought and punched his, Attewell's, Shacklock's and Flowers' bowling all over the place in a stirring knock of 77. The sweetest blow of all was a hit out of the ground off Attewell; the performance overall was described as "perfect".

In the follow-on Stoddart's wait was a long one as W.G. and Abel saved the match with a hundred apiece. Stoddart finally walked to the middle, got off the mark, then was given out l.b.w. to—Peel!

At Hastings the bowlers had it their own way as the North thrashed the South, and in the Gentlemen v Players match Stoddart took 4-51 with Abel's prized wicket and those of bowlers Peel, Ulyett and Lohmann, retaliation that must have been delicious. The amateurs finally had only 73 to get, yet Stoddart and four others were finished with cricket for the season by the luncheon interval.

FOOTNOTE: *Stoddart and Gregor MacGregor also often relaxed at the Conservative Club.*

CHAPTER 6

COUNTY BEFORE COUNTRY

Andrew Stoddart captained England at Dewsbury, when Wales recorded their first ever win over England. The match was played in a sleeting snowstorm, the ground a quagmire which did much towards immobilising England's heavy men up front, Sammy Woods determined and boisterous as any of them.

Stoddart tried kicking his team into a scoring position, but the nimble play of the Welsh threequarters, with the genius Billy Bancroft at full-back, defied all his efforts and reversed the pressure.

The English forwards scrimmaged well, but the conditions were beginning to tell as halftime approached. As they took their oranges in the swirling white storm and trotted into position hoping for more luck, surely the young English captain, with his enormous pants clinging damply to his thighs, must have glimpsed in his mind's eye the lazy sunlit terraces of the cricket grounds last summer; he placed the soggy oval ball and booted it at the fifteen hostile Welshmen awaiting his challenge.

The ball came spinning back, punted by Welsh threequarters sensing the chance of making history. There were tight scrimmages and much heaving and hooking and grasping.

Stadden, the Cardiff half-back, dodged his way through, fooling Fox by bouncing the ball out of touch and gathering it swiftly to go over for a try, not converted.

Now England stormed their opponents' line until a score seemed inevitable. Frenzied tackling kept them at bay, but back came Stoddart in what was amounting almost to a personal duel, loudly and generously appreciated by the crowd.

Those dying minutes saw England's forwards battling blindly to push the heroic Welshmen back, but "no side" was finally called and many a leek was waved delightedly in the chill air.

Four days after his 27th birthday, an injury which kept him out of the Scotland match now cleared, Stoddart returned to the side for the match against Ireland at the Rectory Field where 12,000 people had gathered.

"Stoddy" was to become notoriously poor at calling the toss in cricket Tests, and such was his form on March 15th, 1890, when Ireland chose to take advantage of the wind. England's back-line commanded play during the first half, with occasional spirited runs from the Irish pack, dribbling and pushing their way upfield against the stout wall of Englishmen, Woods, Evershed and Robinson prominent as any.

The first try came when Stoddart made a short run and swung the ball across to Morrison. Morrison penetrated well into the twenty-five, and Evershed took over. He beat three men and crossed the line, only to drop the ball. Rogers pounced on it and England had the try after all. Jowett failed with the wide place-kick.

Soon Mason Scott took the ball from an Irish dribbling attack and got it to Aston. He ran for the line and threw the ball to Stoddart when his path was blocked. The captain grounded try number two, but Jowett was unsuccessful again with a difficult kick.

Early in the second half Morrison scored England's third try with a spectacular run down the right touchline, brushing aside tackle after tackle, and Jowett now missed a kick from almost in front.

The Irishmen were unabashed, and pressed even harder. Johnstone was almost in when tackled by Stoddart, but the record was kept clean and England's victory ensured a share of the title with Scotland.

As captain of Blackheath, Stoddart had scored 7 tries, second on the list of scorers and something of a recovery from the previous year's poverty.

A contemporary pen-picture helps convey his high standing: "Very active and strong, he can well hold his own with heavier and more powerful men, and this he has frequently demonstrated. As for the speed with which he runs with the ball, and the quickness with which he can swerve and dodge without losing way when avoiding an opponent, his extraordinary starts and jumps, the certainty of his fielding, and his mastery of all the tactics of attack, are not these things matters of public notoriety?"

The writer recognised his British pluck and persistency by quoting another admirer: "He is a good-woolled one, and does not curl up after a purler." Take note, ye soccer players of today, if you can comprehend this classic Victorianism.

Even this early he spoke of retiring from the winter game, but the alarmed interviewer trusted that he would "wait until the deterioration which he professes to find in his own powers is perceptible to others."

In February, 1890, he was featured in the fashionable *Sporting Celebrities* journal, which paid him high tribute, and described his rugby play as "scientific" as well as "pretty".

His unselfishness remained forever in the memory of a club-mate who once watched him beat the entire opposition, full-back and all, then pass to a luckless threequarter who had the honour of making the try. He would, recalled the same observer, often fling himself into the thick of his opponents and literally crash his way through. "He seemed not to know the meaning of the word 'fear'."

FOOTNOTE: *Albert Craig, "The Surrey Poet", wrote after the Ireland match:*
May nought on earth that union sever,
May friends of football live for ever.
May all who deserve it rise to fame,
Keep pure and unsullied as Stoddart's name.

The year 1890 initiated a glittering cricket decade notable for the fascinating gallery of players who displayed their gifts daily in all the cricket centres of the land. Their portraits may convey a conforming sameness but their characters were rich and truly Dickensian in variety in an age untouched by the great levelling movement in society.

No television cameras zoomed in on them, and there were few workaday journalists feeling for an angle. A man could be himself; there was room for expression. Rare was the cricketer who took himself too seriously.

Archie MacLaren announced himself this year with a magnificent century at Hove, and F. S. Jackson made his debut for Yorkshire. Gregor MacGregor kept wicket for England while still at Cambridge, where he stood up for the wild slingers of Sammy Woods. And J. T. Hearne qualified both for Middlesex and for the title of the county's greatest bowler ever.

O'Brien, the Reads, Woods, the Palairets, Hawke and the fabulous Graces, pale-faced Shrewsbury and (automatically) Gunn, little Abel and big Barnes, Lohmann, Briggs and Peel, Wainwright, Mold, lisping Jack Brown, Lockwood and Richardson, and the much-loved, sad-eyed Andrew Stoddart. A rousing cavalcade.

After endless hours in their company through photographs, sketches and reports it is with sadness that one has to realise that they are all so long dead. Their deaths were often as spectacular as their lives, and a host of suicides robbed the game of many talents and much mature counsel.

But, for the moment, all was optimism, with Murdoch's side about to arrive from Australia, and the colourful signs of Spring all around—so important to an Englishman.

It was a poor season for Stoddart. Middlesex, having climbed two places in 1889, slipped back again, and more of his thrilling bombardments on those depressingly damp wickets undeniably would have elevated his county.

It was the only year until 1898 that he failed to hit a century for Hampstead, although he got as far as 97 not out. All the same, his 418 runs for the club in 10 completed innings rate as failure according to the Bradman scale.

Seven ducks quacked quite deafeningly at him in 45 innings despite a promising start to the season. In the nippy month of May the Australians opened their tour with a match at Sheffield Park, where Turner and Ferris had his Lordship's pride out for 27 (W.G. 20 of them); and the Australian total of 191 improbably proved sufficient for an innings win, though there was to be more defeat than victory for them in this summer of horrific weather.

Soon Stoddart was playing one of the best innings of his life, for South against North at Lord's. After Shrewsbury had carried his knowing bat through the Northern innings of 90, Stoddart accompanied W.G. to the middle to see what they could make of this sticky pitch and these unrelenting bowlers a second time.

The Doctor concentrated on keeping the ball out and avoiding the kickers, but the young man at the other end was soon banging the ball about to the delight of the crowd and his companions at the balcony of the new pavilion. He cut almost brutally and pulled the short stuff with an elegant swivel. With admirable back-defence to rising balls and a thumping drive against the over-pitched stuff, he made 50 runs while that pillar of Victorian grandiosity, W. G. Grace, made but 3. Probably never was the Champion so eclipsed in half a century at the wicket.

In an hour and a half the opening stand amounted to 111, then W.G. departed for 29. "Stoddy" continued on his chanceless way, and only when his score stood at 115 was he stopped—by a Yorkshire left-hander, Peel by name.

Lohmann carried on the fight, hitting the metal-topped stumps seven times in taking 8-65, and the South had won by 135. It was the first of eight consecutive games at Lord's that season for Stoddart; his 59 was the highest of the match against Kent, but it was followed by the mortification of being run out for 0. Then came the ignominy of defeat by Somerset, not then a first-class county. He took five wickets, but made only 0 and 5.

Against Notts he bowled Shrewsbury for 11, a deed probably worth every bit as much to him as his opening stand of 96 with A. J. Webbe.

Now he top-scored with 46 in another victory over Murdoch's warriors, this time for M.C.C., important opponents for the Australians ever since the 1878 affair. Admission rose to the unprecedented level of one shilling.

Stoddart's restoration took a buffeting throughout June. Ferris, Peel and Mold all had his scalp for 0 in the course of seven innings, the match with the Australians being stiff with sensation: J. T. Hearne and Nepean had them seven wickets for 13 before a last-wicket stand of 80 pulled the "colonials" up to 135.

Middlesex batted and soon the Australians were astounded to find themselves holding a lead of 22.

Then Hearne bowled Murdoch for 0 for the second time, and the Australians were soon 94 for eight; but the tiny Gregory and Barrett played out time and the last day was washed out, which might have saved poor Murdoch, in his current disposition, from making a third duck.

That disastrous June ended with a mauling by Surrey. A fine 60 from Stoddart lifted Middlesex to 140—99 of them for the first wicket with Webbe. Lohmann and Sharpe tipped Middlesex out a second time for 57 on a tacky wicket, Lohmann, who captured 220 wickets this year, taking twelve in this episode.

No batsman could have felt content with this wretched summer, least of all the Australians, notwithstanding the phenomenal success of Turner and Ferris, bowling into the footmarks.

As a batsman Stoddart seldom succeeded in Gentlemen v Players encounters, but at the Oval this year he made a superb 85 on a nasty wicket against Peel, Briggs, Attewell and Lohmann. It was his highest score in 21 contests and one of the finest he ever played. A century was looming fast—and how he must have coveted it—when Lohmann threw himself across the pitch to scoop up the catch.

Today Stoddart House, a block of council flats, looks down on this historic piece of England—Kennington Oval, where a Stoddart straight-drive once removed an umpire's hat—a green expanse which is to the cricket-lover what Hampton Court is to the romantic historian.

The Oval is surely replete with ghosts.

The Lord's contest was spoiled late by rain, but Stoddart once more had the satisfaction of bowling the best professional batsman in the land with a break-back when Shrewsbury was set.

Now Andrew Stoddart was selected to make his home Test debut in the first Test, at Lord's; but he was persuaded to withdraw and assist Middlesex against Kent at Tonbridge.

The Pall Mall Gazette denounced this as a very bad precedent, saying that "the fact of the present Australian team having been found weaker than some of its predecessors does not, in our opinion, excuse the Middlesex executive for departing from a proper and well-established plan."

In assessing Stoddart's own attitude we need to remember that Test matches then were not promoted and conducted under the frenetic spotlight of public attention we know today, and the sacrifice of his services to county before country was considered praiseworthy by some.

W.G. led England to a 7-wicket victory, whilst at Tonbridge Stoddart was making 42 for Middlesex on a hard, true wicket, following up with the bowling figures as Kent went on to win.

He was chosen for the second Test but again withdrew, this time to face Yorkshire at Bradford. When Lord Hawke received word of this he forbade Ulyett and Peel to play against Australia, but the county game was ruined by rain and Stoddart, who almost predictably was dismissed in each innings by Peel, must have wished, for one, that the three of them had been on the same side at the Oval facing the common enemy.

Within a fortnight the England team was named for the final Test, with A. E. Stoddart's name immediately under W. G. Grace's on the list. This time there was no withdrawal, and, alas, no Test match as Manchester suffered a ceaseless downpour. The 1890 season therefore had passed without International laurels for him.

In the second half of the summer there was a superb knock of 42 on a fiery wicket for the Lyric Club, who beat the Australians at Barnes in an intriguing match which, like so many others, was doomed to slip into glass bookcases and remain locked away, forgotten for decades to come.

Middlesex suffered further indignities before Surrey and Gloucestershire, and Stoddart's 15 was the only double-figure score in the last innings. Somerset, moving nearer first-class status, provided a happy talking point with a tie against Middlesex at Taunton, where a frantic run-out terminated the match. September, so often a felicitous month for batsmen, could hardly have been more ghastly for Stoddart. On imperfect pitches he made nine runs in five innings. "Terror" Turner slaughtered Lord Londesborough's XI, and in this battle of the bowlers where Briggs took 15-57 the Australians gratefully scraped home in a sensationally low-scoring game; there were not many triumphs for them in their 28 squelching matches.

Stoddart went for the last first-class game to Hastings, where the castle ruins surmounted a quaint setting. And before a great audience, Stoddart, perhaps appropriately, for the year in question, made a duck. Turner had him at slip, and there was no chance of a second innings.

His penultimate game had been the South v North contest. Although his bat was reduced by Briggs to an inoffensive, ineffectual weapon, he was in at the thrilling climax. Sherwin, last man for the North, might well have hit off the 10 runs required had not a smart pick-up and return from Stoddart sunk him.

Wisden bemoaned his average this season as "decidedly poor" for a player of high class, and conceivably he might have allowed his thoughts to drift to Colorado or somewhere equally distant—but the advantage of being a dual-sportsman is that there is no need to sit over the fire all winter contemplating past miseries.

And in 1890-1 he was busy; he returned to his position atop Blackheath's try-scoring list, and also played in the first Barbarians match, wearing the black skull and crossbones badge over his heart and captaining them to victory against Hartlepool Rovers. But most intriguing of all, he was credited with an England cap this season when, after all, it appears he did not play.

The Pall Mall Gazette stated that the team against Wales took the field as originally selected; The Times listed the team without Stoddart and, as would be expected, without mention of him in the match description. Yet the Rugby Union to this day credits him and fifteen others with caps for this game.

This winter a famous Middlesex v Yorkshire game took place at Richmond, where the home team's superlative threequarter line of Gould, Stoddart, MacGregor and Campbell failed to click because, many said, they were all individualists. Yorkshire, so strong up front, simply crushed the home side, but the one Middlesex touchdown was a classic.

From a scrum near their own line Middlesex broke away. Half-back Orr passed to Gould, who, having drawn several opponents, slipped the ball to MacGregor at top speed. The Scot swerved outwards as if dashing home for a short single, and at the right moment flung the ball to Stoddart, who made breakneck for the Yorkshire line. The crowning movement came at the end of this masterly run: he returned the ball to MacGregor, racing up in thrilling

FOOTNOTE: *Later in the Barbarians' tour Stoddart was running in to score against Bradford when a whistle blew. He stopped in his tracks; but the whistle had been blown by a spectator. Stoddart scored a try in a 6-6 draw.*

support, and the ball was finally flicked to Gould, who broke through a shattered defence quite easily to score the try.

This was what the game of rugby was all about.

He captained Barbarians at Exeter on April Fools' Day, 1891, against Devonshire, and went over for a try and converted three others. Then came the cricket season, and a better year by far.

CHAPTER 7

CARRYING THE BAT

In the alarmingly meagre amount of change I was handed from ten shillings recently for a tin of pipe tobacco there was an 1891 penny, and it was so worn from the years of handling and from contact with various bed-mates in sundry pockets that I felt this smooth, devalued disc to be perhaps as symbolic a chronological yardstick as we are likely to find in everyday dealings. It may even have crossed the palm of Andrew Stoddart: he liked his pipe.

The sun did not always shine in those lustrous days. 1891 was yet another shameful summer and much cricket was lost. Against Yorkshire he made the only "pair" of his career: Wainwright caught him off Peel, and in the last innings Peel bowled him. There would probably have been a shrug and a smile before the dismal trek back to the warmth of the pavilion.

J. T. Hearne was mainly responsible for lifting Middlesex to third place this year, taking 118 wickets at ten each. O'Brien, playing at times under an assumed name but apparently fooling no-one, headed the batting 5 runs per innings in front of Stoddart; and the next match, against Notts, contained a typical display by the robust Irishman—85 off an attack still rated one of the best in the country.

"Stoddy" made 8 and 0 and threatened to outdo all the disastrous starts of previous seasons.

But there came the match against Lancashire, and in glorious sunshine he made 37 out of 96, continuing the good work by almost notching a century in the second innings. Middlesex had won by the end of the second day, and Stoddart had become one of the select few who ever collared Mold.

There were three matches riddled with failure now, only the Gloucestershire game providing the consolation of victory. Against Kent at Beckenham he was mysteriously listed by *Cricket* as "J. J. Evans".

The Oval contest between Gents and Players went conclusively to the Gents, Stoddart opening with W.G. and falling to a very fine catch by Gunn in the deep for 39.

The Lord's sequel was ruined by rain, with the amateurs 89 for five. Rain descended in torrents, and the vivid flashes and deafening thunder-claps seemed to signify the end of cricket for the year at least. Lord's was a lake by the time the splashing had subsided to a forlorn drip-drip; by then the performers had long since gone to their tea and toast.

Now it was mid-July, and the metropolitan team made its way north, hoping for another win over Lancashire. A confident, substantial innings came from Stoddart's bat at last; the weather had brightened, the pitch was good, and he made the highest score of the season. *Wisden's* report, perpetuating the facts, must have given him much quiet pleasure:

"An exceptionally brilliant display of batting on the part of Mr A. E. Stoddart, who, going in first for Middlesex, carried his bat right through the innings, rendered this return engagement particularly noteworthy in the great county matches of the season. The Middlesex amateur may fairly be said to have on this occasion surpassed all his previous efforts, for not only was his score of 215 not out the highest innings played in first-class cricket last summer, but it was, by a considerable number of runs, the biggest score ever obtained in a good match by Mr Stoddart, his previous best having been 151 for England against the Marylebone Club at Lord's in 1887. His innings of 215 lasted five hours, and except for two chances, one at slip when he had made 86 and another at the wicket when his total had reached 109, it was quite free from fault. His hitting at times was remarkably fine, whilst the accuracy with which he got Mold's bowling onto the middle of his bat all the time gave the performance additional value."

The last three batsmen helped him add 214 runs, and it was in these latter stages that Mold suffered such untypical punishment. Hearne and Rawlin, establishing themselves as a pair of bowlers to be feared for most of the 'nineties, twice got rid of Lancashire, ensuring a welcome innings win.

Now at Brighton the page of glory in the scorebook was turned to the next blank sheet, and this time Middlesex were in for a reversal. Stoddart, alive with confidence, made 41, but a second innings breakdown let Sussex in.

In August they went to Sheffield, where according to Hugh Trumble's loving description, "the smoke from the factories is horrible, and they say the big factories always bank their fires when the visiting side goes in to bat." After lying on the grass he noticed black smut on his flannels when he got up.

The factories could not have banked their fires enough this time, for Middlesex ran out winners; Stoddart made only 3 and 9 on this Bramall Lane pitch which was to be blown sky high in World War II.

It must have been pleasant to be home and scoring runs again. He made 90 at Lord's off the Sussex attack before Fred Tate bowled him—the same Tate with the pinned-back ears who in 1902 was to stand excruciatingly centre-stage as England lost to Australia by 3 runs.

The season was an extraordinary one for Stoddart the bowler. For Hampstead he took his all-time best—105 wickets at less than 9 each; but for the county, with Hearne, Rawlin, Phillips and Nepean providing adequate artillery, he had but five overs all season, and they were against the newly-promoted Somerset. He took the wicket of W. N. Roe, who had been a fellow quadruple-century-maker with 415 not out at Cambridge in 1881.

The final county game was at Trent Bridge, and the skies wept once more. Something had upset them greatly this particular year.

Stoddart had been invited to tour Australia again during the forthcoming English winter, this time with Lord Sheffield's side, led by W. G. Grace; the thoughts of all the party during the festival games of September would not unnaturally have been on the delights ahead. Stoddart managed only two innings of note, a 38 and an attractive 71 following a duck and followed by a duck for the Gents when he was caught first ball of the match.

Now for the second time it was goodbye to old England as "Arcadia" pulled out of Albert Docks, explorer H. M. Stanley among her company.

CHAPTER 8

AUSTRALIA AGAIN

Lord Sheffield's men played cricket at Malta and at Colombo, where W.G. soon tired of the fierce sun and gave himself out "hit wicket". Stoddart battled on patriotically for 70 (next highest was 16) and ended with blistered arms and florrid face.

The cricketers finally landed at Adelaide, and "in spite of the seductive dolce far niente of a sea voyage", as one magazine put it, Stoddart stepped ashore fitter than at any stage of his life.

It had been 18 years since W.G.'s last tour of Australia, and there was apprehension as to the Old Man's endurance at the age of 43 through a tour which, although markedly more comfortable than the previous venture now that rail was taking over from coach and horse, was nevertheless a taxing expedition, even if he was being paid £3 000 and had his family with him.

W.G. and Alfred Shaw, the manager, together with all these players who had been but children when W.G. was first establishing himself as champion of the world, were popular everywhere they travelled, retrieving the game from the doldrums where it had languished during the years of Australian ill-success. Though receipts were to fall £2000 short of expenditure, Lord Sheffield was still moved in his appreciation to donate 150 guineas towards the advancement of cricket in Australia, and the following season Victoria won the first Sheffield Shield competition.

Australian wickets were obviously much improved, though W.G.'s own shape and form were soon under less flattering scrutiny: "Great Scott—such feet! He could get £2 a week and his tucker merely to walk about in the grasshopper districts to kill off the pest."

His fun had started on the voyage out, with a Christy minstrel act that featured, naturally, Johnny Briggs, and which had W.G.'s face blackened and the famous beard sacrilegiously powdered.

The team were photographed at Adelaide in the Botanical Gardens, where the flora provided an uncustomary setting for the Englishmen, bedecked in their straw hats and light suits. There sat W.G. in his Derby hat, black beard washed and restored; there he sat with his staff and crew, fit to take his place alongside the other pioneers of the awakening continent.

After a leisurely ten days they opened with an easy win over South Australia, Stoddart making a graceful 78; then on to Melbourne, where all was gaiety: the drags and horses were decorated in the colours of Lord Sheffield, and the cricket match found W.G. in all his commanding glory as he carried his bat for 159.

But the big opposition lay ahead, and at Sydney came the first great tussle, against a star-studded N.S.W. side.

The Englishmen made only 20 more than the home side's 74, and a second innings recovery led by Moses left them 153 to win. When six were back in the pavilion for 88 it looked odds-on N.S.W., but Peel and Lohmann steered safely to victory. Stoddart, falling to Charlie Turner each time, made 4 and 28.

Briggs took 12-38 against Cumberland, but Lohmann outdid him next match again XXII of Camden with 12-17, Bobby Peel bagging the other nine for 36. All but the politer of the English fieldsmen must have found themselves yawning at the monotonous clatter of wickets, but the farmers and settlers were all going through an experience to be told and retold in the months and years ahead.

Next stop was Bowral, where 20 years later the family Bradman were to take up residence, and the tourists beat a "poor lot". Briggs took 24 wickets in the match for 87!

Stoddart, still questing unsuccessfully for runs, had some solace on Boxing Day with 45 runs at Ballarat against shoddy fielding. Then on New Year's Day 1892 the first of the three Tests commenced.

W.G. lumbered onto the Melbourne ground to toss with Blackham—bearded and historic characters both. W.G. made a rueful remark as the coin fell Australia's way.

Alec Bannerman and Jack Lyons opened for "Combined Australia" and took their task so seriously that the crowd of 20,000 became restless. Tight bowling, careful fielding and Bannerman's innate caution restricted the score to 52 for two at lunch, and even the mighty Lyons had been barracked as Lohmann teased him with exaggerated off-theory.

"Hit 'im over the chains, Jack!" rasped one patriot in the outer, but Lyons was caught by W.G. for 19 and Giffen failed. It took Billy Bruce to brighten the play after lunch. Left-handed and tall, he hit his way to a top-score 57, and all the while Bannerman, small, poker-faced, hair parted dead centre, chipped and placed his way to 45 in three hours and a quarter.

On Saturday Australia reached 240, English bowling honours going to Jack Sharpe, who lacked a right eye and always offered a shy profile to the camera.

The day was fine as W.G. took Abel with him to answer for England, and runs were soon coming fast. Bob McLeod shaved W.G.'s stumps once and the Champion fooled the crowd by lifting his head in horror and taking a step towards the pavilion. Yet it was an omen: McLeod bowled him for 50, having already accounted for Abel. Now Stoddart avoided the hat-trick; but he was caught third ball by George Giffen, and McLeod had three of the most auspicious wickets imaginable in just five deliveries.

George Bean made 50, and a riotous 41 from Briggs put England ahead. Yet the eventual lead of 24 was only a morale-flatterer.

It was extremely hot as Bannerman and Lyons commenced Australia's second innings. In faraway Paris Guy de Maupassant had been taken into shelter that day after putting a razor across his throat, but the Australian's shunned suicidal tendencies and proceeded steadily to 33 at lunch. Lyons went on lustily to 51, but Bannerman stayed four hours compiling his 41. Bruce again played a valuable hand, and that afternoon England knew their target: 213.

Saying they would win by about four wickets, W.G. this time took Stoddart out, and they made a competent 60 before W.G. gave Bannerman an easy catch at mid-off. Then at the same total Stoddart tried to drag a long-hop from Callaway and was bowled for 35.

The gate was open and the Australians drove in. At the close of play clouds of dust were rising from the wicket, and the score stood at 104 for seven, with Abel and MacGregor in; and after a further score next day Abel was caught behind off a riser from Turner, and the innings swiftly folded up.

Australia rejoiced in a 54-run win that had been above all the result of determined batting: Australian batsmen had permitted 159 of 343 overs to go unpunished; English batsmen had allowed only 47 maiden overs from 174 bowled by Australia. The modern game of Test cricket was taking shape.

Stoddart must have been taking mental notes, for it was a feature of the batting he took to Australia three years later that any flamboyance was soon anaesthetised. The 1894-5 series, surrounded by intense publicity and played with almost unnerving sincerity, marked the commencement of Test cricket competition as we know it. His own batting approach was transformed in Australia from the free and dashing to the urgent and watchful. A sense of stern responsibility was established.

Six games in Victoria against odds intervened before the second Test at Sydney. Stoddart recorded some modest scores and made a 50 against South Melbourne, who had in their side a certain A. E. Trott, whose life was to cross with his for many years to come.

There was another excellent 50 against XX Melbourne Juniors, and all this time the bowlers had been turning in such outrageous analyses as 9-73 (Briggs), 8-80 (Lohmann), 11-53 (Grace!), 7-7 (Peel), 13-29 (Briggs), 17-64 (Philipson, the wicketkeeper), 12-40, 13-57 and 7-67 (Lohmann), 9-30 (Attewell)—all one-innings figures.

It took a bat full of Australian courage and impertinence to overcome this sort of bowling lust, and small was the number of local men who managed to make a score.

This sort of preparation for a Test match was, of course, hardly in England's interests. Neither were the bushland capers in Gippsland, when Lord Sheffield's team almost went to bed one light after Bobby Abel's horse bolted through bush criss-crossed with wire fencing. The party managed to catch some kangaroos and emus without Abel's assistance, but the dead snake he found curled up in his cricket bag was a reassuring token of his team-mates' affection.

The dwarfish cricketer celebrated his return to the relative safety of the Test match arena by catching Alec Bannerman off Lohmann to start the rot in Australia's first innings, then carrying his bat through England's 5½-hour reply.

The first Test had fired optimism in the Australian camp, and Giffen recalled that even the Englishmen felt Australia would win. That they did so was due to a sterling fight back in the second half of the match after England had seemed as certain of victory as a cricket team could be.

A tremor of controversy rocked this game: Moses was selected in spite of a leg injury sustained in the first Test, and W. G. made it quite clear that Blackham need not expect a substitute if Moses broke down. Further, a Sydney newspaper had printed alleged criticisms made by W.G. on his previous tour, and some sections of the crowd imagined themselves offended.

It was warm and sultry that morning at Sydney, and recent rain had left the wicket soaked. The sun was drying it slowly as George Lohmann flowed in to start the action. Bannerman was his usual unsmiling self, but Lyons thrashed about in scintillating fashion, hitting two successive deliveries over the chains for 5 and quickly running to 41.

This was the only challenge as Lohmann proceeded to harvest 8 wickets for the second time in a Sydney Test match. The expected *contre temps* occurred whilst Moses batted. As they took a sharp single his leg gave way and he had to limp agonisingly on without a runner, with the crowd airing its disapproval, until W.G. caught him for 29.

Australia totalled 144 (*Wisden* mistakenly recorded 145) and that evening the English team made 38 without loss.

Nor was Abel to be shifted. Before an enormous crowd, he batted most of the day for 132 not out of England's 307. Stoddart made 27 in good style, including a massive 5 hit into the reserve off Turner.

Abel, batting beautifully but without risk, had worthwhile support from the tail, and with arrears of 163 Blackham sent in Bannerman and Harry Trott.

It was soon one for one; but Bannerman's dourness and Lyons' hurricane hitting put Australia's nose in front and set the scene for a real game of cricket. They put on 174 of which Lyons pounded 134 in under three hours! The tempo dropped as Giffen and Bannerman built a further 79 to the total before Giffen was trapped by Attewell.

Bannerman's marathon was accepted appreciatively, and even provoked sympathy and good humour. One onlooker cried: "Look out, Alec! W.G.'ll have his hand in your pocket!", so near was England's captain at point. Alec smiled faintly, the gesture itself rendering the match historic.

Another likened the scene to the painting "Anguish", with the crows swarming round a dead lamb while the mother ewe watches in grief. There was the impeccable slips-fielder Lohmann, W.G. close at point, Peel at silly mid-off, Stoddart short mid-off, and Briggs silly mid-on.

The crowd screamed with delight when Bannerman surfaced for an instant to crack a four past W.G.'s ear.

By Monday evening Australia were 263 for three—100 on.

News came through of the death of Bob McLeod's brother, Norman, and the team wore black crêpe as a mark of respect. Bob, greeted in understanding silence, did his duty with 18 runs, then set off for Melbourne on the night express, leaving poor Blackham to ask for a second substitute.

The weather was unsettled on this fourth day, and heavy rain fell. Bruce, with 72, was in fine fettle, and Bannerman, facing Briggs' tantalising slows, was at last caught by W.G. nine short of his hundred, after an occupation of 448 minutes, with three lonely boundary hits and 199 of Attewell's 204 balls to him unproductive. It was like the removal of a sliver of meat from between England's teeth.

An event of some note at the end of the innings drew practically no comment in contemporary reports: Johnny Briggs did the hat-trick! Moses, undergoing a course of electric baths, was unable to bat, and Briggs was thus denied the chance of taking four in four, which might have made the headlines.

Australia had amassed 391, leaving England 229 to win on a wicket that gave decided encouragement to the bowlers. W.G. now made a decision which, like Hutton's at Brisbane and Dexter's at Leeds, glimmers sinisterly from the annals, seeming so wrong in retrospect. Expecting the pitch to worsen, he kept the normal batting order; but to deafening cheers three important wickets toppled that evening for 11 runs before more rain sent the players off.

On Wednesday the wicket rolled out well, and Stoddart and Maurice Read played the bowling comfortably enough. Stoddart swept and cut several boundaries and hit Turner for another 5; the crowd squeezed its way forward in the sunshine, relishing the balance of the match.

Stoddart's strokes were greeted generously, but at 64 he lost Read to the ever-present Giffen. Very soon Peel was stumped, and when Stoddart, trying to pull a ball from the haunting Turner, finally had his stumps spreadeagled after a valiant 69, all hope was lost.

The tireless Giffen took care of the rest: he caught-and-bowled MacGregor and Attewell, and Australia had won the rubber. There was tumultuous gaiety at the end, for Australia's *cricket* troubles were now unquestionably over.

During the seven weeks between Test matches Stoddart had no cricketing to write home about, apart from a couple of characteristic innings in cool

Tasmania, where he passed his 29th birthday.

His contribution against N.S.W. was trifling: not for the first time he was bowled attempting to flay a long-hop which kept low. The game brought further uproar when Charlton was given "not out" to an apparent catch by MacGregor. W.G. said something to umpire Briscoe, who left the field, and Charlie Bannerman had to take his place—Bannerman, scorer of the first Test century, and brother of the "dead lamb" at Sydney.

And so they travelled across to Adelaide for the third and final Test. Drewy Stoddart's hour had come.

The wicket was plumb, and W.G., in persuading Blackham to call, and wrongly at that, won the match and forgot his anger at hearing that the pitch had been covered the day before. A half-holiday had been declared, and 10,000 of Adelaide's 120,000 people were there to see the caricaturist's dream—W.G. Grace and Robert Abel opening for England.

Abel shortly misjudged a high, tempting ball from dreamy-eyed Trott and Blackham did the rest. 47 for one.

Stoddart began streakily: Blackham missed a difficult chance when he had made one. But at lunch the score stood securely at 65—W.G. 32, Stoddart 9.

It was a testing time for Stoddart upon resumption, with Trott's parabolic slow spin at one end and Turner pounding away from the other. But now "Stoddy" met his notorious adversary on level terms. The pitch was innocent, and the English batsmen soon hit Trott and Turner from the firing line. Stoddart gathered two fours off Giffen's first over and W.G. did the same next over to raise 100. The runs were coming fast and W.G. was looking extremely dangerous when McLeod yorked him.

Maurice Read, pride of Thames Ditton village, began shakily, but Stoddart was now in full flight, hitting grandly to leg; and Read, encouraged by the general outlook, square-cut McLeod prettily.

At 138 Trott was brought back, and Stoddart got into a mess with one ball, moving out when back-play (to the eye of the observer in the cool sanctity of the shade) would have dealt with it comfortably enough.

Runs came easily. Then soon after a short tea interval Read was caught for 57. 218 for three, and Bean found things beyond him at first, although Stoddart continued to pile on the runs. The sweetest blows of all were a drive off Turner clean into the Members' Reserve (caught by Lohmann close to the State Governor), and a similar space blast off Giffen. These two 5 s were followed by two glorious square-leg hits off Giffen, and Andrew Stoddart had his first Test century. The ovation was loud and spontaneous, and as his score continued to mount it was suggested to W.G. that his own record 170 might be in danger, a thought which seemed to appeal to the Old Man.

FOOTNOTES: *1. Blackham's miss was both catch and stumping off a ball from Turner which the 'keeper thought had bowled Stoddart.*
2. Stoddart moved from 84 to 94 in two hits off three balls in successive overs.

Bean left, and Peel stayed with Stoddart to the close, when England boasted 272 for four, Stoddart 130 not out, the Australians missing their chance towards the end when Trott missed him. A substantial score now seemed certain.

But any hopes of a long continuation were quickly dashed. After adding 4 and fretting at Giffen's slows Stoddart skipped down the track and was hit on the leg. Up went the umpire's forefinger, and his graceful 230 minutes tenancy was ended. There had been 15 fours and 2 fives, and if ever in middle-age he sat and relived old battles, this careful but attractive knock must have been sharply in focus.

Peel played his highest Test innings, 83, and when Philipson fell it seemed all over—425 for nine. MacGregor and Attewell, however, would not be moved, and the score crept to 490, when a heavy downpour put an end to Friday's play.

Next day MacGregor, rather like Hanif Mohammad, was run out going for a 500th run, and Australia, so cruelly slapped by the elements, started the steep uphill climb against the legendary pair, Briggs and Lohmann.

They bowled unchanged on that wet wicket and Australia fell apart for exactly 100, with tempers not improving as W.G. insisted on quarter-hourly inspections of the wicket during the rainy interruptions.

The Australians followed on, and apart from a good stand by Giffen and Bruce they had no answer to Briggs and, this time, Attewell, on the muddy strip, a feature of this last innings being Stoddart's stretching right-hand catch 100 yards from the bat to dismiss the thunderous Lyons.

Briggs' deadly efforts carried him to his 50th Test wicket, with many more to come, but Australia had now seen the last of Dr W. G. Grace.

The man about to take the helm for these Australian expeditions was A. E. Stoddart.

CHAPTER 9

A WELSH THRILLER

1892 was a dry summer filled with sun, and Surrey carried off its sixth consecutive Championship. Shrewsbury headed the all-England averages, and Stoddart made more runs than anyone else apart from H. T. Hewett, whose 1407 pipped him by four.

Stoddart had now asserted his position among the aristocracy of English batsmen—no longer simply in style but in dependability. For the remainder of his career as a regular player not once was his season's average less than 30, and twice it was over 40: against the background of the times, proof enough of his high achievement.

His legions of admirers could not have failed to appreciate the steeling process which had taken place: it gave them more of him, even if the risks were eschewed.

His caricature ("A Big Hitter") by "Stuff" (magistrate Harold Wright) appeared this year in *Vanity Fair,* a certain pointer to national pre-eminence.

The day after "Valetta" berthed he was taking the English air on the Wormwood Scrubs ground, scoring 132 runs and finding his land-legs with almost rude impatience.

The Nottingham crowd were soon seeing Lord Sheffield's side in a match played for Alfred Shaw's benefit: the touring team were sent back for 89, Stoddart 0.

Showers played an irritating accompaniment to the game, Shaw probably more than anyone wishing for a prolonged sample of that Adelaide weather.

The team were photographed at Trent Bridge, and Stoddart faced the camera and posterity with stony solemnity. The thoughts of most of them might have been many miles away.

The dubious practice of playing benefit matches in May continued at Lord's, where a Married v Single match took place. "Stoddy", still unattached, did his best for Robert Clayton with innings of 42 and 53 against strong bowling, and George Lohmann, every woman's dream, made sure of the match for the bachelors with 12 wickets and a fine 58.

Now for M.C.C. against Kent Stoddart made a brilliant 52 on a damp wicket, with the exciting O'Brien smashing 47.

Stoddart and Webbe opened the Middlesex season against Sussex, but 38-year-old Stanley Scott led them to a substantial first innings lead. This was

Scott's season—top of the Middlesex averages—a careful, unathletic batsman who at times could hit with the best. He made the cricket world sit up with an innings of 224 against Gloucestershire, when Middlesex lengthened a winning streak that put them in the right frame of mind for the derby over the river at the Oval.

Here they suffered a setback against Lockwood and Lohmann, who dispensed with them abruptly for 75 as a wintry wind swept under the awnings. Abel led Surrey to a sizable first innings lead, and it was against these odds that Stoddart gave what *Wisden* considered "one of the finest displays of batting seen in London during the season".

His 91 helped set Surrey 172, never in doubt as Walter Read and Abel, the darlings of South London, hit 117 for the first wicket.

The game with Yorkshire was a wonderful contest. Stoddart and Webbe put on 79 at the start, but Yorkshire, inspired by Ulyett, finally managed a 4-wicket victory, though things might have been different had a catch off Stoddart's bowling been held.

Notts were the next visitors to Lord's—for a famous match. Shrewsbury made 212, and the Notts innings lasted nine hours. On an immaculate wicket it was going to need some exceptional bowling or irresponsible batting to see Middlesex out twice in the remaining time.

But Shacklock, Attewell and Barnes broke through the first time and Middlesex soon had lost four men in the second innings. With over three hours remaining and runs of no consideration Notts seemed to have the game sewn up. As Stoddart and O'Brien tried to mount a counter-attack, "An Old Cricketer" (E. V. Lucas) was walking along St. John's Wood Road in the warm afternoon air:

"Mr T. C. O'Brien—as he was then, he became Sir Timothy later—was bringing off some of his own special late cuts and Mr Stoddart was putting the thick of his bat behind the straight ones and driving them to long-on and long-off as only he could do. His back play could be wonderful! I remember one ball he had to play back to, hitting the Pavilion railings and rebounding forty yards. There's strength for you!"

They put on 97, then Webbe dug in and a draw seemed even more certain as he and Stoddart put on 95 more. Stoddart reached 100 (only two were registered for Middlesex all season) and with only half an hour remaining and 5 wickets to fall, Robinson took the gloves and gave the well-rounded Sherwin a bowl.

It worked: Webbe, so safe, so dependable, was clean bowled. It was, he said as he removed his pads, like being run over by a donkey cart. His downfall had been greeted in stunned silence apart from "a few stray Nottingham yells". Rawlin came in and next over Stoddart was given out leg-before to Attewell for 130, spreading alarm into the home dressing-room.

"You could see in the hush every hand going to the waistcoat pocket. Those were the days before wars and wristwatches, you must remember."

Ten minutes remained and 3 wickets separated Notts from unlikely victory. Thesiger took Stoddart's place, made a single, then faced Mordecai Sherwin, the "donkey cart". Two runs, then he also was bowled by an innocent-looking ball.

Attewell struck a vital blow by bowling Rawlin several minutes later, and with R. S. Lucas looking on helplessly, Jack Hearne was caught off a slash. Notts had won by an innings and 14 runs a mere four minutes from time.

"An Old Cricketer's" thoughts lingered nostalgically: "But when I think of that great match it is not only Mr Webbe's joke that I remember, but the tragic end of the two greatest batsmen: Mr Stoddart and Arthur Shrewsbury. It's odd how cricketers are often not very happy men. I suppose it's got something to do with the disappointments of the game—its glorious uncertainty, as they call it. Uncertainty can be very depressing as well as glorious, and it makes men moody."

For M.C.C. Stoddart made a very powerful 52 and 60 against Oxford University, caught each time by Douglas Jardine's father. One leg-side full-toss ended up in the scorer's box and another was lofted into the outside world. Young C. B. Fry, who started a hat-trick in this match with Stoddart's wicket, several years later vividly described his style: "All Stoddart's hitting is distinguished by a most fascinating elasticity of action; indeed, this quality is what makes his style when at his best so charming."

He thought the drives the choicest of his wares. Sometimes, he said, they were firm-footed, other times he ran to the ball. The right shoulder never dropped, and the left elbow was always well up. When he drove in the air it was never in ballooning fashion, but on a low skimming course.

"He has," wrote Fry, "a hook-stroke that is the despair of all imitators." The cut was grandly played—as good as anyone's—yet often even in a long innings he had seen him refrain from using it at all. To off-break bowling, probably in the manner of Graveney, he used to turn the ball away towards forward short-leg with the turn.

"He makes everything he does look nice, and yet no one was ever freer from any attempt at effect."

The Gents v Players match at Lord's had been shaping into an interesting fight for first innings honours as W.G. and Stoddart made a bright 88 before rain, but Stoddart was bowled first ball next morning by Wainwright for 49, and in the follow-in Attewell trimmed his bails off with a devilish ball.

FOOTNOTE: *In the appendix to* With Bat and Ball *George Giffen refers to Stoddart's "gracefully easy" stance, his "jump or bound" to drive, and splendid forward cut.*

At the Oval, where W.G.'s absence through injury deprived the Gentlemen of their powerful figurehead, Stoddart opened with the elegant Lionel Palairet and posted good totals for the first wicket each time by enchanting stroke-play. Lockwood was unnervingly lively and had Stoddart ducking to avoid trouble. He and Scott had words with the bowler as the ball continually reared back into their faces. Stoddart fell to him both times.

Later that season Palairet was party to sensation by posting 346 with Hewett for Somerset's first wicket against Yorkshire. It sparked off a spate of marathon openings, and before the 19th century was out the record had been passed by Abel and Brockwell, Shrewsbury and Jones, and then, after a dress rehearsal of 378 in 1897, Brown and Tunnicliffe dwarfed them all with 554 at Chesterfield in 1898.

These records were symptomatic of the changes sweeping across the game as pitches enjoyed better preparation and competition intensified. The Universities were now scattering their riches among the counties: carefree young men who injected splashes of glamour into cricket's tapestry.

The men who alternately provided their fodder or cut them down were the army of ripe characters who bowled a cricket ball for a living. Stoddart's next game, against Lancashire at Old Trafford, was played out by four of the best of them: J. T. Hearne and J. T. Rawlin, who took 18 wickets between them; and Mold and Briggs, who achieved the same, all serving up satisfactory production figures to their respective employers, and finding the wicket a handy selling aid.

During this match MacGregor, playing his first game for Middlesex, suggested to Stoddart that a catch at the wicket might result if the bowlers pounded them down short outside the off-stump, but Johnny Briggs' blazing cuts caused O'Brien to remonstrate with skipper Stoddart, who abandoned the tactics. Briggs slashed his way to 98 and helped set Middlesex a stiff target. In the end the last Middlesex pair held out for a nail-biting draw.

The Yorkshire match was another bowlers' feast on a soft wicket, though Stoddart kept Peel at bay and made 46, the chroniclers yet again looking for suitable classification and coming up only with the repetitious "brilliant". Yorkshire subsided for 46 in their second innings.

He came back to London and took part in a spectacular sequence of club matches for Hampstead, making centuries against Crystal Palace and Hendon, and leading the club on tour, making centuries off Bournemouth and Hampshire Hogs. He made 500 runs at an average of 100.00 during this club cricket sojourn, and during the periods on tour when his open-ribbed pads were off, this Club Colossus grabbed 31 wickets in the three games, including a hat-trick against Bournemouth, who were 0 for five wickets at one amusing stage.

Low-scoring August was all Hearne and Rawlin, and Middlesex in seven matches managed wins over Lancashire and Sussex only. Stoddart's best innings of the month was an 88 off Kent, and later there was a 41 against

FOOTNOTE: *A.O. Jones, of Notts, was compared in Australia, when he toured in 1901-02, with the Stoddart of 1888, who "used to jump in and smack the ball in brilliant style".*

W.G. and his yeomen, pursued by a fast 43 pulled and swept off the short bowling of Sussex at Brighton.

And so the county programme was complete, with Middlesex disappointingly in fifth place; and the festival matches were enacted like a wake over yet another dead cricket season. At Scarborough Stoddart dealt Lohmann one monumental blow and had an enjoyable partnership with W. L. Murdoch against the county champions, Surrey, before rain again drifted across.

For South v North he made 32 runs in even time off Spofforth, Attewell, Wainwright and Peel on a bad wicket, and the Saturday was devoted to a match played with broomsticks.

Then, against the Players, the Gents curiously had only one regular bowler in their ranks, the doughty Sammy Woods, who worked a small miracle in the first innings, taking 8-46 and sending the professionals out for 109. One man was run out and the other wicket went to Stoddart, who drank Woods' health over dinner that night, remarking "Well bowled, we two!"

In the follow-on the inevitable happened: Abel and Lohmann got runs, Peel, Attewell and Bean lent support, and poor S. M. J. Woods wheeled down 65 overs to take 3-201. W.G. strained his knee and the only other bowler in sight was one, A. E. Stoddart, who duly carried 40 overs to the enemy and took 1-96. The Gents salvaged a draw in the end, and Stoddart, after what was probably a tired stroke of Lohmann, packed his sweat-soaked gear and prepared for football.

He had captained Blackheath for two seasons and missed the last owing to the tour of Australia. Now W. P. "Tottie" Carpmael led the Club, and Stoddart sat by his side in the team photograph, moustache luxuriant as ever, eyes fixed distantly beyond the camera. This was the year of his final appearance for England on the rugby field; it was also the season when "A Country Vicar" first saw him play:

"He was drawing near the end of his football career, and wore the badges of long service and many injuries—elastic knee-caps on both knees, anklets on both ankles, and a rubber bandage on one elbow! But he played beautifully—tackled, passed, kicked, and ran in the grand manner of the finished master. We undergraduates had gathered in force on the Corpus ground, where the University matches were then played, and we had all gone with the idea of 'seeing Stoddart'. He showed us a perfect performance by a wing-threequarter—how and when to part with the ball, and what to do when he kept it. I still see two runs of his—one, from half-way, when he was pushed into touch just the right side (from our point of view) of the Cambridge goal-line—one, of about thirty yards, when he flashed down the field and scored in the extreme corner. That game was played in a tornado of cheers, but it was

Stoddart's try that brought the longest and loudest applause—Stoddart himself, limping a little, who received the great ovation at the end."

He played for Barbarians against Cardiff on Boxing Day, but throughout the first week of 1893 Britain suffered blizzards, and it was only late on the Friday afternoon, January 6th, that the English team decided to leave for Cardiff for the International. They arrived in a raging snowstorm and went straight to he shelter of the hotel.

In polar conditions they went down to the Arms Park after dining and beheld one of the strangest sights conceivable on a sporting surface: numerous braziers full of hot coals glowed across the frozen expanse of the ground, with children darting gleefully about like junior citizens of Hell.

The Englishmen returned to their rooms holding out meagre expectations of play. There was no relief the next morning; it was still extremely cold. But the braziers had done their work, and the ground was declared playable.

The players changed at the hotel and walked to the ground through hordes of admiring boys, each trying to place a cold hand on the great men for a fleeting moment of magic.

England were fielding three threequarters and nine forwards, Wales, with eight Newport players, four threequarters and eight in the pack.

Stoddart and Gould tossed, and the English captain chose to have the wind advantage; and his back-line soon started a movement which ended with Lohden, his club-mate, falling on the ball for a try within minutes of his International debut.

Woods missed the conversion, but England kept up the pressure: Stoddart missed an easy penalty which may not have seemed important when Marshall soon followed through a forward rush and touched down for England's second try, Lockwood converting. But the additional points would have been invaluable later on.

At the interval England were comfortably placed after superb work by its great pack, Woods, "the father of modern wing-forwards", so formidable among them. His tackling was crushingly effective, and he was famous for quick breaking and relentless dribbling—as fast bowler or rugby opponent, an awesome competitor.

The Welsh backs had been starved of the ball, but now with the wind helping, they and their forwards stormed into the English half and pressed hard until Field gathered a high punt near his own line and raced out through the Welshmen. He was brought down after a stupendous run, and Marshall scooped up the ball to plant another try for England, unconverted.

Now Wales came back. The 17,000 welcomed the chance to clap their numb hands together as Gould raced over for Wales' first try and Bancroft kicked a wonderful conversion.

Wales took heart. The back-line responded, and Phillips and Biggs set up another try for Gould which Bancroft only narrowly missed converting.

Soon one of the English forwards got the ball away to Stoddart who made ground and fed Marshall. Playing his only International, Marshall slid over for his third try. Woods missed with the kick.

This seemed to seal the match for England; but a sudden move down the flank let in Gould for *his* third try. Bancroft from the touchline was unsuccessful.

The game moved on towards its hysterical finish, when confusion after the final whistle was so great that the result of the match was not known for some time. It began when England conceded a penalty and young Bancroft, not knowing the score, was called up by Gould to take the kick. As no firm instruction seemed forthcoming and as the crowd yelled for some action, Bancroft picked up the ball, took three strides, and drop-kicked.

"It's there, Arthur!" he called to his captain as the ball sailed through the uprights.

The difficulty was that only two days previously the system of points-scoring had been rearranged by the International Board. A try was now worth 2 points, not 3; a conversion was worth 3, not 2; and a penalty was 3 as before. There must have been widespread arithmetical distraction as the final furious minutes were played out in the biting wind.

Wales held on and, indeed, went on to win their first Triple Crown. The English boys, if the match had been played a week earlier, would have earned a draw, and without the blizzard's chorus.

A month later Rowland Hill was informed that A. E. Stoddart would be unable to play for England in Dublin; but a further month saw the England team assembled at Headingley to tackle Scotland.

In fine weather and before a crowd of 20,000 Stoddart led out the national team for the last time. For him it was to be a disastrous event.

Boswell won the toss and took the wind on Scotland's back. Among Stoddart's opposing threequarters was his dark-haired friend, Gregor MacGregor, and it was he who relieved the initial pressure on the Scottish line with a good run that put Scotland on the attack.

The English players, without Woods up front, tried desperately to push the Scots upfield. Scotland's scrimmaging was strong, however, with McMillan and Boswell outstanding; and it was the unlikely defence of England's halves, Duckett and C. M. Wells, that kept them at bay, tackling heroically and making short runs to relieve the danger.

England made progress. Dyson claimed a lot of territory with a penalty, Simpson returned the ball, then Mitchell sent a penetrative kick into Scotland's half. Wells had the ball and ran for the line; he passed to Stoddart, who had a fairly clear run, but he dropped the ball. And the Scottish forwards seized the opportunity to surge forward. In seconds England were defending desperately.

Play was balanced for a time, then Scotland rushed, and rushed ferociously. Stoddart again failed at a critical moment and Boswell had the ball just within kicking range. He dropped a lovely goal, the ball bouncing over off the crossbar.

The same pattern fell over the second half as the Scottish forwards marauded and harassed. Before long Campbell was gathering a loose ball and dropping another goal.

The monotonous tidal attacks continued, with England's forwards being outgunned and the backs playing themselves into the ground. Only a penalty by Stoddart gave breathing room, though not for long.

A Boswell penalty sparked off another sharp attack, and as the curtain was about to fall Stoddart, filled with remorse, made several long drop-kicks which caused Scotland to fall back.

Two dropped goals (8 points) to nil gave little idea of the disparity between the sides, and with Scottish reports justifiably rapturous, one English journal summed up by saying that "generally the English game was disappointing, and the threequarters were weak".

Looking back many years later Sammy Woods remarked with cryptic brevity that Stoddart was "alas, a little too gentle when playing against Scotland". Was it fear of injury to his bosom pal, Gregor MacGregor?

Thus exit A. E. Stoddart, one week away from his 30th birthday, greatest of threequarter backs, most agile and finished rugby footballer of his generation.

Within days word came through that "Orizaba", carrying the Australian cricket team to England, had sailed from Melbourne. This kind of report— every touring year—sends a thrill of anticipation through cricketers everywhere.

CHAPTER 10

ENGLAND CAPTAIN AT LORD'S

Wisden for 1893 honoured him with inclusion in its Five Batsmen of the Year. Concise words of praise were now indelibly inscribed in the gospel: "He continually gets runs under conditions that find most batsmen at fault, his play both on slow and fiery wickets being quite exceptional".

The panegyric ground to a brutal halt with passing comment on his football career, lamenting that "he is now rather past his best"; but for lovers of the summer game "Stoddy" was in vogue.

It was again generally warm and sunny this year, and after the customary early practice at Mitcham the Australians went to salubrious Sheffield Park for the opening match of their tour, which they lost by 8 wickets. One scribe, looking for signs of sophistication in this eighth Australian touring team, wrote cheerlessly that the visitors had, as before, failed to please the critics with their batting style, although he granted that they amply demonstrated its effectiveness. The erratic performances of some of the Australians this season was put down to the periodical bulletins from Melbourne, where the land boom, in which many of them had speculated quite heavily, was collapsing.

Stoddart was welcomed at the Hampstead ground, and initiated a dazzling club season with 75. In his seven matches for the club he was to average 111, with a century and a double-century and not a defeat. MacGregor joined Hampstead this year and shared comfortable bachelor accommodation with Stoddart at 30 Lithos Road, on the breezy slopes of South Hampstead, where from the rear window they could see across to the ground down in Lymington Road.

Stoddart stroked his way to 62 in less than an hour for M.C.C. against Sussex. Then when M.C.C. played the Australians, W.G. posted 41 with him for the opening stand. The pitch was at its worst during this early period, and again a promising start had been made before Stoddart was caught for a determined 58.

M.C.C. ran up 424 and soon had the Australians following on. Jack Lyons now played a phenomenal innings—persistently battering the bowling into the crowd and onto the awnings of the covered enclosures. His staggering hitting had the crowd and fielders silent with awe. Only the clang of the ball's landing disturbed the spell. He thrashed J. T. Hearne for four gigantic blows in an over, and shouldered his way greedily into Attewell's and Nepean's servings.

His century came in 55 minutes, with the score 125 without loss; and the pace sagged momentarily as the giant seemed to step back and savour his destruction. ("When I taps 'em they hit the fence!") Then it was on again,

FOOTNOTE: *For M.C.C. against Sussex Stoddart bowled leg-breaks to Fred Tate, who "hit at them with immense energy" but could not connect.*

and the figures on the scoreboard (Bannerman's excepted) were no sooner up than they were making way for higher numerals.

He steamrollered his way to 149, when the arrears were exactly accounted for, then with fine dramatic sense he was instantly caught in the deep.

M.C.C. eventually needed 167 to win. W.G. and Stoddart settled down, and there were hopes that Stoddart might do something similar to Lyons. He hit one ball over the stand near the new scoring-box at square-leg, and 72 was quickly posted before rain began to fall again.

Upon resumption both men were caught, and a collapse had to be checked. Though drawn, it was another of those matches which, if ever played over again in the fields of asphodel, simply *must* be televised, regardless of cost.

Stoddart was in spanking form in the Whitsun match against Somerset, and Surrey were beaten comfortably at the Oval, always a worthy feat. Middlesex seemed fairly placed against Gloucestershire, too, until Stoddart was hit by Roberts in the last innings. Unsettled, he was caught straight away by W.G., and the side crumbled to defeat. His first innings of 74 had tingled with all the well-known artistry.

On the first of June, Hirst got a swinger through him for 2, but a second effort of 88 plus a solid Scott innings left Yorkshire a few to get after all; they scraped home, and ultimately took the title this season.

Middlesex next met Notts, and Stoddart accomplished the very rare distinction of a century in each innings, a deifying performance in Victorian times. Not since William Lambert in 1817 had a batsman made two centuries in a game at Lord's.

The match began with a stand of 50 in only 20 minutes with Webbe, but no more support came until F. G. J. Ford batted, followed by MacGregor's useful 31.

All the while Stoddart was taking the experienced Notts attack and placing it expertly through the field. Last man Jack Hearne came in, hoping desperately to see him to his double-century, but Dixon bowled him, and Stoddart had carried his bat for 195.

Billy Gunn, tall and commanding as any military leader, led the reply with 120, and Middlesex had to make another big score to escape defeat. At the end of the second day they were 184 for two wickets, Stoddart 94 not out, a careful innings so far, no loose ball wasted.

Now, with overnight rain having sprinkled the wicket, the crowd came early to make sure of seeing the hero of St John's Wood get his second century.

It soon came—to storms of cheering and waving of boaters, though it is not recorded whether anyone ran out to kiss him or hoist him aloft. There was widespread conjecture as to his limits this day, with 300 runs under his belt already off this highly professional bowling, and all day to bat. His manner was increasingly radiant with confidence, but finally, at 124, Mee, who had done most of the work with Attewell, forced a catch.

FOOTNOTE: *Stoddart later secured the two balls, off which he had made his twin centuries, with the object of getting them mounted as mementoes. His second hundred came with a cut for three off Mee after 2½ hours' batting. A boy ran out to him with a telegram, probably of congratulations, but he stuffed it into his pocket unread.*

Notts wickets fell all afternoon, and Middlesex clinched a 57-run win 10 minutes from the end. For a long time afterwards Stoddart's performance was a talking point of great delight. "Verily," said *The Cricket Field,* "we are lucky who are living to see such things."

The Australians faced MCC again, and this time Lyons made a competent 83 which would have been exceptional from the bat of any other man. He had to face Kortright's lightning, and as with Tyson 60 years later, the practically invisible onslaught cast a paleness across Australian faces.

Stoddart, the man of the hour, played on to Turner early, but late on the second day, reminded the tourists of his powers. Needing 175 to win, he ran up the majority of 83 with W.G. in only 45 minutes, taking the stand to 120 next morning. "Stoddy" eventually played on for 74. The 7-wicket victory was a promising augury for the first Test match.

The Cricket Field paid him a prim compliment at this time: "His is the best sort of cricket to watch. All he does is done without effort; he rarely seems to have a difficult ball to play, because he plays it so easily; he is a comfortable bat to watch".

E. V. Lucas, recalling the way Stoddart often moved down the pitch to a bowler, branded him as the immortal Billy Beldham's worthiest disciple.

On a sub-standard wicket he now made 95 in Brighton's salty air, MacGregor attracting attention with his splendid 'keeping as Hearne and Rawlin bundled Sussex out. At Gravesend, he made a fine half-century on a bumpy wicket. Then it was back to Lord's to meet Surrey.

He took the bowling honours with 3-45, and topped a disastrous first innings with 31, falling to the strapping new fast bowler, Tom Richardson. Soon Stoddart and O'Brien were walking out through the gateway, a pair to make the pulse throb even when their side was trailing by 179 runs.

In 140 minutes Stoddart hit 125 runs and the pair lashed 228 in partnership. O'Brien's 113 contained some rumbustious strokes, including some controversial drives past the wicketkeeper (sic) off Walter Read's teasing legside lobs. When the dust had settled after one of these absurdities a bail was on the ground, and a sharp discussion ensued between the principal parties, As neither umpire had seen things clearly O'Brien settled the issue with characteristic decision: "Anyhow, I'm not going out!" And the game went on.

The faithful Hearne and Rawlin saw to it that Surrey fell well short of the required 199, and at the end the crowd swarmed round the pavilion calling for the Middlesex cricketers.

FOOTNOTE: *Against Surrey Stoddart caused amusement by running in to bowl, then stopping for something in his eye. At the end of the match the crowd rushed the Lord's pavilion and shouted his name for five minutes before a man in a tall hat ran inside: "Soon afterwards the hero of the great match appeared at the entrance-door, cap in hand, while his admirers shouted themselves into a perfect frenzy of delight." Stoddart acknowledged with "a profound bow"*

There was no stopping Stoddart now. Against the Australians he hit a magnificent 94 on a perfect Trent Bridge wicket that spoiled after overnight rain and cheated the visitors into an innings defeat. Again he had posted a century for the first wicket with W.G.—114 this time for Arthur Shrewsbury's deserving benefit.

Then came a sojourn into club cricket. Spofforth, now with Hampstead, arrived late for the Uxbridge match, so Stoddart and George Thornton bowled Uxbridge out cheaply. "The Demon" then amazed everyone with an innings of 155 that put Stoddart's 68 in the shade.

Soon Spofforth hit the headlines against Marlow by taking 10-20 and 7-20. There is a suspicion that some of these wickets were surrendered to his reputation, even though this fire-breathing monster was already mellowing into the well-liked gentleman who, in his sixties and seventies, was exhibiting chrysanthemums in Surbiton.

Stoddart made one further score of note before the first Test—a 68 against Sussex—and failed to make his mark in yet another Gents and Players encounter, running himself out for 13 and falling for 11 on the final day of thunderstorms.

The cricket world was shocked at the news, a week before the Test, of Bill Scotton's suicide. This sensitive, heavy-lidded man, dourest of left-handers, had lodgings in St John's Wood Terrace, and after umpiring at Clifton College he returned to London depressed, and stayed in bed all day, rambling, incoherent.

At the inquest one of his friends said that Scotton, who was a sly tippler, would weep at the slightest provocation. It was his belief that the famous stonewaller had cut his throat because Notts had not engaged him that season.

Scotton had been photographed only days before, and approved of the portrait sufficiently to order copies for friends and relatives. Now those friends and relatives were invited to view his body instead when the coffin was unlidded on the railway station at Nottingham.

So the legendary Scotton was laid to rest as rain fell in torrents, and now two other tragic figures walked to the wicket at Lord's to open for England: Stoddart, the lad from South Shields, playing his first home Test and captaining England (W.G. was out with a broken finger) for the first time, emulating "Monkey" Hornby's achievement of leading England at both cricket and rugby; and Shrewsbury, the batsman W.G. placed highest of all others, now about to compile his third and final Test century against Australia.

A hot sun smiled derisively on the damp pitch, posing Stoddart a dilemma when he won the toss. He had to take first innings: if the first unpredictable overs could be piloted through England could perhaps make a tall score.

15,000 people were there as Turner ran in with the bell-toppers and frock-coats darkening the pavilion behind him. He hurled the first ball down, and hearts leapt when the second delivery flew to slip as Shrewsbury aimed to

FOOTNOTE: *Stoddart was run out while batting for the Gentlemen when he hit a ball straight to Briggs at cover and bolted; W.G. at the other end did not leave his crease.*

turn to leg. By the last ball of the over Stoddart was facing the most formidable of his personal cricket enemies. He played him square for three.

Soon he made a stirring off-drive that panicked the crowd at the Nursery end. He hit Bruce again next over—a thumping blow that once more gave a handful of spectators at square-leg the chance of inspecting the bright red ball. His score spun round to 20 out of 21 in twelve minutes, but trouble overtook England in Turner's next over. Stoddart took an agonising crack on the elbow which hurt him beyond concealment. The joint stiffened up, obstructing his freedom of movement when play resumed: he was almost caught at point from a desperate parry, and minutes later played forward to Turner and failed to cover a sharp cutter that hit the off-stump.

First blood at 29; Stoddart 24.

Gunn made only two, then F. S. Jackson walked out for his first Test innings. Shrewsbury existed without causing the Australians much concern, though they must have yearned for the sight of his sloping shoulders receding into the pavilion. He reached double figures after an hour's grafting.

Jackson, meanwhile, was delighting the crowd with leg shots and drives. Shrewsbury stirred himself occasionally, but the style and approach of Jackson proclaimed him a species apart.

Harry Trott for once failed to drop a length and Jackson punished him with three fours to leg; so Blackham hurriedly withdrew him.

It was tense and engrossing cricket as the Englishmen took the score to 168 before Jackson was caught nine short of his hundred. The pitch had settled down apart from certain antics at the Nursery end, and it was now up to the middle order to consolidate.

Maurice Read failed, however, and as Peel tried to push things along the crowd became restive. It may have gained Australia a wicket, for Peel let fly at Trumble and skied to Bruce. Five were out for 213.

When Shrewsbury fell at last to Turner for 106 he had been in over four hours, with late cuts and leg placements mixed with great care that endeared him to all patriots.

The innings ended at 334 and Australia had an awkward session to see out, Lockwood taking Lyons' leg-stump and Giffen suffering a similar fate without scoring. Two down for 7, little Bannerman Sphinx-like at the other end.

No-one envied MacGregor as he tried standing up and was constantly driven back by the ferocity of Mold and Lockwood, and 13 extras helped make up Australia's 33 as Bannerman and Trott marched off at the end. Stoddart was well content with the situation.

Tuesday was bright, and the pitch appeared to have eased, yet Shrewsbury was soon dropping on his left elbow to catch Bannerman for 17, and Bob

McLeod was beaten by a sizzler from Lockwood.

At 75 the fifth wicket fell, and Lockwood had all five—almost six as he dropped a return catch from Graham which would have made a staggering difference to this Test match.

Stoddart had got all he could out of Lockwood, and the Surrey bowler made way for Mold after a stretch of almost two hours of potential devastation. Yet the last overs had been played with growing confidence by the youthful little Graham, in his first Test innings, and tiny Syd Gregory, still to show his true worth in the highest class.

Like so many subsequent captains of England, Drewy Stoddart had to face criticism from many angles: he had kept Lockwood on too long; Jackson should have had more to do; it was not so much determined batting as a slight case of mismanagement.

Perceptive romantics wondered what might have happened had Graham's catch been held, but it was past, and now the Australians took runs easily.

Sturdy Lockwood, the likely match-winner, was granted only half an hour of rest before taking up the attack at the Nursery end, and Shrewsbury, undoing so much of his good work, missed a high one at point off Graham, who was scoring much faster than Gregory.

The hundred stand came in little over an hour, and Gregory was finally out to an excellent high catch by MacGregor off Lockwood. At 217 for six, Australia were right back in the match.

"Grummy" Graham, boyish face flushed, reached 98, and the whole of Lord's tensed. He played uppishly to point and Shrewsbury put his right hand to the ball and dropped it. The century came, warmly applauded, and when MacGregor finally snared him off Mold his 107 had been made in only 140 minutes; Australia finished a mere 65 behind.

Stoddart shaped better in the second innings, and the early sensations centred around Shrewsbury, who, as Trott missed him at point, smiled innocently and took a couple of boundaries. From a Stoddart late-cut they ran four swift runs, but with 27 on the board Turner yet again broke through the England captain, this time for 13.

Gunn came in and the Nottingham men took it to 113 by the day's end—Shrewsbury 45, hitting Turner over the fieldsmen's heads and picking the gaps as fast as they were created. Gunn once more fell into step behind his business-like little mentor.

They wore the bowling down on the final day, and as the grey clouds came across, the run-rate began to accelerate. Shrewsbury was heading remorselessly towards his second century of the match when Gunn was caught near the ropes.

Jackson knew what was needed. He hoicked and was missed by Bruce, who compensated with a catch almost immediately. Read made only a single, and, after rain, Shrewsbury was bowled for 81. Lockwood went, and suddenly it was 198 for six.

Stoddart's thoughts were now on the weather and the clock as Wainwright, the bluff Yorkshireman, hit hard. Eight were down for 234 at lunch, leaving Australia exactly 300 to win. But not till 3.15 p.m., when the drizzle had ceased, did Stoddart declare the innings closed.

Blackham had the wicket rolled, but rain fell again, and the match was finally given up. The people, cheated miserably by the weather, drifted away from the dreary roped-off space.

At Old Trafford, O'Brien and Stoddart hit Briggs over the railings repeatedly before being stumped off him one after the other. Briggs, the laughter-maker with the tell-tale "grimace of Grimaldi", as Cardus saw it, gathered seven wickets with his ingenuous and persistent deliveries. Mold took twelve as Lancashire, so often the bridesmaid in the Championships of the 'nineties, chalked up a win over Middlesex.

Stoddart took the ball in this game, too, and did something with it: 4-23 and 2-23 helped render the trip worthwhile.

Then for Hampstead he thrashed Hampstead Nondescripts for 129 runs, and within days was hitting 40 boundaries in an innings of 210 which helped his side to a lead of 400 over Willesden!

The Middlesex men went to Taunton in August, and in the blazing sunshine there was a feast of run-getting. Stoddart was reported lame when Middlesex fielded (the football injury?), but he managed 34 before Woods had him in the slips. One memorable hit had been a drive into the river off Hedley. And it took an astonishing catch by Woods to end his second innings in the scorching heat at 25.

At Bristol, against the puzzling spin of Townsend, the precocious schoolboy, a typical 75 from Stoddart led Middlesex to 385. Then Gloucestershire crashed before Rawlin after misty rain and sun on the Saturday.

Thick attendances on the first two golden days of the second Test match at the Oval helped swell Maurice Read's benefit fund.

There was the usual rumble before the Test got under way. Wainwright was retained by Yorkshire for the Middlesex match though Stoddart and MacGregor played for their country. Fortunately for the Oval crowd Jackson represented England, but this thing was coming to a head. There was a feeling that the priorities (particularly Lord Hawke's) ought to be reviewed.

W.G. was fit again, and resumed his position on the mount, succeeding in his first obligation by winning the toss. A smile creased his face as he came down the steps, but Stoddart seemed tense with the responsibility of opening for

FOOTNOTE: *Stoddart's declaration at Lord's was the first ever in Test cricket.*

England.

Turner measured out his run from the pavilion end, but in truth the threat of intimidation seemed to stem from the batting, for the "Terror's" field was as respectful as that of a mere change bowler. Only two slips and a third man stood behind the bat; Trott crouched at point; then, challenging the driving power of Stoddart, whose right hand gripped the bat-handle so unusually low, was an array of off-side fielders.

It was not easy at the start. Turner caused frowns after W.G. had set things going with a lofty square-cut. Trumble, tall and commanding, had almost the same field setting, and for six stringent overs these bowlers tied down England's openers.

Stoddart was dropped at slip when 1, but in the same over he got his off-drive away; then he was missed by Trott off an easy chance. He was mistiming Turner embarrassingly, and W.G. himself was surprised by a kicker from Trumble which hit the top of his bat-handle.

Stoddart edged through slips—and then came the break from bonds that comes often to batsmen in the horrors: he saw a short ball early and swept it serenely to the chains. It heralded a string of thrilling strokes played without inhibition to all sections of the shirt-sleeved crowd. Forty came up fairly promptly after all, and W. G. pulled Turner masterfully for four. Stoddart drove McLeod beautifully through mid-off, reaching 30, and then was dropped again. His luck was almost unbelievable.

The crowd gasped as W.G. edged Giffen over slip to the boundary to raise 50, and now runs came thick and fast, especially from a fatalistic Stoddart, who reached his own 50 in 70 minutes.

W.G. slammed Harry Trott through the cover field, then galloped a swift single. The 100 partnership came as Stoddart lifted Trott over long-off for another four and hit him to leg for three—the century stand in 90 minutes.

Trumble bowled some maiden overs, but W.G. made a fine stroke to leg to register his own 50. Giffen ended a model spell of bowling which had continually brought W.G. tentatively forward and forced the less rangy Stoddart very often to drop down late on the ball. They went to lunch 134 for no wicket, the aggrieved Australians following thoughtfully.

The English pair were late coming out after the break, and stories circulated that W.G.'s finger had let him down, and that his partner had been stricken with sunstroke; but the rumours probably started in the Oval bars, for the batsmen came out in due course, and the battle was taken up.

There was a confident howl as W.G.'s pads were rapped, but Stoddart restored confidence with an on-drive for four quickly supported by a cut and a pull to the ropes. 150 was posted, and things became quiet. Then Stoddart was put down at short-leg and McLeod muffed an easy catch at second slip off Turner, and the crowd murmured. It was as if the proverbial cat had donned flannels.

Yet the fortunes had exhausted themselves, and Stoddart played the next ball from Turner into his stumps. The flukiest of all his innings, an innings he declared he was positively ashamed to go on with, was at an end. There had been 11 boundaries in his 83 made out of 151 (W.G. and he had now raised over 100 in each of their last three openings against the Australians) on a wicket which had interested the bowlers all the while. There had been frequent errors, but also some explosive hits, and although an artist considers first the quality of his work, this innings, his highest ever in a Test in England, had gone into the book with enough weight to ensure the likelihood of victory.

Now, at the other end, and without a run added, the Champion was caught by Giffen. Shrewsbury and Gunn were now together, and the game changed colour. Shrewsbury was in commanding, almost flamboyant, mood. The 200 came up, and Giffen returned to his domain, the bowling crease. With his second ball he bowled Gunn for a worthy 50th Test wicket.

When Albert Ward, in his first Test, snicked a four through slips, that o her serious man, Giffen, pretended to examine his bat for holes. Then Shrewsbury reached 50, and celebrated with 12 off an over of Trot's leg-breaks, and Ward cut cleanly and hit to leg. In the sunshine the runs mounted up.

A stand of 103 had been made before Shrewsbury was tempted to hit out once too often. Ward soon fell for 55, and Jackson strode in at number 7.

Calamitous fielding cost Australia heavily again as Gregory missed Jackson in the outfield, and by the end he and Read (W. W.) had added 67, England waxing fat at 378 for five.

In the high heat of the day Jackson drove Trumble's third ball to reach 50 in only 45 minutes, and the eager crowd saw Read let go at last with a characteristic pull-drive. The 400 was rolled onto the board, and English eyes were smiling.

The cricket sparkled until Read finally played back and was bowled, the stand worth 131. Someone moved behind the bowler's arm as Briggs faced Giffen. His off-stump was hit, and Lockwood prevented a hat-trick. But soon the eternal Giffen trapped him; and now MacGregor ran "Jacker's" quick singles and watched him drive with Olympian power.

At 98 Jackson lost his penultimate partner, and Mold, almost the world's worst batsman, played out the over with legs and bat. Then the ground settled to watch Jackson hoist his century. The ball ran to third man, and Mold came stampeding down the wicket. Jackson unselfishly consummated the run, and it was left to Mold to see out another nerve-racking over.

He managed, and Jackson faced Giffen. He drove mightily at the third ball, and the clunk as it hit the pavilion was lost in the hubbub of jubilation in the crowd.

Mold, who was not thinking at all clearly, ran him out straight afterwards, and England wound up with 483, their highest so far in England.

The cream figures in their assorted hats played out the second act of this game of Test cricket under the gaze of the gasometers in August of 1893, when Victoria was ruling with loving supremacy, Gladstone was enjoying his fourth and final term as Prime Minister, and the occasional "four-wheeled petroleum gig" could be seen and heard along the Queen's highway.

Australia started well, but Briggs had Lyons playing across the line at 30. Trott and Bannerman were snapped up by Lockwood before lunch, and Graham was caught behind second ball after the break. Thus Australia were soon in deep trouble.

MacGregor moved up to the stumps to take Lockwood and was rewarded for his pluck by a full-toss which smashed him on the knee. But these things were forgotten (except perhaps by MacGregor) as Briggs dealt Gregory his fate, and Australia had lost five for 40.

Giffen and Bruce made a bright little stand that promised much until Giffen fell to England's bowler of the series, Lockwood, and the collapse continued unchecked as Briggs chimed in with a series of tail-end wickets.

Jackson finally ran out Blackham after the last-wicket 32 had taken Australian up to 91, a tired performance. The deficit could hardly have been more dispiriting.

But Billy Bruce, spurning the deficit, hit away when the second innings got going at half past four. Boundaries flew in all directions and in half an hour 50 was on the board. Then Mold's first ball flew from the edge of Bruce's lightweight bat to Jackson, who made a fine catch at slip.

Big Gunn nearly ran out little Bannerman as he scrambled to open Giffen's score, and when Lockwood dropped a few short Bannerman suffered some stinging blows, walking rhetorically down the pitch and patting a spot.

Slowly it became clear that the match would not be quite so simple. The pitch was holding well and the other Australians were resting up in the dressing room whilst W.G. and his army sweated it out. The fieldsmen's tiredness was showing: a misfield gave Australia the 100th run. Soon Giffen was dropped and disdainfully cut the next ball for four, perhaps hoping that Stoddart's lucky star now hung over him.

Then Bannerman, 55, was caught by Read running back at mid-on, and two were down for 126.

Australia at the close were 234 behind, with eight wickets left. It was going to need something exceptional from Giffen on the morrow.

The public gave little for Australia's chances; only 2000 turned up to see

Briggs and Lockwood spearhead the attack. The only runs Giffen made today were given him: he cut, but MacGregor failed to take the return and four overthrows resulted. Lockwood then yorked him for 53.

Gregory's dreadful run continued, with Shrewsbury toppling over to catch him for 6. Graham, on a "pair", was soon liberated, and the runs came quickly. He pulled Lockwood defiantly to post a speedy 200 for four wickets.

Graham, moving down the wicket as Briggs moved in to bowl, and clubbing a slowed-down Mold, had the crowd in ecstacy. Trott reached 50, and W.G.'s tactics, not for the first time, were queried. Why not Read with his strange lobs? Or Stoddart? Or some cunning from the Old Man himself?

Trott and Graham put on 106 in little more than an hour, but soon Briggs was looking very pleased with himself as he turned away, hands in pockets, after bowling Graham for 42.

Lyons' first ball was sent comfortably up to Jackson at mid-off and was dropped. The 300 was reached, but soon Trott's gem-like 92 was terminated like so many innings in an age of robust driving—by a catch at mid-on.

Lyons, with little to lose, struck out at Briggs, then turned his attention to Bill Lockwood, hitting him for 4, his third successive boundary; Read was sent to field in front of the members, but Lyons' next effortless stroke lifted the ball onto the pavilion roof. Lockwood bowled again, and the mighty Lyons got underneath with a huge heave. Read rubbed his hands together, but the ball zoomed well over him as he leaned back on the railings. This was Lyons' fifth 4 in a row, and to the next delivery he drove to mid-off where W.G. surprised everyone with a wonderful catch low to his left. It nearly rocked him off his feet, but for Australia it really was the end.

Jackson aptly finished the game by catching McLeod, and England had won by an innings and 43 runs.

Next day "Stoddy" was bowled for 0 by the six foot four inch Mee of Notts.

The Windsor Magazine once looked at cricketers' fingers, and Stoddart's were found to bear no trace of rough usage. Most bowlers had fingers of considerable length; Stoddart had not. His hands were on the small side, well-proportioned, characteristic of their owner: "thoroughly neat and work-manlike". They had done a goodly share of work in this game with Notts. He held five catches and took three wickets.

There was one more match before the third and final Test. It was against Lancashire, who needed a win to stay in the race for the Championship, and Lord's was filled on the showery Monday morning.

Middlesex made 304 (Stoddart 12), then Lancashire twice fell apart at the seams against Hearne; and with time running out after rainy interruptions Middlesex went out to get 29 in the slithery conditions. Stoddart, swinging a short one from Mold for what seemed a certain four, stood nonplussed as MacLaren made a catch of it, dismissing him for 0.

Webbe finally sealed Lancashire's fate for another season by applying the whip to Briggs.

At Old Trafford England now had to resist Australia's attempt to level the series.

Manchester had been drenched, but a drying wind left the wicket suitable for a prompt commencement Thursday morning. This time Lord Hawke kept Jackson and Peel in the Yorkshire ranks.

There were 8000 present to see W.G. lead out an England side containing two new faces—Surrey's Billy Brockwell and Tom Richardson. The doubling of admission prices may have had something to do with the poor attendance, yet those who saved their money missed an entertaining day's cricket, initiated by the incorrigible Lyons.

It all began with a boundary first ball of the match to Bannerman—surely a freakish beginning—then for 15 thrilling minutes it was Lyons unlimited. He made 27 of the 32 for the first wicket, thrashing Mold and Briggs, bowling before their own crowd with a defensive field.

MacGregor eventually caught Lyons, then at 59 the colossus from Mitcham, Tom Richardson, took his first wicket in Tests. The uncompromising Giffen was a good one to start with.

When Bannerman unhappily went to a touch off the glove, Australia were three down for 69.

Richardson thundered up again and had Trott edging to W.G., who grasped the ball low down. Four down for 73, Harry Graham in; and the score moved gradually to 100 at the luncheon break.

Mold hurt Graham twice, then hit his boot and gained an l.b.w. decision. Half the side out for 129, and Stoddart at mid-off feeling happy with life and exchanging pleasantries with the skipper as they crossed between overs.

Swarthy little Gregory was bowled first ball by Briggs and drooped off, probably wondering why International matches were always so perverse, and how the English could be so inhuman as to select this Briggs match after match.

Now Bruce and Trumble set about restoring the situation. The left-hander clubbed Briggs for 16 in an over, and Trumble used his distinctive cut. 150 came up, with Mold and Briggs making way for Richardson and Brockwell, who today lie in close proximity to each other in Richmond cemetery— Richardson beneath a broken wicket of marble, and Brockwell anonymous beneath a grassy patch.

In 1893, with blood coursing urgently through their veins, they strove to increase England's advantage as Bruce and Trumble dug in. Bruce drove

Brockwell through the field for four to bring up his own well-earned 50, then cut Richardson and hit him to leg.

As the 200 loomed, Bruce was well caught by Read, and the tail went quickly when W.G. brought Briggs back. Richardson strode off with 5-49, Briggs with four wickets. Australia had a paltry 204 that soon seemed far more comfortable as England squandered their position.

Giffen opened the bowling without a slip, and the other end was taken by Charles Thomas Biass Turner, also with men plotted out against the lofted drive, and Trumble now bestriding the slips area.

W.G. drove to mid-off and started a run. Stoddart, still scoreless and perhaps not impatient to come to grips with Turner, was not backing up very well; he was a long way from home as Gregory broke the wicket with his punctual return—a nauseating way to go, and it seems W.G. was upset too as he grafted into the thirties by close of play. Shrewsbury made only a fearfully slow dozen.

On Friday Gunn and W.G. began confidently, cutting boundaries and off-driving. Then a ball from Bruce kept low, thumped W.G.'s pad, and disturbed the leg stump. 73 for three wickets.

Gunn took matters most seriously. His first hour provided him with 14 runs, and Bannerman at mid-off must have squinted across with mixed emotions. Resolute Ward was caught behind, and Read, after two spanking boundaries, was bowled by Giffen. Now, with an end to bowl at, the Australians still led by over 90.

Brockwell stayed a while, then made way for Briggs. This fascinating partnership saw Gunn find his strokes. Then Briggs, unable to stand by any longer, tried to hit Giffen and was bowled for 2.

Eventually the Australian total was passed, and once more Mold, for all the satirical remarks, stayed long enough to see a batsman to his century. When he fell for a duck Gunn had reached 102, and England with 243 had a token lead of 39.

Bannerman and Lyons soon wiped off the arrears, but Mold got Lyons at 56, the muscleman having hit 33 in even time. Giffen went to a good slip catch by Brockwell, and near the end Trott was bowled by a shooter from Mold. Australia led by 54 with seven wickets in hand and a day to play. The balance was delicate.

It was the first Saturday of the Test series, yet, probably owing to the weather, only 5000 came to the ground to see Bannerman and McLeod resume. After a shower of rain, McLeod was caught off Richardson, who was getting the ball to kick off the damp Old Trafford turf.

Bruce raised some excitement with four fours and a two off a Briggs over, and after another weather break he edged one close to Stoddart at third man. Then he played to point and Shrewsbury made certain of the catch.

England had to get wickets quickly, but Bannerman seemed immovable:

after two hours and a half he reached 50, and was dropped by Read at slip. Johnny Briggs was called up again and had Graham stumped, then 3 runs later Gregory went l.b.w. to Richardson, and Australia were 173 for seven. Trumble had to stay with Bannerman now that time was as important as runs.

But only nine were added before Bannerman refused a call and tall Trumble slipped in reversing. Australia, with two wickets left, led by 143.

Soon after lunch Richardson smashed a ball into Turner's hand. He made the run, but went straight to W.G., who pulled the finger into place.

The 200 was posted, then Richardson took his 10th wicket of the match: Bannerman, with 60 in 205 minutes of grim defiance lightened by eight boundaries.

Turner and Blackham now swung the mathematics of the game around.

This last wicket, so often the most crucial in an innings, realised a quick 36, and when W.G. came out with Stoddart, England needed 198 in 130 minutes, with the wicket playing truly.

Both openers hit fours early, and twice Stoddart pulled Trumble to the boundary almost off his face; then he drove Turner deep. Hopes rose around the ground as W.G. lustily drove Turner into the crowd, losing the ball.

In 70 minutes they had 78 up, but it was hardly good enough. Stoddart, after eight stirring fours, tried to place Trumble to leg and was snapped up for 42.

Shrewsbury punished Trumble, then, as the pointlessness of the enterprise became obvious, he became quiet. At 5.30 W.G. was caught for a 45 which had taken almost two hours, and the game had long since been doomed to stalemate. Gunn, the hero of the first innings, made only 11, and Trumble bowled Ward next ball.

Thus England, with the Oval victory, had won their fifth home rubber in succession, and eager eyes looked forward to the next compelling chapter of Anglo-Australian competition.

The first game of the Scarborough festival provided Stoddart with memories gloomier than he might have prescribed for himself. The Rev. Mr Holmes had urged him to make a tall score, but the response was a doleful shaking of the head and a gentle protest that he was worn out; Hirst gave him a hectic time in both innings.

Then recovery: for the South he and Hewett made a cracking century stand, and although Stoddart fell to Hirst both times he took 77 runs away with him.

Then, for C. I. Thornton's XI against the Australians, in beautiful weather and in front of a capacity house, Jackson, the local god, and Stoddart, the champion from the South, played out a stern opening spell from Turner, then began to play strokes.

Similar in appearance, the pair accelerated the rate of scoring the longer they were in. Stoddart soon relaxed into carefree cricket. He outscored Jackson practically two runs to one, and had his century by lunch, when the total was 170.

He finally fell for 127, and the Australians more than matched the eventual total of 345. Jackson made runs again, and in the end there was time only for another brief sample of Lyons' heavy-footed homicide.

The season was wound up at Hastings with the big talking point being Stoddart's 2000 for the year. In two games would he get the 35 runs necessary? After batting for the South against the Australians the odds lengthened. Turner, as if to remind him of the personal jinx, had him caught for four, and the well-informed girls in their puffed-sleeve dresses felt sad at heart. Stoddart had been obviously oppressed by the thought of completing his 2000, an achievement hitherto the boast of only W.G. and, this very season, Billy Gunn; whilst he dithered over his four runs W.G. had compiled 24, one of the rare instances of the elder outscoring the younger.

The Australians collapsed for 64, but in the follow-on Lyons gave another Herculean display, and the South, after all, needed 111 to win.

There was a sense of urgency this time, and Stoddart and Hewett made runs fast. The 2000 edged teasingly within reach: one boundary shot would do it. After all the hooks and square-drives, the skimming off-drives and cuts of 1893, "Stoddy" wanted just one more well-placed stroke and the momentous prize was his.

Turner purred in and bowled. The ball was through, the stumps were down. Stoddart, bowled Turner, 27. Season total: 1996.

For the cream of English cricket there was one more first-class match before the leaves began to fall. It was mid-September, and the gaiety of Hastings was tinged with the poignancy of farewell.

W.G. and Stoddart commenced the South's reply to the North in mid-afternoon. Stoddart played the first ball away and they ran a three which might have been four with a younger, swifter running mate. Season's aggregate now 1999.

W.G. played the remaining four balls, then it was Briggs to Stoddart, a half-volley floated outside the leg-stump; Stoddart opened his shoulders, the umpire flinched, long-leg peered eagerly, but the ball was through to Sherwin, and a murmur of disappointment went up.

The next ball was short, and Stoddart hit it for four. The 2000 was his at last, a rare and grand accomplishment.

England's father figure recorded a duck, and Stoddart soon followed for 13, but a lead of almost 100 accrued, and in the final innings the South had to get 261 runs. W.G. again went cheaply, but Stoddart, with the monkey off his back, made a pulsating 63 for which Nicolls, the batmakers, awarded him a

FOOTNOTE: *Stoddart's 63 included 11 fours and five threes, and took 55 minutes.*

new blade.

The season closed with Andrew Stoddart top of the aggregates for the only time in his life. His total was 2072; his average of 42.29 was .56 behind Gunn's; Shrewsbury's tally of 1686 was third best.

Middlesex C.C.C. presented him with an elegant silver bowl at the end of this wonderful season, "in appreciation of his splendid cricket for the county"; over 50 years later it stood on his widow's sideboard, bright and pleasing as the man's own batting.

1893 was also the year of his retirement from rugby football, a gap that was felt sorely at club as well as national level. Henceforth it was to be cricket first, and dalliance with golf and racquets, lawn tennis and winter skating, between times.

CHAPTER 11

THE COUNTY GRIND

"Who is the greatest cricketer, please?"
And Mr Simon of course replied, "Dr W. G. Grace".
"And the second greatest?"
"Perhaps," the minister answered, "A. E. Stoddart".

In 1894 Stoddart was elected Vice-president of Hampstead C.C.; once more every game in which he played resulted in victory for the club, his contributions with the ball surpassing much of his batting.

Against Beckenham, considered strong at least until this particular match, he and Spofforth swept the opposing batting away for 13 and 21. "Spoff" took 8-7 and 4-4, "Stod" 2-5 and 6-7. Hampstead made 269—Stoddart 148.

He made a century off Emeriti, and chopped Willesden about with 226 not out (having hit 210 against them the previous year, and 238 in 1887).

Yet in spite of these pyrotechnics, his club average was restricted to a modest 64; his 37 wickets cost only 5.5 each.

His Middlesex form was less satisfying. *The Cricket Field* remarked in mid-season that "centuries in first-class matches have become quite common, and almost the only man who has not greatly profited is Stoddart, the best batsman of all".

Early in the year, after Lord Sheffield had declined their invitation, the Melbourne and Sydney authorities asked Stoddart to gather a team to tour Australia at the close of the English season. The job of seeking a balanced talent for the party was probably responsible for a certain distraction as the season progressed from one damp week to the next.

The curtain-raiser at Lord's was a curious game between M.C.C. and Sussex which commenced at five minutes past noon on May 2nd and finished at 5.25 p.m. the same day.

Sussex crashed for 42, Stoddart hit 44 out of 103, and Sussex fell again for 59. Could this be the solution for those who demand bright cricket?

Stoddart gave the customers value during the dawn of this cricket season: 32 in Sherwin's low-scoring benefit, a magnificent 81 for M.C.C. against a strong Kent attack, 41 against Lockwood and Richardson's unpatronising stuff at the Oval, a tortured 45 in the brief Gloucestershire match (W.G. 0 and 1)— all this before May was out.

Middlesex did well in June, the bowlers generally having things to their

FOOTNOTE: *Stoddart's 41 at The Oval took 40 minutes. When he bowled, he was hit for a seven to leg by Abel.*

liking. Stoddart had a 70 at Brighton, but the big innings came in Billy Barnes' benefit at Trent Bridge: for the Gentlemen of England he made 148—all style and charm—helping build a total of 340; yet Notts got to within one run, and by the time Stoddart and Hornby had made forties in the second innings there was no time to complete the match. The attendance was poor, but Barnes sought out Woods and Stoddart after the game and bought them a grateful drink out of his meagre takings.

Against Oxford University Stoddart again found himself seeing the ball clearly. His 78 was easily the highest score of the match, which was made notable in a way by "Shrimp" Leveson Gower's "pair". Stoddart caught him the second time, and comforted the victim as he passed by saying: "Congratulations! W.G. maintains that no-one is a first-class bat till he has made 'spectacles'!"

W.G. and Stoddart made a quick 56 for the first Gentlemen's wicket at Lord's; but the historic performance came from Jackson and Woods, who bowled through both Players' innings unchanged as the professionals slid to an innings defeat.

The Somerset game gave Middlesex their last victory of the season, with O'Brien hitting and hooking 110 not out, the only century recorded for the county in the entire season. This was also Plum Warner's first county match, and later he was to describe his introduction to the team at the Castle Hotel, Taunton:

"It was a very shy and strange boy who walked into the sitting-room. I can see Webbe getting up at once, coming forward and shaking hands with me, and welcoming me in the most affectionate manner. In the room were Stoddart, O'Brien, and MacGregor, and I was delighted when any of them spoke to me. I thought them all heroes. In later years when I became captain I always, when a new man came to play, had in mind the way Webbie first met me. To know Webbie is to love him".

Stoddart's reaction upon making the big-time nine years previously had been identical.

August, 1894, was a cheerless month, with only the Lancashire match touched by the Stoddart personality. Against Briggs and Mold he dominated both Middlesex innings with 68 and an 84 which took him past his thousand for the season. The game was lost, however, and it might have been after this debacle that the team photograph was taken.

They look glum, those nine men, with Webbe and Foley in inset. Rawlin, with his inverted-horseshoe moustache; Pawling, once Stoddart's school opponent, tall and solemn; MacGregor in his insubstantial gloves; the frail Henery, the muscular O'Brien, arms folded truculently, cap-peak vertical as a guardsman's; Hayman, who modelled himself on Stoddart, the Hampstead favourite; Andrew Stoddart himself, tenderly nursing a piebald kitten, thinking perhaps of the task ahead, the trip to faraway Australia, this time as Chief of

Staff.

Lord's would soon be abandoned for another winter, and the kitten would have to find affection elsewhere.

Stoddart's three games in September were all rain-affected. Yet he came up with an amazing performance for the Gents at Hastings. On a dampish wicket W.G. persuaded him to open the bowling, and he and Ferris sent the Players back for 85. In 25 overs Stoddart had Abel, Brockwell, Ward, Alec Hearne and Peel for 34.

Now W.G. made a hundred, and the Gentlemen built up a lead, though Stoddart fell to J. T. Hearne that evening, to the general regret of those who had booked seats for the following day.

This time the Players made no mistake, and Stoddart, bowling 26 overs this innings, was cut down to size with 0-47. Gunn's declaration made a game of it, but W.G. could not resist altering the batting order. At the close his side had lost seven for 73, though Stoddart had still to unsheath his sword.

About this time he began to take a keener interest in golf, and the spectacle of the three beginners, Stoddart, Murdoch and Grace, thrashing through the bunkers of Rye with the slightly more experienced Woods must have been a rare sight indeed.

As time went by he became a long hitter. He often practised for hours, and it was said in later years that he was yet another cricketer to be swallowed up by the golf-course.

His Middlesex average fell by half this year, and his first-class aggregate was hardly more than half; yet he stood top of the Middlesex aggregates. It was the county's mighty bowling attack of Hearne and Rawlin that had carried the day.

Perhaps this was the season he cut the shoulders off his bat after a series of dismissals in the slips. The surgery had little effect on his fortunes, and finally he gave the implement to Spofforth, who donated it many years after to a charity auction at Lord's. The "Bat of Misfortune" fetched just two guineas for St Dunstan's Hostel for Blinded Soldiers and Sailors under the hammer of George Robey in 1917.

William Caffyn was another to put the magnifying glass on Stoddart: "I have always, from the fact of his having been so closely associated with Australian cricket, taken a peculiar interest in the career of Mr Stoddart".

Caffyn considered his style unique: "I always think that Mr Stoddart drives more with the arms and less with the whole body than any other hitter of note that I have seen".

He was not to know that his final assessment would be wide of the mark: "His defence is equal to his hitting powers, and his name will be handed down to posterity as one of the greatest batsmen that has ever been".

FOOTNOTE: *Sir Home Gordon, asked (Cricket, 1908) whose cricket he had most enjoyed, replied: "Unquestionably Trumper's. Next to his Ranjitsinhji's, Stoddart's and Jessop's."*

CHAPTER 12

ENGLAND ON TOP

There were thirteen men in this 13th English side to tour Australia. On September 18th a colossal crowd at Fenchurch Street Station wished the uniformed cricketers a back-slapping bon voyage, a crowd made up of "all sorts and conditions of men who, whilst not cricketers themselves, can get much pleasure out of seeing celebrated cricketers in mufti".

Stoddart had been given a send-off dinner at the Hampstead Constitutional Club, where the first of many quiet, slightly nervous speeches of thanks passed his lips, followed as the evening progressed by a rendition of "Tommy Atkins", the hit song of the hour. Now the team sailed away in "Ophir" (which became the Royal Yacht in 1901), with the Hon. Mrs Ivo Bligh a fellow passenger.

If Stephenson and Caffyn and Lawrence, with their companions of the 1861-2 expedition, joined with Australia in the conception of big cricket in the continent, Stoddart and his staff assisted in the delivery of a bonny child. The 1894-5 rubber sparked off the frenzied interest which has always since surrounded Test matches between England and Australia; it saw a new dedication and application by the players involved; the Press gave the public what it wanted—detailed coverage, with comments by retired cricketing warriors; the *Pall Mall Gazette* gave the word "test" a capital "T", and spent large sums telegraphing the action across the world every few minutes. The English, from their Queen down, loved it.

Events were to ridicule yet again the forecasts of contemporary judges. *The Cricket Field,* for one, had stated that Stoddart's contingent, lacking several leading players, seemed hardly strong enough to play matches under the title of "England v Australia". Yet we are told that the surname "Stoddart" derives from "stud-herd" or "keeper of a stud", and the cricketers who set sail looked a healthy enough herd to most people, though Johnny Briggs had to battle to control his weeping wife. The last the huge gathering heard from them was Lockwood's shrill whistling across the water.

In Australia excitement was widespread. Stoddart became instantly popular as a courteous leader, (his manner "contrasts distinctly with the bombastic way in which old W.G. used to swagger about. Stoddy moves among the crowd most unpretentiously, as if he were walking upon velvet") and his men brought in with them a fascinating gust of youthful dash and mature, awesome experience.

The Test series was to be as gripping as any before or since.

The batting depended upon Stoddart, Archie MacLaren, Albert Ward, Francis Ford (whom Major Wardill admired), and Jack Brown (whose technique Major Wardill condemned: "He won't get ten runs in five months, and had better go home").

Billy Brockwell was a utility all-rounder; and the fast bowlers were Lockwood and Richardson, with Peel and Briggs crafty left-arm, and Humphreys (underhand lob bowler), apparently requested by the Melbourne Club, and fairly fit at 45 because he rode a tricycle.

Leslie Gay, England's soccer goalie the previous winter, was taken as first wicketkeeper, although Stoddart allegedly had never seen him keep wicket. The second 'keeper was Hylton "Punch" Philipson, born at Tynemouth, across the river from South Shields, and a few years later reported as Stoddart's prospective brother-in-law. As it happened, Miss Philipson never did become Mrs Stoddart (life might have been longer and sweeter for him if she had), nor did any of the other numerous handsome women whose portraits appeared in the England captain's book of cuttings.

The voyage was interesting. They arranged games of cricket in the nets on deck, and played a match at Colombo, where the local colt, Raffel, took 9-43 and 5-44 against them, bowling fast left-arm into a "shifting sand" wicket pitched on the barrack square.

The 7000-ton "Ophir" behaved nicely in a tremendous swell, and Brockwell recorded that Stoddart, a good sailor, was "most assiduous in his assistance to those who have suffered from sea-sickness".

Finally the rollers and the flying fish and the games with the lady passengers were mere memories, and they docked at Albany. Then, at Adelaide, Stoddart explained that he had brought more professionals than planned because he could not engage enough amateurs of the required standard. A local observer was quick to note that the amateurs and pro's stayed at separate hotels, in the "old obnoxious English tradition".

The team picnicked at Mount Lofty, unburdened by any real threat of personal recognition, and their appetites for cricket were eager by the time they made their way up to Gawler, where Albert Ward made a century first try in Australia, and Stoddart made 13 on the asphalt.

Now, in their white sunhats, they met South Australia at Adelaide, where George Giffen, having trained all winter, was bursting to get at the old enemy.

Jack Brown made a century as Giffen operated inexhaustibly from one end or the other, taking 5-175, and Stoddart got into his stride with 66; the Englishmen totalled 477, surely a safe figure.

But the young wonder, Joe Darling, scored 117, and South Australia climbed to 383. Giffen now struck with 6-49, and his team were set only 225 to win after all. Reedman's 83 helped him into the first Test team, and Giffen's 58 not out repaid him sweetly for the hard winter's effort with a 6-wicket win.

Stoddart disliked being interviewed, but one reporter managed to corner him and asked for an explanation for the collapse. "I don't think I could give you a reason if I tried," was the laughing reply. Later, however, he is supposed to have stated weightily: "We took risks; your men took none".

FOOTNOTE: *The* Ophir *weighed 6910 tons and carried 602 passengers.*

He had an excellent match against Victoria, although MacLaren stole the bouquets with his 228. Again Stoddart's XI made over 400, but with Richardson injured the attack failed to contain Victoria, who made 306.

With a double of 77 and 78 (appreciated by a little old man in a tall hat who came out and shook his hand), Stoddart made sure Victoria had plenty to chase, and the home team went down by 145 runs. "Felix" and his fellow onlookers were enchanted by the MacLaren-Stoddart partnership: he actually regretted Stoddart's downfall, trying to "send the ball to Jericho", and added his own warm tribute to the "Stoddartian plaudits".

Further eastwards, N.S.W. made a tedious 293, and Frank Iredale clinched his place in Australia's team with a watchful 133; but it was not enough. Stoddart's men made 394 before Saturday's huge crowd, Brown once more hitting a century, and Brockwell, finding his English form and subjugating his journalistic and photographic duties, making 81.

Stoddart continued a strange sequence of scores with 79, this time taking nearly three hours over the runs. The exasperated crowd often called out to him to open his shoulders, but he was serving notice that he had made up his mind to play purposeful cricket. The bowling was not cheap. Callaway bounced them aggressively around the ribs, and Stoddart, standing, as a woman columnist noted, "with quite a Piccadilly manner", stroked the ball away calmly and smoothly. His old adversary, Turner, tempted him with some innocent-looking deliveries, but he was not to be seduced. His drives were hit hard along the grass. Perhaps a chance to Callaway from a cut early on had steadied him, and the home side must have cursed the lapse as the English skipper hit McKibbin three times in a row to the chains, the invective swinging towards Howell as he missed the third at square-leg.

When Howell finally bowled him there was a shriek of excitement from the masses.

Next day, Sunday, they relaxed on Sydney Harbour. After lunch their launch moored in an inlet, and Lockwood, restless as ever, decided to swim, heedless of the warnings of the shark danger. Whilst Stoddart and Ford shot at objects in the water, Lockwood dived over the other side and began to stroke his way towards shore; but halfway across he was letting out gurgling cries. Some of the players thought it a clever impersonation of a drowning man, but England's great fast bowler was in serious trouble.

A yacht happened to glide past, and a lifebuoy was thrown to the thrashing figure; for a moment only his upturned feet showed. It took some dynamic action from two of the yachtsmen to get him ashore, where he was revived with brandy. The atmosphere was ruefully uncomfortable for the rest of the day.

Back at the cricket ground, however, Stoddart's men pressed on to victory in 97° heat, swamping N.S.W. for 180 in their second innings, when Syd Gregory played *his* way into the Test side with 87.

There was a hearty banquet at Sydney, and, before they moved on, there came an invitation for "Mr Storade" to play an aboriginal team from Shellharbour. Their secretary wanted to play on the Sydney Cricket Ground, and offered to put on a corroborree afterwards!

The tourists almost came unstuck at Armidale, where at Stoddart's behest their sleeping car was shunted into a siding to allow them extra rest after the night journey north. They drew lots to decide the batting order, and collapsed for 67. Ford and MacLaren saved them in the second innings, and a visit to Baker's Creek goldmine, richest in N.S.W., gave them something else by which to remember this stop.

The mayor and M.P. were predictably at Toowoomba railway station to meet them, and, sent in to bat, Stoddart's men made 216 on another matting wicket. Toowoomba tumbled twice rapidly, just avoiding the innings defeat, but Stoddart good-naturedly declined the offer of extra time to hit off the three runs for victory.

Now for the first time Queensland faced an English team on even terms. Stoddart won the toss at Brisbane Exhibition Ground and, batting number 3, showed his colours straight away by lashing all the bowlers, Pierce (slow lobs) and Arthur Coningham in particular.

Volatile Coningham was building up an irritability that was due to erupt in Brisbane towards the end of the season. Here and now "Stoddy" did not help matters by stroking him for 4 4 5 4 then a massive 6 out of the ground.

He finally stepped out to McGlinchy and mis-hit to slip for 149 made in even time. Ward made 107, their partnership was worth well over 200, and they eventually set Queensland 494. The persevering Coningham had 5-152 for his labours.

Tom Richardson now came through with a show of strength. His 8-52 (seven bowled) sent Queensland crumbling for 121, and Lockwood, his lungs now clear of water, stole the figures in the second innings of 99.

Now Stoddart and his men braced themselves with playing-cards at the ready for the 29-hour trip to Sydney. A truly historic Test match lay ahead.

"Someone will be swearing directly, Jack," Stoddart said as he watched Blackham flip the coin, "I hope it's you!"

Australia's captain took first innings for his men, who had been practising for four days. Enthusiasm in Sydney was at a keen pitch even though there were five South Australians in the side; and under a hot sun a huge crowd waited tensely for the contest to start.

Thunder was in the air, but rain fell on other areas where it was more welcome. The strong shapes of Jack Lyons and Harry Trott were reassuring to Australians as they commuted to the centre, just as Colin McDonald and Peter Burge have been in our own times. And not even Fred Trueman could symbolise

FOOTNOTE: *The stand between Ward and Stoddart against Queensland amounted to 255 in 167 minutes. On 98, Stoddart was beaten by a ball from W. Hoare which touched the bails without shifting them.*

greater dramatic menace than black-haired Tom Richardson at the extremity of his run.

Stoddart arranged his field, and Richardson got the 1894-5 series under way with a terrifying maiden over to Lyons. Peel opened the other end, then Richardson hit Lyons' knee with an express delivery which clattered into the stumps.

Giffen came in and the score eased up to 21; then Richardson smashed the top off Trott's off-stump. Darling in his first Test innings, was yorked first ball, and Australia staggered at 21 for three wickets. It was a powerful statement from Richardson, who was expected to miss his English pitches.

Giffen and Iredale now had the weight of the continent on their shoulders. The wicket was sound, but Richardson's deliveries were rearing at knuckles and shoulder-blades. There was less danger at the other end, where runs came freely from Peel and the others.

Giffen once found himself with Iredale at the bowler's end, but Gay fumbled and Australia escaped. At 75 Giffen was missed by the wretched Gay, who repeated the tragedy a few minutes later. Runs came swiftly in celebration and relief, with Giffen striking Briggs straight into the crowd for 5.

The ball seemed to be following Gay: a fast one from Richardson flew off the bat's edge and was grassed. It was a difficult chance, but Stoddart was beginning to wonder where the next wicket was coming from. The partnership reached 100, and Ward missed Giffen in the deep. Stoddart decided to have a bowl himself, but two overs produced 18 runs.

Seven bowlers were tried in quick bursts during the afternoon, yet Australia rose courageously to 192 before a wicket fell. Iredale was caught at mid-off by the England captain for a faultless 81.

After tea runs came faster. Gregory, who had made only 100 runs against England in ten completed innings, now whipped Peel for 14 off a 6-ball over and, with Giffen, added 53 in half an hour. The ball sped all over the Sydney ground like a crazy cat's-cradle. With Lockwood's shoulder ricked, most of the work fell upon Richardson and Peel as Giffen raced well past his century and "Tich" Gregory executed one vengeful stroke after another.

Gregory reached 50 and was dropped by Ford at slip; with the 300 up, the sensation half-hour at the day's outset was the most distant of memories. Giffen rode high on 150.

In ten minutes the curtain would be dropped and the actors could rest for the night. Who knew then what feats they might perform with strength renewed? Brockwell was bowling—hoping to achieve something worthy of report in his newsletters. And now the drought broke: he had Giffen taken at slip for 161, the greatest innings of his life, and Australia were 331 for five, Reedman joining Gregory, who was 85 at the end.

Stoddart had worries that evening, with Lockwood hurt and Richardson, though tireless, unable to master the high bounce of the wicket. Peel and Briggs, such important weapons, had been fearfully expensive whilst failing to take a wicket. And Gay's confidence was in ribbons: it was as if he'd let in six goals against Scotland.

A new day, the grass sparkling in the sunshine, a record crowd at the Sydney Cricket Ground to see what the national team could make of its cosy posture: Stoddart led out his cricketers.

Richardson kept bumping the ball head-high to Reedman. Something was bound to happen: he cut it towards Brockwell and was dropped. Soon Richardson clouted Reedman on the head. Within minutes the batsman was counter-attacking with a hit off Peel into the crowd, and every person present must have considered the journey worthwhile.

Syd Gregory was inching towards his century, but Reedman fell to Peel, and Charlie McLeod came in. Gregory, after crouching as passive witness to long periods of off-theory and seeing 99 beckoningly beside his name, finally cut a ball to the fence and had his century. The sustained applause was heartfelt, but Gregory contained himself, scoring only when ready chances arose.

400 came, and McLeod had the base of his stumps battered by Richardson. Turner, after one run in 15 minutes, was eventually caught by the grateful Gay.

Blackham divulged hopes of a massive total. Gregory put his bat cleanly to square-cuts and, when the length was full, reached out and drove splendidly through the field, or stole singles with his captain. The fielding, Brown apart, had become loose; the match was running away from England. Gay dropped Gregory at 131, and Blackham seemed to be run out, but received the umpire's blessing.

Richardson and Peel, in one of the longest spells in history, had bowled all day until lunch and for some time after while 132 runs had been made, and it was killing Richardson, whose pace slowly slackened until the batsmen were hitting him to leg hard and often.

Briggs and Ford took over, and in mid-afternoon Blackham snicked a ball to raise 500. The stand blistered on at two runs a minute till Australia's previous highest score—551 at the Oval in 1884—was surpassed.

Gregory on 194 hoisted Ford high out to Ward, who failed to hold it. From the next stroke Gregory had his double-century, and the lace parasols, handkerchiefs and straw hats were waved in frantic acclaim. In the members' enclosure they collected £103 for him, presented by the recently-elected State Premier, the corpulent, often vulgar George Houstoun Reid.

The applause apparently lasted 5 minutes; then Stoddart, who had put Peel on the long-off boundary, bowled to Gregory, who belted the ball and was this time caught by Peel. His 201, taking only 244 minutes, contained 28 boundaries, and the record stand of 154 with Blackham has survived to this day—through over 500 subsequent stands for the ninth wicket in Tests between England and Australia.

Ernie Jones, the new fast bowler, smote 11 off Stoddart, and only when Richardson whipped through Blackham with a 6-inch break-back were the Englishmen out of their misery. Veteran Jack Blackham had made a gallant 74 in what proved his final Test match, his side surely safe at 586.

In my boyhood I often sat high in the Sheridan Stand at Sydney, and after my light-footed hero Neil Harvey had been dismissed I sometimes found myself gazing across at the towering tiers of the Noble Stand, with the desiccated rainbow of white shirts and coloured dresses.

At the top of the edifice, where steel girders span the ultimate height, pigeons strutted with a proprietary swagger or glided through the humid air. And I used to thrill at the belief that these same cricket-loving birds must have watched from their heavenly perches the batting of Archie MacLaren and Clem Hill and Victor Trumper and this A. E. Stoddart, whose acquaintance I had recently made in the record book: whose christian names I knew not—but whose Test runs, four short of 1000, filled my tidy young mind with regret.

Seasons later it occurred to me that the M.A. Noble Stand was constructed many years after MacLaren had left this favourite ground of his forever; and his spectator-pigeons, according to normal life-span patterns, had long since deserted the arena.

On Saturday afternoon, December 15th, 1894, there may have been more seagulls than pigeons in the outfield as heavy clouds blotted out the sun and diluted the colours all around. MacLaren and Ward opened England's innings to the bowling of Turner and Jones.

At 14 MacLaren played a wretched shot off Turner and was caught at cover. Stoddart took guard, and whilst Ward scored methodically and steadily he moved cautiously into position against both the fast bowlers and showed clearly that responsibility was pressing on him. He showed signs of fatigue after his exertions in the field (it had been noted that he usually placed himself where there was most work to be one).

After making 12 he offered a feeble shot at Giffen, and Jones at slip held the catch.

Belligerent Brown made little headway at first against Harry Trott's leg-breaks, then suddenly cut a cracking four and drove another; Ward also cut strongly.

Then a cardinal rule was broken—Ward called for a quick run after a misfield. Lyons recovered, and his throw ran Brown out. After so much promise England were 78 for three, and the all-rounders were lining up.

Jones was thumping them down, but Ward stood calm and resolute, and

Brockwell fought desperately in the failing light; the hundred came, built to 130 by stumps, Ward's 67 brim-full of courage.

Heavy rain fell that night and Sunday, but Monday broke fine, and the wicket, though softened, was undamaged. Turner and Jones opened the attack at noon.

Ward enjoyed an early reprieve by McLeod, and soon it was raining hard and play was held up; then soon after resumption Ward's vigil ended ironically in a boundary catch. Soon Peel was gone, and with the weather cooling Ford blazed away in his finest Lord's manner for 30 before skipping out to Giffen and missing; Brockwell fell at the same total for 49, giving Ernie Jones his first Test wicket, and England headed towards certain follow-on.

Then, during Briggs and Lockwood's stand of 41, Blackham's thumb was split by a ball from Lyons.

Briggs (57) fell to a Giffen daisycutter, and with Gay managing 33 England were all out for 325 as play drew to a peaceful close. For the moment it was not altogether obvious just how crucial was each run.

By the fourth day the wicket was still in good shape, but the outfield had thickened and runs had to be earned the hard way. Giffen, acting captain, gave Jones only a short burst against Ward and MacLaren before taking over himself. Turner needed careful watching with his variable break and changes of pace.

Gradually the run-rate accelerated and the opening stand kindled hope, until a slow ball from Giffen puzzled MacLaren and clipped the middle stump. First loss at 44.

Stoddart made ten extremely cautious runs before lunch, and afterwards the runs began to come, as they sometimes do in a follow-on. Jones dropped a few short and both batsmen hooked savagely; Giffen was accurate and varied, but Stoddart hit him to the fence twice in an over and Trott was called back. The hundred was passed. The captain was finding his feet and all sorts of things suddenly seemed possible.

Then Stoddart took three nonchalant singles to reach 36, and, facing Turner, lifted a ball towards cover, where Giffen caught it almost at grass level, giving Turner "Stoddy's" wicket for the seventh time in Tests. 115 for two. Chunky Jack Brown in.

The century stand which followed melted all the plastic preconceptions about the match. The magnificent bombardment by Albert Ward and J. T. Brown took their side almost up with Australia, and further stiff resistance would set the home side some sort of target after all.

Giffen threw all his resources against them as the game slowly shifted axis. It was far from inclining England's way, yet the counter-challenge was on— turning it into an exceptional game of cricket. The score ticked past 200, and Ward had his great century.

Giffen finally beat him playing back, and Brockwell joined Brown, who drove Giffen to the boundary to reach 50.

Brown, recalled by a later generation as they watched Hendren bat, hit Giffen hard and high to the longfield, but Jones hurtled across to bring off an astonishing catch, and England were perched indecisively on 245, with the four top men out.

Our smug advantage is that we may calmly examine every run and every wicket wasted as destiny took its course. Peel, for instance, benefited from a critical miss by Jones five yards from the bat, and went on to be 9 not out at stumps, when England were 7 runs ahead with six wickets to fall. Brockwell, with much depending on him, made 20 in the last drizzly overs.

Skies were still grey on Wednesday, but it was darker still in England, where no news had come through, and would not be coming through until the match was over. The cable delay meant that an unbelieving English public received the story of the last three days in one sensational report.

Jones did for Brockwell (37) with a "bailer", and Peel was bowled off his foot by Giffen. 296 for six—a mere 35 ahead.

Briggs held himself in check; no slashes yet, no pillaging square drives. Ford ("Six foot two of don't care") had one escape, and in the cricketer's idiom for a nervous chuckle hit a couple of fours. Briggs' caution dissolved as he slammed Giffen, then was dropped by Graham, substituting at square-leg; the score at lunch was 344 for six.

The crowd swelled after the interval and saw some of the best of Ford, who hit freely to all points of the driving compass and shared a priceless stand of 89 with Briggs.

Lockwood also played a vital part, scoring well off the ubiquitous Giffen and gleefully snicking McLeod, who forced Briggs to play on for 42. Eight gone for 398, and England's captain clapping every run.

Gay raised 400 then became the only man to fall short of double figures. With one wicket remaining England were 159 ahead.

Tom Richardson, heavy with flu, flayed 12 useful runs, then Lockwood was bowled, leaving Australia to make 177 on a good, firm pitch.

At four o'clock Lyons and Trott started the task and in 15 minutes 25 were on the board to Lyons, a single to Trott. Then Richardson again hit the knee of Lyons (who was distracted by the three men placed near square on the leg side). The thrust of the ball carried it into the stumps. It was Richardson's last gasp for the day; he retired at 32 for one wicket.

Giffen was circumspect, and with Trott "ridiculously cramped" Australia seemed to be looking to the following day. Peel now rolled over a delivery of deceptive flight, and Trott, playing off-line, gave Gay a catch. Darling got off his "pair" but at 14 gave a one-handed chance to Stoddart which he could not hold. As the clouds banked up Darling began hitting in all directions. Giffen made most of his runs from a back-cut, but there was no mistaking that he was to be anchor man. Darling raced to 44 by the close, but all "Giff" had for his hour and three quarters was 30 and a tender knee after a bang from Lockwood.

Australia, 113 for two wickets, needed only 64 more. It could have been even fewer if the ball had been cracked more firmly.

For the first time a game entered the sixth day, and the players awoke to streaming sunlight. Giffen has recorded his delight at seeing the blue sky, yet only half the scene was visible: millions of raindrops had fallen during the small hours. Somewhere the aboriginal rainmakers had exceeded the bounds of patriotic decency.

Blackham had feared rain ever since the last evening and now, his "coffee-pot" face becoming forever part of Australian folklore, he lamented his team's fate with Giffen as their drag left furrows in the damp ground in front of the Baden Baden Hotel.

For once the Australians detested the sun's burning rays, feared their effect on the saturated wicket. The job would not be easy now. If only another 30 or 40 had been banked last evening.

For Stoddart's team, some of whom had "relaxed" the previous night thinking the match lost, the task still lay ahead—though Peel and Briggs recognised well enough the favours awaiting them in the dark-stained pitch. Peel thought someone had watered it!

"Give me the ball, Mr Stoddart," he is supposed to have said, "and I'll get t'boogers out before loonch." The extraction of five teeth just before the match no longer bothered him, and his skipper had steadied him up after the indulgences of the previous night by ordering him under the cold shower.

An 11 o'clock start might have given Australia a chance, but when the cream figures did eventually spill out into the sunlight the stickiness was acute. (MacLaren recalled that Peel and Lockwood both arrived late, having overslept. With Blackham's generous forebearance the Englishmen took the field late). Within 20 minutes the wicket was cut through and virtually unplayable.

With only a few hundred people present, the ground was like "some silent cemetery" after the previous five days of packed stands and cheering ranks; Richardson, bumping all over the place, opened with Peel.

One kept low and Giffen edged it for four, and at the other end Darling, realising the urgency of his mission, whacked Peel for 5. At 130 he tried to repeat the shot, but Brockwell in front of the two and sixpenny seats clung to probably the most important catch of his life. Darling's 53 had been a courageous effort—in the manner of Harvey's 92 not out also at Sydney 60 years later. In either case the batsman's genius, if supported, could have won the day.

After Brown had missed Giffen badly, and with cabs and carriages being pulled at the gallop across Moore Park to the Cricket Ground as news came through, snub-nosed Briggs ceased licking his lips and took over at Richardson's end. In his first over Giffen slipped and was leg-before for 41.

Iredale did all he could against the leaping, creeping ball, and Gregory, revitalised by his 201, stroked masterfully despite the hazards. But Iredale mis-hit Briggs, who took the high catch gladly.

Reedman drove and Gregory snicked and cut. The total reached 158 for five wickets. Only nineteen runs and Australia would be home—on little Gregory's back.

Alas, he edged Peel and Gay made no mistake this time. MacLaren suffered anguish in dropping Reedman, but without further damage the South Australian jumped out desperately at Peel and was stumped. Eighteen to win and three wickets to fall. "Observer" observed Blackham pacing the balcony, muttering "Cruel luck" over and over again; Giffen standing stunned, singlet and shirt in hand; Graham, head in hands, a helpless 12th man; Lyons sighing in vain now that his own lines were spoken.

Visualise the situation: Charlie Turner can bowl, Stoddart knows well enough; he can also bat, and a few well-timed blows could finish the match. The captain surveys the field. Turner makes two runs then lifts a ball towards cover and Briggs secures the catch. Jones hits Briggs into the outfield, and this time MacLaren holds it. Nine down for 162. Blackham, injured, walks to the centre. The ball is sent up unerringly at the off stump. McLeod spars, takes a single; Blackham plays and winces at the pain. Stoddart peers anxiously. The bowlers, Peel then Briggs, saunter to the crease, dispatch the ball, not daring to pitch even as close as middle stump. The ball spits away into Gay's gloves.

A single here and there, and Blackham wishes so fervently that he could use both hands on the bat-handle. Peel in again. Blackham prods the ball back and Peel catches it. England have won!

They had won the match impossible to win. It ended two minutes before lunch, and the final margin was ten silly runs. Peel had 6-67 off 30 overs, Briggs 3-25 off 11.

Andrew Stoddart, at the function which followed, acknowledged Australia's foul fortune with the weather, but expressed the greatest pride in his "team of triers". They had fully justified his most sanguine expectations. "There'll be a good deal said about this match," he predicted.

By the strangest quirk of fate, at the tiny Victorian township of Jeparit, Australia's greatest statesman, Robert Gordon Menzies, had chosen this topsy-turvy sporting day upon which to make his entry into the world.

FOOTNOTES: *1. MacLaren dropped Reedman at second slip, and later recalled Brown at point "nodding his head and clicking his tongue until both might have dropped off"*
2. This is the only England-Australia Test won by a side after following on.

After Friday's rest the team faced 18 Sydney Juniors, who rattled up 442. A youngster named Noble made a solid 152 not out, and a respectful 17-year-old called Trumper played a pretty 67. Ward and MacLaren made runs but Stoddart was caught off Noble for 13.

Christmas for the travelling cricketers meant warm, pleasant hours in the Botanical Gardens, then a traditional roast beef dinner, with Humphreys wielding the carving knife.

They did Randwick races on Boxing Day, then found themselves in damp Melbourne for the second Test match.

Stoddart's hand left an impression in the pitch, and when he pressed his foot down on a good bowling length moisture came up. All the while, according to one report, the Australians were inside choosing a leader. Giffen finally emerged and said "Let's look at that pitch, Stoddy, before we toss". And they walked in silence to the middle, where Giffen got on his haunches and prodded and gazed at the battle strip whilst the Englishman stood by, hands behind back.

The toss was made, and Giffen went into a prolonged huddle with his seniors before issuing an irrefutable invitation to England to take first innings.

Giffen's tactics paid off, though rather too rapidly and emphatically, for England were out in two hours for 75 and Australia had to bat on a wicket still a trifle unhealthy.

Bowlers dictated events right from the first ball, delivered swiftly by Coningham in his only Test match. It reared, and MacLaren popped it into Trott's hands at point.

Stoddart, uncomfortable with the sharply kicking deliveries, for ten minutes exercised great care against Coningham and Turner. Suddenly he opened out, as if to push the enemy's high ladders off the battlements. Lofting the ball over the crowded infield, he took a couple of twos and a single, while Ward grafted. Then at 10 "Stoddy" attempted to pull a short one from Turner and was bowled as it kept low: 19 for two wickets.

Brown fell to Turner also, and Brockwell pottered desperately before bursting into indiscretion, lofting Coningham for a catch. Three ducks sat uncomfortably alongside their grim-faced skipper.

Ward was now a Test cricketer of stature. To him must be accorded the greatest credit for the first Test triumph, and now, with runs no less highly-priced, he played sensibly, creating runs. Then Trumble came on, and at 44 England's central pillar was lost: Ward on 30 cut, and Darling took the catch at short third. Ford found trouble with the deliveries of fellow-giant, Trumble, but caned Turner to the cover fence. Peel made only six; and soon Ford cut and set off for a run, only to see Giffen leap from slip and pluck the ball out of the air. Seven down for 60.

FOOTNOTE: *At Melbourne Turner hit Stoddart "just above the elbow, drawing from him an involuntary exclamation that could be heard all over the ground."*

Briggs made five lucky runs, and Philipson, winning the 'keeper's position from Gay, hit wildly. Richardson, keen to get the pads off and the ball in his strong fingers, lashed yet another outfield catch, and they trooped off soon after 3 p.m.

Turner's 5-32 and Trumble's 3-15 had denied Giffen the chance of a bowl, but the new Australian captain soon had to face a hostile Richardson as his star hitter, Lyons, was bowled for two.

Billy Bruce swung at Peel and was caught at slip, and Gregory was also taken behind the bat off another Richardson thunderbolt. At 15 for three Darling and Giffen tried to keep out of trouble by letting Richardson's bouncers fly harmlessly past. Twice in succession Darling made that collector's piece, the left-hander's cover-drive off an express delivery, then hit a fast half-volley from Lockwood over the fence for 5; but a near-shooter snapped back wickedly and bowled him after a 38-run partnership which was the highest of the day: 32 of them had come from Darling's bat.

With Iredale in, England were passed, but Richardson came back and bowled him with a beautiful ball; and at 96 Giffen fell at last to a smart catch by Philipson. Trott and Coningham hoisted 100, but life was fleeting and another snap catch accounted for the fast bowler, and Trott was run out in some confusion with Jarvis.

So, as the crowd wended its way out into the world again, Australia, at 123, led by 48.

The last day of 1894, Monday, was sunny and bright, with a cool breeze holding a tolerable temperature. The pitch soon proved a batsman's strip as MacLaren and Ward opened England's second innings, MacLaren playing Coningham away to exorcise the spectre of a "pair". Both men scored freely off Coningham, but Turner soon knocked MacLaren's off stump out of the ground.

Stoddart started with a three cut off Turner and a four off Giffen; then all was reticence as he and Ward set about investing for the future. Stoddart took a single to wipe off the arrears, and finally lofted Turner grandly over the fence onto the asphalt. It seemed to encourage both batsmen, and the total reached 78 at lunch, Stoddart 35, Ward 28. "The Englishmen mean business today," many a man was remarking to his neighbour.

Soon Stoddart enlivened the day with four to leg off Turner. Ward edged Trumble's faster one for three, but with 100 up he was bowled off his pads for 41 and Brown came out to make a shaky start.

Stoddart was thrilling spectators and team-mates alike with his free stroking. At last he was applying his intrinsic skills to the supreme occasion; at last he dominated—not for several overs, nor for a tantalising sunlit half-hour. Now, against the full battery of Australia's Test team—Giffen, Trumble, Trott, Coningham and Turner, especially Turner—he had the satisfaction of playing a prolonged hand when his side most needed it.

Looking back many years, MacLaren wrote: "It was one of those days when he convinced you from the commencement of his innings that nothing could get past his bat, that there was no ball that could not be hit to the exact spot he selected. He stood out supremely great so often, and I experienced some of my greatest treats when his partner. A courteous gentleman, his delight over the success of any member of his side was beautiful to behold. His kindness to me was such that I always felt I could never do enough to make myself worthy of his affection."

He elicited much affection this day. He had the greater share of a 90 partnership with Jack Brown, and stood 93 not out as Brockwell struck his first ball for four. Then Turner came on, and soon, with a four to leg, Stoddart reached his second century against Australia, and the crowd paid its resounding tribute.

Some years later Stoddart recorded that this innings was "*the* century of my career. As I felt that I had contributed a small share to England's victory, nothing I have ever done in cricket gives me the same lasting pleasure to look back on as that innings".

He continued on his stylish way till the day's end, when he had reached 150. Peel succeeded Brockwell and played perfectly to orders: the loose ball was punished, but risks were avoided as England ground towards a winning total. It was said that Stoddart's style was unrecognisable in that quiet final session. His comment: "I had to buck up for England, home and beauty".

He was given a tremendous ovation as he returned to the pavilion that evening, and Giffen, as he clapped, knew that his opposite number had gathered the game well into his own territory with a lead of 239 for the loss of only four men. The Australians had bowled well and fielded almost faultlessly, but an early breakthrough in the morning was their only hope.

But on New Year's Day, with a huge holiday crowd raising dust all along the approaches to the ground, England consolidated. After three quarters of an hour Stoddart had added only 13 to his overnight score. Peel had seldom been so restrained either. It was almost a shock when Stoddart hit Giffen to square-leg for four and next over drove another boundary.

It was the last jewel in this monumental innings: at 173 he chopped down on a faster ball from Giffen and played on. He had been determined, vigilant, even cramped, only once lifting the ball over the fence. The crowd rose and the gloved ladies clapped their English hero, who, when Tom Horan congratulated him, seemed cool and fresh enough to start another marathon innings.

His stand was considered slow because it stretched over 320 minutes: such were his dynamic standards. Yet he had worn down the opposition. This was a Test match and he had a responsibility. W.G.'s English Test record had been beaten almost incidentally, and three quarters of a century later no England captain has yet exceeded Stoddart's score in Australia in a Test.

F. G. J. Ford, hitting freely, was just the man to step into his place now, with England 320 for five. Giffen eventually deceived him, and with Briggs in, Peel,

FOOTNOTE: *Stoddart's record 173 was exceeded by Mike Denness, England's captain, who made 188 at Melbourne in the final Test of the 1974-75 series.*

batting with surprising patience and sobriety (not having overdone the New Year's celebrations), began to put some meat into his shots. In no time at all he fell to Jarvis, stumped, his taxing performance of 53 containing 37 singles and not a single boundary—truly national devotion.

Now the Australian fielding cracked: against Briggs and Lockwood first Iredale then Gregory missed catches. Tireless Giffen supplied the answer: a full-toss passed Briggs' cross-bat and found him l.b.w.

402 for eight, and the end surely in sight.

But now Lockwood and Philipson put together 53 valuable runs, then Lockwood and Richardson added 20 more, and with England's final total 475, Giffen's men needed 428 to win. The captain had taken 6 wickets in 470 balls, but now, the marathon over, he had to reorientate his thoughts. His decision was to send in Bruce and Trott for a final session that could ruin everything or provide a base upon which to build next day.

Australia romped to 86 that evening, and Bruce reached 50 off Peel's opening over next day. It was looking good for Australia, but a miscalculation against Peel stopped things short: Bruce drove, hitting the ground with his bat, and Stoddart at mid-off made the catch. Australia 98 for one.

Giffen joined Trott and the hitting policy went on. By lunch 149 was on the board: Giffen 28, Trott 67. With care, on this first-class pitch there seemed no reason why Australia should not grind away to victory. Soon it was 190, almost halfway, lots of batting to come.

And Stoddart called up Brockwell, his erratic but often useful change bowler. He held one back and Giffen cocked it easily up to Brown at point. Two overs later Trott, five short of his century, drove Brockwell like lightning and the bowler dropped to pick up a wonderful catch near his boots. Now Darling was in, and before long Brockwell produced a suitable delivery for him, pitching leg-stump and taking the off. Surrey's Billy Brockwell, to the delight of all his team-mates, had cracked Australia's foundations with three fine wickets for eight runs, and England were now back on top.

Gregory played on to Richardson and it was 216 for five. Lyons and Iredale stopped the rot momentarily, but at 241 Lyons clipped Peel into the stumps. Jarvis, Coningham and Trumble were all disposed of quickly and Turner came in last—Iredale 30 not out.

The first ball all but bowled Turner, but unaffectedly he kept the bowlers at bay, and as the minutes ticked by and Stoddart rang the changes the frustration mounted. At one point Lockwood threw at Turner's wicket as he stood out of his ground and hit his bat. Phillips rejected the appeal for obstruction, having already called "over", but there was agitation in the crowd, and Turner was indignant.

Iredale cut charmingly and Turner hit straight confidently, and 61 runs were added by this pair of non-conformists; the entire cast had to report back the following day to claim the last wicket.

Stoddart spoke to Peel "with the little touch of humour which would put Bobby into the frame of mind". Bobby then bowled Iredale with a straight good-length ball which kept a shade low, and England had won her Test match at last by 94 runs, going two-up in the series.

Stoddart, the *Pall Mall Gazette* commented, had gained honours "not so much international as immortal".

The teams gathered in the Melbourne pavilion, and Brockwell was presented the ball with which he had tilted England's fortunes. Both captains made speeches, then thoughts turned to the third contest.

CHAPTER 13

AUSTRALIA ON TOP

At Ballarat, where Humphreys, shirt-sleeve flapping, took 10-51, they strolled through the glorious Gardens; they went horse-riding; they went down the Last Chance gold-mine at midnight; then they moved on to Adelaide to meet a much-changed Australian team.

Turner was omitted in view of Adelaide's fast strip: nowhere is there record of Stoddart's reaction. Lyons, with flu, was an absentee, and Trumble was also missing. Ambidextrous Jack Harry was selected, as was Callaway and young Jack Worrall; but the most interesting newcomer was the brother whose claims Harry Trott had been promoting.

Young Albert, strong and wild, had his own way of training. W.G. had his apple-orchard, Grimmett his faithful dog, but Albert Trott spun the ball past a large wooden box representing George Giffen, the most obstinate batsman in the land. And now "Albatrott" was in Adelaide to show what he could do for his country.

The enclosures were filled as Giffen, the local idol, flipped the coin. It was a good day for him to win the toss: over 100° in the shade and 155° out of it.

The original wicket had been too near one side, and the revised strip may not have enjoyed adequate preparation, yet after five electric minutes Australia had 22 on the board. After this bludgeoning by Harry Trott and Bill Bruce all sorts of things seemed possible.

But it had to stop: Bruce played on to Richardson with the total 31, and in came Giffen. Nevertheless, 50 appeared in only 35 minutes play, and the English players squinted at the sun and hated its fury.

After an l.b.w. shout against Trott, Giffen called for a run: Trott, bemused by the appeal, set off late and sacrificed his wicket. His quick 48 was an inspiration to the younger brother waiting in the wings.

Brockwell came on without working the same trick as at Melbourne, and Australia lunched at 80 for two.

Richardson bowled Iredale second ball after the interval, but Peel left the field with a sprained ankle and England's stocks slumped. Briggs bobbed up and conceded a series of singles, and excitement rose as Darling showed his willingness to pull. The little left-hander sent the ball swirling up over the 'keeper. Philipson positioned himself under it and held it.

Now Gregory and Harry fell rapidly, and at 124 for six sweat-soaked Richardson had earned four wickets and his captain's undying admiration.

Worrall was jittery. He hit hard to Richardson at cover and streaked up the pitch, but the ball was back in Philipson's gloves even before Worrall was halfway.

Giffen brought up 150 with a "quarter-off drive". By now the heat had driven an exhausted Tom Richardson from the field, and it was left to Lockwood to chip in with a wicket—a fine caught-and-bowled off Jarvis. They took tea.

The dehydrated Englishmen, temporarily relieved, set about winding up the innings. Brockwell took his valuable wicket: Giffen (58) after eight partners in almost three hours; 157 for nine.

Only Callaway and Albert Trott stood between England and the comforts of the pavilion now, but they resisted and even repelled the experienced attack. Callaway cut 16 off two overs from Lockwood, and Trott picked him off his toes in the grand manner, landing the ball in a buggy in the driveway.

The score passed 200 and Trott mis-cued on the leg-side, sending the ball spiralling into the blue. Richardson, back in the fray, lumbered across but just failed to get under it.

Under the expanse of cloudless sky the Surrey giant now bowled again, and young Trott drove him far into the outfield, with the fieldsmen transfixed; they scampered five hoarsely-applauded runs!

Finally Richardson, aching all over, bowled Callaway after a stand of 81. Australia rested at 238. MacLaren and Briggs (his former coach) gathered five token runs in those last ten minutes.

There were hours of sleeplessness ahead for all of them, a night of over-powering heat, damp sheets, throbbing heads, hopeless tossing and turning. Some of the Englishmen unwisely took showers during the night ("Stoddy" was seen walking down the corridor of the hotel after taking bath number four), and all the unwitting indiscretions took toll next day as their batting was dismembered with horrific deadliness.

Stoddart had the iron roller pulled only once up and down the wicket for fear of crumbling it, and with hopes of making 350 despite Jack Blackham's sombre forecast of 200, England went into the steamy cauldron and faced up to Albert Trott and Syd Callaway, both medium-pace, breaking sharply.

Briggs soon cut Trott away for two boundaries, and Giffen readily took it as the signal to bowl himself. Callaway sent down six successive maidens, in the third of which he bowled Briggs.

Brockwell hit Giffen, but against Callaway there was no breathing space, and in his seventh over Brockwell tried to lift a ball clear and Harry leapt to hold it. Soon MacLaren was given "not out" after touching Callaway to Jarvis; then he swept Callaway to break a remarkable spell: after one hour Callaway had had 2-3 off 12 overs.

Ward, carrying so many of England's hopes, was tempted by Giffen to swing uppishly to square-leg, and now England were 49 for three. Stoddart, holding himself back to number 5, took a single off Callaway. Then, after playing five successive off-cutters from Giffen, to a great shout from the crowd he fell to a fast straight ball. White umbrellas danced about "like demon toadstools".

Bristling with pride, MacLaren tried to defeat the swarming off-side field by hitting Callaway to leg but the ball barely rose, crashed into the stumps, and half the side were out for 56.

After lunch Peel was bowled for 0, giving Callaway 4-14. A determined stand by Brown and Ford saw 100 up, always a relief in such ominous conditions, but Giffen, at 111, lured Ford under an off-drive.

Then Lockwood lashed out and Worrall turned, ran and caught him. Eight down for 111. Stoddart had rejected the suggestion that England might let the compulsory follow-on materialise in these stifling conditions. His men were instructed to strive for every run.

The tail did curl up, but without connivance. Worrall took his third catch as Richardson swiped, and defiant Jack Brown was left 39 not out, made in great style. Curiously, eight of England's wickets had fallen to the final ball of an over. The follow-on had been averted by six runs.

Harry Trott, scoreless, helped a yorker from Peel into his stumps as Australia set about building up the lead. Giffen and Bruce carried the score to 44, then Ford clasped a hard cut by the Australian captain.

Bruce thrashed Brockwell for 13 in an over and took 4 4 and 3 off Lockwood; when Iredale struck two more successive fours it was suggested that Stoddart might have served as a model for a statue of Melancholy.

Briggs came on as the partnership approached a hectic 100, and Bruce, fairly worn out, hit the first alluring delivery into square-leg's hands. It was 5.50 p.m. and in that mood a night's rest for him could have set the stage for one of history's greatest innings. As it was, the Melbourne solicitor's slashing 80 pleased his skipper, who feared a change in the weather.

Darling failed to bridge those last minutes. Lockwood, after taking so much punishment, beat him, and the Englishmen trooped off in the evening heat.

A half-holiday was granted on Monday, so keen was Adelaide's interest, and right well did the oppulation savour the day's play. First Gregory, under an overcast sky, sent the ball speeding away through the cover field. Iredale went soberly to 40 before the first discordant note was sounded: Peel dropped a hard return. Soon he snicked Richardson through Philipson's hands, and then split Lockwood's finger with a cover shot. Albert Trott, of all people, came out as substitute.

Gregory suffered a common fate when a ball rebounded from his foot into the wicket, and Australia at 197 for five already led by 311.

Richardson bowled Jack Harry out of Test cricket, and as Stoddart swung his bowling about, Briggs got Worrall; Jarvis hit well, seeing Iredale to his century and eventually holing out just before lunch.

Albert Trott and Iredale completed England's demoralisation afterwards. They took runs freely, and it was only a tired shot by Iredale on 140 that ended it all. A looping full-toss from Peel finished up in the bowler's grateful palms, and neither batsman nor bowler could keep a serious face.

347, with one to fall. And it was the heroism and the agony of the first innings all over again. Callaway and Trott hammered 64 runs against a weary and aching attack.

Brockwell, for one, probably yearned for a quiet corner with pen and paper where he could chronicle the day's events, reaching for a drink between paragraphs. Trott (72) did most of the damage. Richardson at last got one through Callaway, with Australia 411. For England victory was a mountainous 526 runs away.

MacLaren and Ward set about keeping Australia in the field for an age, but the thought was a vain one, even if given weight by an encouraging beginning. MacLaren made a majestic 35 out of 52 before being caught in the longfield.

Albert Edwin Trott had his first wicket, and with appetite whetted he immediately took another, and decisively at that. Ward's stump was broken from top to butt by a murderous delivery.

Philipson, nightwatchman, was bowled by Giffen, and three wickets had fallen for one run. Stoddart and Brown were watchful as the minutes crept grimly by. Trott bowled again and hurt Brown, and as the end of play was drawing near Giffen mercifully led his men off, with England 56 for three.

The wicket's surface was broken here and there but generally played true, and the day was fine as Trott and Giffen took up the attack as men might sit themselves at a lavish dinner with all evening ahead of them.

The batsmen were ill at ease from the start, and shortly Trott, kicking sharply from the off, found the stumps off Brown's pads.

Brockwell was steady, and with Stoddart looking confident, there were fleeting visions of a revival; but Brockwell could not contain himself, letting fly at Trott: the new man had smelt success, and no hit, however well struck, was going to elude his grasp.

Peel, first ball, suffered the same fate, registering a "pair".

Stoddart tried to launch an assault on Trott, but soon he went back to watchful, crouching batsmanship. Ford tipped an impossible ball into point's hands, and the Trott brothers had gained a wicket for Australia family-style.

Briggs went third ball, bowled Trott, while Stoddart stood firm, feeling each rapid dismissal like the lash of a whip. Lockwood went after Trott, but in this match of great catches Iredale took it deep on the drive, and after a dozen aimless runs belted by the trojan Richardson the innings was laid to rest at 143.

Stoddart was stranded on 34 not out made in 100 minutes of faultless technique; but the most amazing figures, together with the cleverest verse, were:

A. E. Trott 27 overs, 10 maidens, 43 runs, 8 wickets

> *You didn't expect it, my sonny?*
> *Yet, truly, complain you must not;*

For you wanted "a run" for your money,
And, complying, I gave you "A. Trott".

(The Kangaroo to Mr Stoddart—by "Lika Joko")

The youngster was given an uproarious ovation for his performance following his unbeaten 38 and 72. Cash and gifts were heaped upon him, and an English player bet him a new hat he would be in the next Australian side to tour England. He did not win the hat, as we know. Possibly with Stoddart's encouragement, Trott went in his disappointment to join Middlesex, and today a forlorn tumulus identified as P613 in Willesden Cemetery marks his final resting place. Less than a week before the outbreak of World War I, Albert Trott, depressed by dropsy, shot himself through the head with a Browning pistol. His will, written on the back of a laundry bill, bequeathed his wardrobe to his landlady; the Coroner's officer found £4 in cash.

The English team visited Broken Hill, where the miners chipped away at the huge silver-ore faces, so important to the future of the young continent. One of the cricketers saw a chunk of worthless galena ("new chum silver") and, thinking it to be the real thing, asked Stoddart excitedly if he could take some. He was told drily that he could take a pocketful if he wished.

Stoddart treated the locals to 55, and again the old deceiver Humphreys bagged a host of wickets. Brockwell took 7-35 and 7-7, and Philipson astonished everyone with his huge spin.

There was good shooting to be had at May Bell station: the kill included wallabies, lizards, rabbits and hawks, plus a cat shot in error by Bobby Peel.

A special train took them into the Dandenong hills, where Stoddart was at his best with 81; then on the first of February they went back to the serious stuff in Sydney, where rain threatened to continue as the 4th Test match began.

It was Stoddart's choice of innings, a choice he declined to make immediately, to the annoyance of many onlookers. After taking Peel and Briggs to inspect the wicket, he asked Australia to bat.

Harry Graham, Australia's hero at Lord's in '93, was in for his first Test on home soil, and Harry Moses was back, with much expected of him. Charlie Turner also returned to the side for what proved to be his last Test—a game which could hardly have been much shorter.

The third Harry—Trott—walked out with Bruce to see if the wicket would react as soggily as it appeared. They took a single each before Trott was caught off Peel. Richardson at the other end started to bump in lively style, sometimes

FOOTNOTE: *Trott was also encouraged by Jim Phillips to try his luck with Middlesex.*

breaking a foot or more from the off, and Bruce took evasive action. But Peel got him when he lifted a ball to Brockwell at deep square-leg.

Moses came in ahead of time, and in 20 critical minutes six runs crystallised; then Peel beat Giffen with an unexpected straight one, and Australia were 26 for three.

Moses was bowled for 0, and it was 26 for four as Graham took up position. Richardson roared in and hurled them down, rearing impossibly to shoulder height and creating terrible problems for Syd Gregory. Graham flung back the challenge with two leaping hits to the chains off the fast bowler, dropping to his knees when the deadly bouncer roared at him.

The sun was through now, hardening the wicket into a perfect batting strip. It seemed England were through when Gregory was stumped off Briggs and Iredale was caught first ball by the same delighted bowler. It was 51 for six wickets, and whatever happened thereafter, Stoddart's policy of sending Australia in had paid off.

Now Darling came in, an exceptional batsman at number 8; and the direness of the situation was an ideal problem with which the armchair critic might test him. The clear-eyed young man from Adelaide got straight into it: runs off Peel, then a hit over the heads of the meagre crowd into the tennis courts off Briggs. Graham became infected: flowing drives, pull-strokes to quicken the pulse of even the indifferent dispenser of refreshments.

Stoddart brought back Richardson and switched Briggs, and soon Graham was edging the ball at a nice height straight to Brockwell, who dropped it.

Now Darling had to clap on pace as MacLaren's return was beating him home, but Philipson fumbled. Graham had another let-off as a steepling catch was misjudged by Briggs, running back after delivery and receiving the forthright views of Peel, who could easily have taken it. A tactful word from Stoddart sent Briggs back to his bowling mark, but with runs coming fast there was an air of desperation about England in the field.

Darling hoisted a ball out to long-on into MacLaren's hands—and out again. Richardson's next ball was a horrifying loose one at Darling's face; he diverted it into his wicket, and the sensational 66-run stand was over.

The latest idol came out now, for whom the *Melbourne Argus* smilingly visualised canonisation: "Saint Albert Trott would look well in a coloured window". Certainly his innings was once more full of vivid colour. First Richardson hit him sickeningly, and several fielders worked for some time to bring him round; then he and Graham played brilliant cricket, punishing all the bowlers on that smooth, firm slab of a pitch.

At 192 Brockwell erred again: he might have caught Graham off his own bowling. But at tea Graham was 87 and "Albatrott" had already rustled up 40. It took Graham very few hits to raise his hundred after the break, and the "Little Dasher", who was to die a lonely death in Dunedin asylum, still stands alone as the man who made a century in his first Test innings in both England

and Australia.

At 105 he jumped out at Briggs once too often and Philipson removed the bails; his timely innings had Australia now tolerably placed at 231 for eight.

Jarvis edged to Philipson, and Turner assisted Trott in the fourth consecutive abnormal final stand for Australia; 45 runs were added. Trott, still undefeated, had 86 by his name—196 Test runs unbeaten against this star-studded bowling line-up; this was the zenith.

The fielding had been "shocking", only Stoddart, now at slip, maintaining a standard of efficiency.

England had to bat through ten tense minutes, and almost immediately MacLaren was stumped off Harry Trott. Rain began to fall soon after the field had emptied.

The boisterous weather continued and there was wide expectation of seeing England caught on a sticky; but a noisy deluge did irreparable damage and Saturday's play was abandoned at 2.30 p.m.

On that sunny Sunday evening Stoddart drove to the Australian camp at Coogee, but after the fraternisation was done with rain splattered the pavements. It fell all night. As if manipulated by some fiendish playwright the sun broke through Monday morning, warming the cricket pitch to an evil, gluey tackiness. The crowd was building up rapidly as Ward and Briggs of the red rose county faced up.

Harry Trott bowled impeccably and faster than usual; and Turner looked venomous, but presented less menace as his short stuff flew over the bat into the gauntlets of Jarvis. At 20 Ward made the first error against Turner; then Briggs played round a ball from Trott, and England stood alarmingly at 24 for three.

Stoddart was watchful, making a stirring hit or two, and trying desperately hard to counter the drunken antics of the ball as it bounded at all angles, marking his shirt-front more than his bat. He had recently had an affectionate little note from an 8-year-old English girl begging him to "make your usual big score". He thought enough of this letter to retain it, but the infant in the "big stand near the Governor's box" was in for disappointment.

Trott bowled one short, and Stoddart jumped out; it spun sharply from leg and Jarvis fetched it and stumped England's captain for 7, though his bat flashed round hastily.

"It's the worst wicket I've ever seen," he told his men, "absolutely the worst. And not only is it the worst I've seen, but it's miles the worst!" He felt England would not survive the day.

There seemed no answer. Poor Brockwell again succumbed to a miraculous finger-tip catch; and Ford, Giffen's "bunny", became the sixth casualty at 43. Brown, jaw set, sadly surveyed the destruction. Peel aimed an almighty blow at Turner and gave Jarvis a third stumping, and by lunch England were 59 for seven.

Giffen was cutting the ball prodigiously, often beating his 'keeper as well as the helpless man with the bat. Philipson was caught close in, and with accident-prone Lockwood, hand in sling after a bottle burst, unable to bat, Richardson was last man, and he was mortified to see Giffen turn a hefty off-drive into a left-handed catch.

Thus in an hour and three quarters England had collapsed helplessly for 65. Jack Brown, 20 not out, did not even bother unbuckling his pads: he and Ward marched out for the follow-on on a pitch no less treacherous than when they had first cast eyes on it that morning.

Giffen's fourth ball bowled Brown, and Stoddart made only one unproductive hit before holing out to Iredale in the deep; for the last time in a Test Turner had been his executioner. Two out for 5—both last men 0.

MacLaren had had enough of this nonsense, and when Giffen gave him half a chance he hooked—but straight into Bruce's hands. Three down for 5: three ducks! Britannia's trident trembled.

Ward's turn came as Darling gathered a lofted drive off Giffen; and Peel, stepping out to Turner, slipped on the greasy turf and was stumped for his second consecutive "pair".

It was 14 for five wickets, and the series was all but level at 2-all as Ford strove with Brockwell to implant some decency into the scorebook. The total stuttered to 29, at which point Turner claimed his 100th Test wicket against England in only his 17th match.

At 47, Bruce, still menacing at silly mid-on, brilliantly caught Briggs, and Ford was taken in the outfield, where most of the fielders were waiting expectantly. Still the ball behaved unpredictably, and Jarvis drew applause for his saves. It was considered salutory that only 12 byes had slipped into the combined total of 137 runs.

Philipson and Richardson made the highest stand of the day with 20 for the ninth and last wicket, and the carnage ended as Turner caught the 'keeper and tossed the ball to Giffen to present to a lady in the reserve.

Hats were flung in the air and cheers echoed all around. Australia had won by an innings and 147 runs in two days of play. Turner and Giffen had bowled unchanged throughout the second innings and Albert Trott, after his 8-43 in the previous Test, had stood idly by and observed it all through his oriental eyes.

Long after the conclusion of the match a big crowd waited outside the members' gate at the Sydney ground, hoping for a glimpse of the players, to "settle whether they were different to other men" Brockwell, whose home was the Oval, eyed this gathering with suspicion: "It is a demonstrative, ribald crowd that, especially the boy section of it, has so much to say in a way that is personal that even a big man like Lyons won't face it alone".

There was almost a month between this Test and the decider in Melbourne. Stoddart, the newest rumour linking his name with a girl from Sydney's North Shore ("his future home", miscued the correspondent), took his team to Armidale, and himself made 88 in fairly sedate style, relishing the relaxed atmosphere and the chance to practise on a fair pitch, striving to rebuild team confidence.

Against a N.S.W. & Queensland side England's champion had reached a stylish 40 when an unhappy chapter unfolded, best described by an eye-witness:

"Mr Bannerman, one of the umpires, gave a no-ball against Coningham. That mercurial individual lost his head, and in his annoyance deliberately threw the next at Stoddart. The English captain wisely and firmly called upon Coningham to apologise to the umpire and himself, and this the bowler ultimately did, but not for some time. The incident put Stoddart clean 'off', Coningham's next ball bowled him off his pads".

Coningham's must be a fidgety ghost. This lively left-hander was adept at billiards, an oarsman of renown, a good shot, and as a rugby footballer not even "Stoddy" unaided could have caught him. Further, he had earned a medal for saving a boy's life in the Thames in 1893, and as a fast bowler he could be quite unpalatable, as he had proved on this warm February day in Brisbane.

But all this came to seem dull fare indeed beside the conspiracy sensation of 1900, when "Conny", revolver at his hip, conducted his own scandalous and unsuccessful divorce case with an eminent priest as the alleged "other man".

They left Brisbane at the earliest opportunity, seeking relief from the sub-tropical conditions in Armidale's pretty setting (at home the Thames was frozen over, and people were skating on the ponds at Hampstead).

Andrew Stoddart gave the scribes of Newcastle something to write about with a hit for six straight out of the ground and a wicket with his first ball.

Packed steamers and trains and horseback riders were now converging on Melbourne for the greatest show on earth. A frenzy had swept the land as the kangaroo shaped up to the lion in newspaper and over meal-table.

Crowds gathered in unprecedented numbers, even for the preliminary net practices. All was set for the Match of the Century.

FOOTNOTE: *Against N.S.W. & Queensland, Stoddart was dropped before he had scored.*

CHAPTER 14

TEST MATCH CLASSIC

Some momentous quotes have come down to us through the ages. Turner said: "I'll never play cricket again!" when the startling news of his omission came through.

"It's no use talking like that, Charlie," said Jack Lyons, whose position in the team was secure. "You'll have to go to England if we go next year". (They did, but Turner didn't).

And George Giffen has recorded his own thoughts at the time: "I knew that when Stoddart and I went into the ring to toss and arrange preliminaries, he was as white as a sheet, and I have been told that the pallor of my own countenance matched his".

Major Ben Wardill, secretary of the Melbourne Club, escorted the captains out, linked arm in arm with them. They stood by the glossy wicket, and as Giffen made the most of these last seconds free of responsibility Wardill could contain himself no longer.

"For Heaven's sake, toss and get it over with!"

"Keep cool, Major," "Stoddy" soothed.

Giffen's hand was unsteady as he flipped the coin. "Heads!" Stoddart commanded, but the Australian gave a delighted little skip as it came to rest "tails". Stoddart's look of despair seemed to say "It's all over", and the packed house cheered the home skipper to the echo.

Trott (G.H.S.) and Bruce opened Australia's batting, the latter having dashed down from duty at North Melbourne police court and soon cutting Peel to the boundary with typical audacity and perfect legal right. Trott also punched the ball hard, especially off Peel. They put on 40 before Bruce was caught.

Giffen, almost 36, his hair grey as ash, walked to the middle fixing his glove; he represented the most formidable obstacle to his opponents.

Soon he was jumping out to Peel and sending carpet-drives speeding into the wide outfield, and Trott began to time his leg shots off Richardson.

Lockwood and Briggs took over, but after lunch when Australia were 76 for one wicket, the pair hit strongly again; Trott was driving with immense power. The hundred came, then Briggs lured Trott out and bowled him.

Iredale was not very well, though his grace and ease under his new white quilted hat were ominous. But at 112 Richardson celebrated his breather by crashing through him with a good length ball. The last 25 runs had taken 45 minutes.

Australia soon suffered another blow as Peel returned to the front line and Giffen (57) played a yorker into his stumps. The innings was now perched

FOOTNOTE: *Stoddart had looked "rather uneasy" as he went out to toss, with Ford and Philipson alongside him, but the "generous applause of the public seemed to brighten him up a bit".*

noncommitally at 142 for four. It was ten minutes to four as Joe Darling joined Gregory and held on nervously.

Ford missed a difficult one at slip after tea, and Gregory celebrated with a drive and a hit to leg, both for four. Darling, for his part, gave the crowd the sweet-sounding cuts and enchanting drives which always seem so unexpected from a small man facing fast bowling on a hard pitch. The afternoon ticked away and the runs began to come—200 rapidly posted and forgotten as the 250 was applauded rapturously. All the bowlers were being roughly handled.

With Gregory 70 and Darling 72 at the end, Australia were well set at 282 for four, and the odds on this decider were easing towards the home team.

Darling, due to receive a gold watch from his father when his expected century was achieved, added only two runs next day before edging Peel low to slip (the paternal prize was his after all for top-scoring). England had the early breakthrough so eagerly hoped for.

The *Argus* man took his eyes off the play long enough to paint an enthusiastic picture.

"Stoddart ought to make an excellent agent-general when he returns and looks in at the Royal Exchange and tells some of the haughty financiers of that poorly-informed institution that Australia is most prosperous, that a happier, better-spirited, better-dressed, and better-behaved crowd could not have been seen than he saw at the Melbourne ground".

England now had the muscular Lyons to contend with, but further excitement came next over as Gregory touched one from Richardson, and Philipson completed the job. At 286 for six, things had taken an abrupt turn.

Lyons pushed the total to 300, but Richardson unleashed a wonderful ball at Graham which cut back and broke the wicket. Albert Trott, the phenomenon, took his place and made ten before being caught at cover, at last registering a Test batting average—206!

Jack Lyons was aided by the equally husky Jarvis in adding 32, but when Lyons fell for a splendid even-time 55 it was the dapper McKibbin, who took his country past 400 and made runs apace with Jarvis. It was Australia's *fifth* freak last-wicket stand in a row, and raised their effort to a reassuring 414.

At 3.10 p.m. Ward and Brockwell set about England's reply. Ward took a single, then Brockwell placed Giffen away for 2 and 3. Facing Trott's first ball, he advanced to hit, fell, and was stumped.

So Stoddart walked out sooner than he would have wished, to the staccato music of 28,000 clapping pairs of hands, and was soon playing the ball away for runs. Hitting to leg with assurance, he soon had 20 to his name; then he daringly late-cut Giffen for the first boundary. He settled down: he swung his opposite number to the square-leg chains and forced Giffen to miss his length. As the Australian captain wavered in accuracy Stoddart won this personal duel of the leaders with strokes that thrilled those watching and went, otherwise unrecorded, amongst their memories to their graves.

FOOTNOTE: *One drive by Lyons hissed through the air and reached Stoddart in the deep first bounce, giving him a ''very nasty crack on the leg''.*

Albert Trott came on, and for a while McKibbin's pace and movement puzzled both batsmen. Stoddart, however, got several exquisite leg-glances away, and some spanking leg-side shots; and Ward ventured forward, and three times claimed four through the covers.

Stoddart was master of this bowling now, so Giffen brought back Harry Trott in the hope of encouraging a mis-hit. The England captain welcomed the change with a disdainful shot through the field, but with 100 up Giffen's gamble paid off as Stoddart stepped out a pace but failed to make contact. Jarvis stumped him, and the crowd jumped to its feet with joy at the important capture.

His 68 had occupied 90 minutes of all that was best in batting—and at a time when it mattered most. England were now 110 for two.

"Well played, Mr Thtoddart," Jack Brown might have said as he stubbed his cigarette and marched out determinedly to carry on the campaign, but almost instantly Ward was bowled by McKibbin for 32. With two new men in, Australia went for the kill.

MacLaren played Harry Trott's looping spin charmingly to leg and had him replaced by his brother, who enhanced his reputation by clean-bowling Brown for 30. The stand had promised much with its 54 positively-made runs, but now no more wickets could be afforded, and surely and safely MacLaren and Peel saw the day out. England, 214 behind, had six wickets left.

On Monday MacLaren and Peel showed fine touch, the lordly Lancastrian forcing good-length balls, and Peel, with less of a regal air but equal authority, cutting Albert Trott's fizzers breezily.

Giffen removed his felt hat and took over; Peel clouted him square. And when Albert Trott flung one wide it bumped over the dry grass to the boundary, and a touch of anxiety sounded among the people assembled under the glaring sun. The runs were coming, but two chances went begging, and at lunch England boasted 295 without further loss. The match was already deserving high classification.

The punishing batting continued, and at 322 Albert Trott came back. MacLaren drove him imperiously through the covers and had his century.

At 104 he was missed by Jarvis, but a ball finally went to hand when the gallant Peel (73) lifted Giffen to Gregory. The 162 partnership had almost doubled the score.

Lockwood lasted only a few fidgety minutes and Giffen dismissed Ford. At 364 for seven the betting in the outer was against England equalling Australia's 414, and the likelihood slumped further when MacLaren's great stand finally ended as he trod on his wicket, a sad end presaged by several near misses. His 120 had included some beautifully-timed strokes, each majestic as any he was

FOOTNOTE: *Near the start of his innings of 68 Stoddart played Giffen uppishly to point. This prompted him to "try his bat very carefully" but he was evidently satisfied, as he went on with it.*

to stroke in the glorious if unvictorious years ahead.

An extraordinary catch by Harry Trott gave Briggs the first duck of the match, and Richardson was out when ten minutes more of the blacksmith treatment would have stolen a first innings lead. As it was, England were only 29 behind at 385.

There was some very determined batting in the closing phases as Australia increased the lead by 69 for the loss of Bruce, whose eleven took the best part of an hour. The sky clouded over as Giffen started batting, and while Harry Trott hit freely, the captain happened upon one solitary run in half an hour, Lockwood's eight overs so far having consisted of seven maidens and two runs.

The match was in the melting pot in a sense besides the meteorological.

On the fourth day a stifling dust-storm caused terrible discomfort to players and spectators alike. The awning over the Ladies' reserve was torn away and Charlie Turner's girlfriend's parasol was blown inside out. Poor Johnny Briggs had a fit of stringhalt and was placed at point until the spasm passed.

The dust may have helped Peel when Trott missed a straight one and was bowled.

There was then a 50 partnership between Iredale and Giffen, who drove Lockwood from the attack; Richardson bowled with the choking wind now coming in gusts across the wicket. Iredale played on to Richardson, and Gregory saw his captain to lunch at 50 not out. At 139 for three Australia led by 168.

Giffen eventually played over a Richardson yorker, having made 51 in 3 hours.

Darling and Gregory eased the score along without the spectacular pillaging of the first innings. Every stolen run made England's ultimate target the more remote, and for what must have seemed a long time to Stoddart the two elegant little men waited for the bad ball.

Gregory finally went for 30, and as Lyons commenced one of the most important innings of his life by dealing some thunderous blows at Richardson, England's captain exhorted his key bowler not to flag, to draw on his innermost energies.

Briggs did the trick, flicking down a faster ball to Lyons which veered from middle to off. With Australia's Hercules gone, it was 200 for six wickets; and soon Graham, hitting out wildly at the relentless Richardson, was leg-before.

Albert Trott infuriated statisticians by making 0, halving his average to 103 for ever after.

So Australia, with two wickets left, led by 248. Darling was still there, and with Jarvis he stretched the lead; Bobby Peel was called up to finish the innings, but more precious runs came as Darling cut and drove Richardson. He reached a faultless 50, then, aiming a huge hit at Peel, was bowled. 248 for nine. McKibbin soon went, and England needed 297 to win the match and the series.

Richardson had bowled 45 overs and taken 6-104—a superlative performance;

FOOTNOTE: *On the third day Stoddart led his men out at 4.15 p.m. as dark clouds approached from the north-west. He "watched them from time to time with considerable anxiety."*

1. *Andrew Stoddart's parents*

2. *His birthplace, South Shields*

A. E. STODDART.

BORN 1863.

MR. ANDREW ERNEST STOD-DART is a native of Durham. His cricket career, which is most brilliant, practically commenced when he joined the Hampstead Club in 1885. He made no fewer than five

the highest individual innings (485) for Hampstead v. Stoics, and three days later made 207 for the same club. As a batsman he has great strength, and plays very hard. He is also a fair change bowler, and an excellent field anywhere. He has gained the highest honours on the football field, and made his first appearance in International

football in the season of 1884–85. Mr. Stoddart went to Australia with Lord Sheffield's cricketers 1891–92, for whom he did brilliant work. Last year he became one of the holders of the rare record of two hundreds in a match.

centuries for that club in July and August of that year. In the following year he hit up

3. *The child, the youth, and the man (from* The Strand Magazine, *volume VII)*

4. "A most fascinating elasticity of action"

5. "He seemed not to know the meaning of the word 'fear'"

6. *Blackheath 1892-93. Back row: H. Marshall, F.C. Lohden, H.W. Finlinson, A. Robinson, G.J. Mordaunt, P. Maud, A. Allport. Seated: M.H. Toller, A.E. Stoddart, W.P. Carpmael, J. Hammond, W.B. Thomson. Front: E. Bonham Carter, W.H. Devonshire, R.F.C. de Winton, R.G. Baiss*

7. *England at Lord's, 1893 (Stoddart, although captain, has moved over to make way for W.G. Grace, who missed the match through injury). Back Row: E. Wainwright, A. Mold, W. Gunn, J.M. Read. Seated: R. Peel, A.E. Stoddart, W.G. Grace, W.H. Lockwood, A. Shrewsbury. In front: G. MacGregor, F.S. Jackson, W. Flowers*

3. *A relaxing pipe before an innings at Lord's*

9. *Middlesex 1894. Back row: S.S. Pawling, J.T. Rawlin. Seated: G. MacGregor, P.J.T. Henery, T.C. O'Brien, A.E. Stoddart, H.B. Hayman. Front: J.T. Hearne, R.S. Lucas. Insets: A.J. Webbe, C.P. Foley*

10. *Stoddart (with stick) talks with the Hon. Ivo Bligh aboard* Ophir *prior to sailing to Australia. Lady Bligh was a passenger*

11. *The 1894-95 team in Australia. Centre: A.E. Stoddart (captain). Clockwise from top left: T. Richardson, A. Ward, L.H. Gay, F.G.J. Ford, J. Briggs, W.H. Lockwood, H. Philipson, W. Brockwell, J.T. Brown, A.C. MacLaren, W.A. Humphreys, R. Peel*

12. The Sydney ground during the first Test of the 1894–95 series, with the large Gregory-Blackham partnership developing

13. Stoddart's 1897-98 touring side at Hastings the following summer, when they defeated a Rest of England side. Standing: A. Priestley (companion), J.R. Mason, E. Wainwright, T.W. Hayward, J.H. Board. Seated: G.H. Hirst, A.C. MacLaren, A.E. Stoddart, W. Storer, J. Briggs. In front: J.T. Hearne, T. Richardson. Absent, K.S. Ranjitsinhji, N.F. Druce

15. *"Boo hoo! This rude fellow is calling me names."* A sample of Australian Press reaction to Stoddart's criticism of the barracking

14. Tossing with Harry Trott, left, *during the 1897-98 series*

16. *The Middlesex amateurs, led by A.E. Stoddart, emerge from the pavilion*

17. *Kanji's mixed bunch in North America, 1899. Standing: G. Woolley (umpire), S.M.J. Woods, B.J.T. Bosanquet, A. Priestley, V.A. Barton, F. Luffman (umpire). Seated: G. Brann, A.C. MacLaren, K.S. Ranjitsinhji, A.E. Stoddart, C. Robson. In front: G.L. Jessop, W.P. Robertson, C.B. Llewellyn, C.L. Townsend*

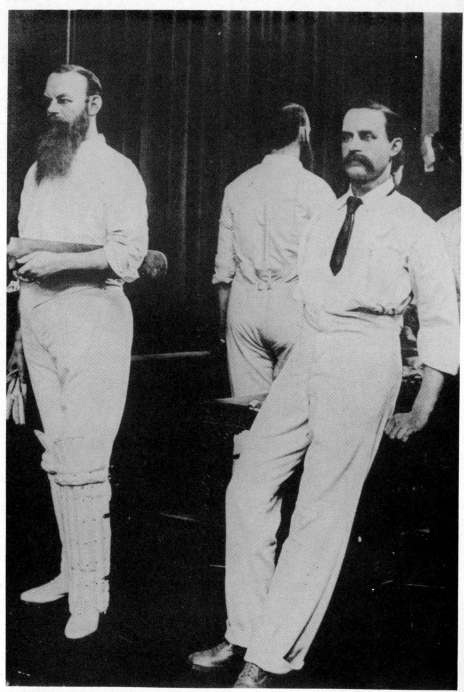

18. *Wax models of W.G. Grace and A.E. Stoddart at Madame Tussauds, at the turn of the century*

19. *In front of the pavilion at Lord's around 1900*

20. *Stoddart (partially obscured) welcomes Prince Albert (later King George VI) to Queen's Club in 1908*

22. The ageing batsman takes a net

21. Stoddart, left, has a gentle game of tennis at Queen's

23. The last gathering of the brothers and sisters (about 1913, when Harry visited from the U.S.A.). Left to right: Minnie, Drewy, Harry, Connie, Cissie

25. All that remains: the base of his gravestone

24. 115 Clifton Hill. A.E. Stoddard died in the small room above the hall

now the batsmen had to follow it up by completing an assignment rather too bulky for comfort.

Brockwell and Ward set about it.

As in the first innings, Brockwell took five from the opening over and succumbed to the first ball of the second. During the series he had been proverbially unlucky, but this time a bad pull-stroke cost him his wicket.

Stoddart came in when more casualties would have unbalanced the match, but in company with Ward he saw it through till close of play, with the score 28 for one.

England needed 269 runs more on a pitch that was holding. The series was about to be decided. All Melbourne, all Australia, all the Empire, was agog.

The epic entered its fifth day, a morning of tranquilising drizzle. Play got under way sensationally: in pin-dropping silence Harry Trott's first ball to Stoddart (11) hit the pad as he played to the on-side. Cries of "Zat!" went up and Stoddart's Middlesex colleague, Jim Phillips, raised his finger. England's chances seemed suddenly to have been sliced in half as the crest-fallen captain walked off midst roars of delight.

But Jack Brown now came nonchalantly to the crease to play a phenomenal innings. Under an overcast sky and with the precious objective so very distant, he flung down his challenge with a square-drive over cover's head first ball and a hook for four off the next—11 off Giffen's first over, followed by a stream of red-blooded strokes all over the slippery field.

Somebody in the crowd played "Rule Britannia" on a tin whistle that afternoon as the robust Yorkshireman chopped the ball through slip, cut it lethally through the cover area, and stirred even his opponents with short-arm pull shots. In less than half an hour he made 50 while Ward, watching the back door, picked up five. The bowling was changed constantly, but Giffen, Lyons and the Trotts, McKibbin and Bruce all came the same.

Soon after 1 p.m. the hundred came up—Brown 60. Now Ward, born at a village called Waterloo, with all its dramatic implications, took equal billing as the score climbed to 145 by lunch.

Ward seemed to edge to Jarvis, but Phillips, unsighted, had to reject the appeal, and soon Jack Brown had scorched to his wonderful century in even time. The game was tilting pulsatingly towards Stoddart, who sat with Lady Hopetoun, "cool as a cucumber, applauding both sides impartially".

Brown on 114 gave a faint chance to slip, but Ward was soon performing the stroke of the match, a superb drive off Giffen clean over the fence, supplying Giffen's critics with demonstrable evidence that he was bowling far too long.

"Better stay on," "Giff" claimed Harry Trott told him.

Affie Jarvis missed Brown on 125, and soon the 200 partnership blossomed—

FOOTNOTE: *As Stoddart returned after superintending the rolling of the pitch at the start of the fifth day he said: "I think it (the pitch) is all right." After his dismissal, the gatekeeper was heard to say that "Trotty" had bowled a plain ball because Stoddart was so fond of hooking him.*

in little more than two hours. Then the record for all partnerships in England v Australia Tests went by the board, and with 210 added in a most astonishing 145 minutes, Brown's great effort was ended by a Giffen catch.

Never, it was said, had Australian bowling been more completely collared, and years later the innings was classified Trumperesque when such comparisons were jealously allocated. Lord Hawke thought Brown's "head was turned" by his success here, yet only the strongest and most retiring of men could have remained unaffected under the glitter of this deed, coming at the exact moment England called for it.

Ten years later the hero was dead; he had once tipped all his beer down the sink and with typical resolve became a teetotaller; but cigarettes he could not, would not, forego. King Edward, upon hearing of Brown's heart attack, sent his own physician to tend him, but at the age of 35 he was lost.

MacLaren took his place this day in Melbourne, with 59 now wanted, seven wickets in hand, and the score mounting confidently. Ward was grinding away towards a priceless century. But at 278, seven short of his reward, the opener fell to a yorker from Harry Trott. He had done his job magnificently and left England sailing safely into victory.

Peel was in at the kill for the third time, having finished off the 1st and 2nd Tests: he made the rest of the runs in no-nonsense fashion, cutting a full-toss from Harry Trott at 4.12 p.m. as generous applause went up all round the enclosures.

When news reached Ballarat Stock Exchange, an Englishman unfurled a Union Jack and burst lustily into "Rule Britannia", at which the Southern Cross was hoisted and his Australian colleagues attempted to drown him out with "The Men of Australia". They all ended up singing "God Save the Queen". Everywhere newspaper offices were jammed as progress boards recorded Brown and Ward's fantastic stand. Today enthusiasts would all be by their radio or television sets, and the fervid group excitement and togetherness of the pavements would be—is—missing.

The 298 runs had taken only 215 minutes from 88 6-ball overs.

Giffen's emotions almost got the better of him as he shook Stoddart's hand: "It's hard to have to congratulate you, Stoddy, old boy". He apologised for the hesitancy in his words, but he had written a victory speech!

Peel gave his bat to Charlie Turner, whom Stoddart had thanked for helping England—by being absent; but the greatest prize, the ball itself, ended up in McKibbin's joyful clutches.

"Do you think there is a possible chance of getting that ball?" Stoddart said to Blackham. "I'd give my very soul to get it, upon my word I would."

Blackham probed the possibilities.

FOOTNOTE: *At the conclusion of the Test match the crowd besieged the pavilion and called loudly for Stoddart, who appeared at last at the window and bowed and smiled.*

"The ball's very valuable to me," said young McKibbin. "I prize it greatly." But a look at "Stoddy's" hopeful eyes was enough.

"If you give me your photo, " McKibbin relented, "I'll give you the ball." So the dressing room transaction took place, and the England captain showed delight at "the nice way in which McKibbin met him". That ball should have had a preservation order put on it, but it seems to have gone the way of all things.

George Giffen, for his efforts this season, received something rather more material—400 sovereigns from the cricket public for his services to Australian cricket.

The most absorbing Test series to date was concluded, the last frantic cable sent off; and *The Times* announced ENGLISH VICTORY IN AUSTRALIA with characteristic restraint.

The Rev. R. S. Holmes wrote in *Cricket*: "Well, England won the rubber. Yet it may be open to question whether on the whole our men did as well as the Australians in the test matches. True, the luck was against us in the choice of innings; Stoddart won the toss only once, and then he was foolish enough to put his opponents in, with the result that England lost that match by an innings and 147 runs. I wonder if it ever pays to do this?"

The question echoes hauntingly down the decades.

"Let me offer my sincerest congratulations to A. E. Stoddart and his gallant band," he concluded. "In a letter to myself before leaving he spoke in the highest terms of the fibre of his men; they have deserved all that was said. The captain has never played better, perhaps never so well when we take into account the burden of responsibility he has borne throughout in an office to which he was almost a stranger."

To modern eyes it seems that A. E. Stoddart was born expressly to govern this fabulous series of Test matches. Nothing in his life before or after seemed as important.

But now it was time to let the hair down; it was almost as if Shakespeare were there:

> *Upon a chair in that big banquet hall*
> *Sate Stoddart, England's captain; he did hear*
> *That sound the first amidst the festival,*
> *And whispered in a portly waiter's ear,*
> *To fill Brown's glass who sat so thirsty near,*
> *Humphreys' and Ward's: he knew that Peel, too, well*
> *Liked it, preferring it to muddy beer;*
> *And so the aforesaid waiter he did tell*
> *To put a magnum near, on which he promptly fell.*
> (*Douglas Moffat*)

FOOTNOTE: *"Mr Stoddart, during his recent visit to N.S.W., although the recipient of a plethora of hospitable invitations from his influential Sydney friends, invariably preferred the elegant comforts, the unparalleled spaciousness, and the surrounding quietude of the Hotel Australia to all the attractions of private Sydney hospitality, great and variously acceptable though they were."*

Briggs was pitched out of his bunk on the way to Tasmania, where they played two games against odds, the first at Launceston where Stoddart made 73 and the girls surprised him with a birthday cake; and the second in Hobart, six hours away through mountainous country ablaze with bushfires.

The cake, iced in team colours, was greatly appreciated by this warm and gentle man who was so many miles from home and family.

The gossip columns still oozed with theories on the cricketers' romances, and an enquiry into the status of the English amateurs resulted in the following par: "Stoddart and Philipson are the only ones with any money at all, each possessing an income of five or six hundred a year. The former is a stockbroker in London, and the latter does nothing."

They crossed the turbulent Straits again without Stoddart, who was suffering from a chill caught batting in the rain at Hobart. He followed later, missing the game with Victoria.

Philipson was put in to bat by Harry Trott and the Englishmen virtually lost the game with a first day total of 131 as the Victorian captain rammed his decision home with 8-63.

Now the action was almost done with, and a farewell banquet was thrown for Stoddart and his fellows in the luncheon room at Melbourne (with "Stoddart pudding" among the entremets).

Mr Justice a'Beckett proposed the toast to "Our Guests", recalling that everyone had followed that final Test as a father would watch over the progress of a child seriously ill. Bulletins had been handed up to him at the bench; such excitements may even have interfered with his understanding of what the witnesses were saying! (Surely the judicial tongue was in the judicial cheek?).

England, he said, had won esteem for their steadfastness in an uphill battle and for the affability with which they had accepted defeat. The Australian people were saying farewell to thorough sportsmen, and although they may have to wait for Federation of the Australian states, federation in sport was an accomplished fact.

"For They are Jolly Good Fellows!" boomed round the room, the liquor flowed, and the cheering was prolonged. When the cheers had died, the Chairman commended the professionals for their "uprightness of conduct" and fine play. Drewy Stoddart rose to respond.

He had to wait a long time for the cheering to subside, and was obviously moved by it. He thanked Melbourne for its kindness. Their lot as cricketers had been a very happy one from the time they set foot in Australia, and he felt certain all the players regretted most sincerely that it was almost time to leave.

As a member of Lord Hawke's team he had thought the trip near perfection; Lord Sheffield's tour was also most enjoyable; but the hospitality extended them on the present trip eclipsed all else.

And the cheers echoed again.

In thanking Melbourne and Sydney for the delightful venture he could not

help mentioning two of the best fellows it had ever been his lot to meet—
Major Wardill and Mr Sheridan.

Australian visits did much good for English cricket; he said he would like to
see a tour each two years. Moreover (diplomatically) he hoped it would always
be under the auspices of the Melbourne and Sydney Clubs.

Australians could congratulate themselves upon having three of the best
umpires in the world: Jim Phillips, Charlie Bannerman and Tom Flynn
(cheers), and he acknowledged the great service rendered his team by Phillips.

Finally, he could only hope the next English XI would have half as good a
time as his team had experienced. If only he could have known how chillingly
real and literal this equivocally uttered wish would become.

The last match of the tour, against South Australia, was fittingly sensational.
Again Stoddart remained in the wings, and this time his side piled on the runs.

Clem Hill had celebrated what was thought to be his 18th birthday with a
wonderful 150 not out, and the Giffens scored well.

Then as the Englishmen dwarfed the South Australian 397 with an innings
of 609, George Giffen, with Jarvis badly injured after being thrown from a trap,
must have wondered how he could have offended cricket's Great Puppeteer.

Ford made an entertaining hundred, Brown carried on from his Melbourne
delights, and Ward made certain of his century this time, and after 6 hours
batting had converted it into 200. Tireless Giffen bowled 87 overs to take
five wickets for (could this be right?—the scoresheet says so) 309 runs!

Hill made another fifty, but Richardson, Peel and Briggs had them out the
second time for 255, and Brockwell and Ford chased 44 for victory in the
remaining 20 minutes.

It took them 17 minutes.

On the eve of departure they were entertained by Governor Sir Edwin Smith,
and Stoddart exclaimed that, much as he disliked speechifying, he almost
regretted that this would be the last of the many occasions on which he had
got to his feet.

George Giffen wished them all God speed.

The professionals, prompted by "feelings of love" as well as respect for their
skipper, privately presented Stoddart with a silver tobacco jar as a parting
tribute, and he was too choked to say more than a word or two in thanking
Johnny Briggs.

The small boats taking them out to "Ophir" were all caught in a rain squall
which drenched the players and showered possible foreboding on Stoddart,

FOOTNOTE: *"Well, I never want to meet three better fellows or more pleasant companions than
Tom Richardson, Albert Ward, and Brockwell."* — *Stoddart quoted by Ranjitsinhji in* The Jubilee
Book of Cricket.

MacLaren, Briggs and Richardson, who were all destined to return in three years.

In London the bronzed captain, banjo conspicuous in his luggage, was greeted by cries of "Well done" and "Bravo Blackheath". He lost no time in visiting the Hampstead ground where, oddly enough, a game against Stoics was in progress.

The jubilant aftermath of the tour lasted a full month, Brown getting a tumultuous home-town reception, and Members of the House of Commons collecting £100 for equal division between him, Peel, Richardson and Ward.

The bat with which Brown made his grander-than-fiction 140 was displayed in Wisden's window in Cranbourn Street, and eventually found its way into the Wisden museum, where he sometimes held it again, recalling his hours in the sun.

As for Andrew Ernest, celebrations culminated in a memorable evening at the Café Monico in Piccadilly Circus later that month. W.G., having just notched his 100th century, was there, as were Sir J. M. Barrie and the Rev. R. S. Holmes, indulgent towards the huge array of magnums and bottles:

"We had the usual loyal toasts and much singing one could have dispensed with, good though it was. But we had come to hear Stoddart and W.G.; and we were getting impatient at the interval between their speeches, although a recitation entitled 'The Cricket Club of Red Nose Flat' brought down the house, and the editor of the Pall Mall, along with the Hon. Justice Stephen from Sydney, were well worth listening to.

"But Stoddart and W.G. bore off all the honours. It was more than generous for W.G. to hurry off from Bristol to do honour to a brother sportsman. What a reception we gave him as he rolled in a few minutes late, as fresh as a new pin, and as brown as a berry, although I would have preferred to see him in flannels rather than a swallow tail.

"Stoddart's speech was modest, and very happy. I couldn't help wondering how this singularly quiet, mellifluous talker could be the mighty smiter we all know him to be. He assured us that two factors made his stay in Australia the happiest eight months in his life. The first was the loyalty of his team; the second, Australia's boundless hospitality. He thanked his old club, the Hampstead, by whom the banquet was given, for the introduction it had given him to first-class cricket, and he perorated by a very appreciative note of thanksgiving to the enterprise of the Pall Mall and the services they rendered to his team and the cricket-loving public at home.

"W.G.'s speech was like his cricket, entirely devoid of all meretricious ornamentation. It was the man, and was effective just because it was guilelessly natural."

The Champion spoke of his past association with "Stoddy" in England and Australia, and referred to the sensation the recent Test matches had created.

"Who else was present? Well, I forget; or rather I saw only two persons out of the company of nearly 300, and their names were A. E. STODDART and W. G. GRACE. Other names I heard mentioned, or read them in the paper on Monday."

There had been "a heartiness and spontaneity about the proceedings which those who were present are not likely to forget".

FOOTNOTE: *As a further tribute to his eminence and popularity a wax model of Andrew Stoddart was installed at Madame Tussaud's in 1895. It remained on exhibition until 1905, an unusually long time for a sportsman.*

CHAPTER 15

W.G.'s YEAR

And the score is running up as the rays are running down,
"Old Grace" is at one wicket, and "young Stoddart" at the other;
And they both have got their eyes in, and the bowlers are done brown,
Grace has hit ten fours already, and by Jove, there goes another!

(*E. J. Milliken*)

1895 was, of course, the year of Grace. The 47-year-old monarch of cricket enjoyed a second wind which amounted to something of a tornado—1000 in May, his 100th century (288 to make quite sure before the champagne corks popped), nine centuries and well over 2000 runs in a summer not without its damp wickets.

Early in the season he and Stoddart opened together for the Gentlemen against Cambridge University and raised 100 in an hour, Stoddart going on to 84.

At Oxford H. T. Hewett dealt out the punishment with "Stoddy". The hard-hitting left-hander made two speedy centuries that week.

So things initially were looking good for Stoddart; but it was to be a year of frustration as continually he appeared well set only to fall unexpectedly. He bowled a good deal, but unpenetratively, and each wicket for Middlesex cost him over 30. His followers had to be patient and wait for the luck to run.

He was out of form at net practice after the sea voyage, and withdrew from the M.C.C. game with Yorkshire. Indeed most of the tourists suffered a reaction and performed modestly for at least the first half of the season.

The first time Middlesex ever opposed Essex he was bowled fourth ball by Walter Mead, but made up for it in the last innings with a 67 that ensured victory.

The next game went down boldly in the annals. Gloucestershire came up to Lord's on May 30th with W.G. needing 153 runs to become the first person ever to make 1000 in May.

The Old Man won the toss and took advantage of a good-looking wicket upon which the spin of "Nipper" Nepean troubled him most. He sweated through the crisis, and settled down as the afternoon wore on. Hearne and Rawlin in particular were difficult to score from, but W.G. was watchful, taking every chance to drive and cut authoritatively.

His 100 came in three hours, and the pressure built up as the four-figure target drew closer. At last, towards the end of this long day, palpably fatigued, he swept a long-hop away for the 1000th run, and the ever-attentive crowd stormed its acclaim and the members stood as the champagne was brought out. It rained heavily that night and Middlesex fell twice for around 200, with Stoddart offering only 2 each time. Gloucestershire lost five men chasing the 43 required, but so long as the mighty Doctor waited in the pavilion there was little serious anxiety.

Stoddart, like W.G., had a propensity for high scoring in benefit matches, and this time it was to Tom Mycroft's advantage. There had never been such a crowd at Lord's before on a Whit Monday—over 16,000 paid—and both Palairets captivated their audience with centuries. Middlesex, however, passed the 337 as Stoddart needed only an hour to make 50, and a further hour and a half to reach his century. Vernon Hill missed him twice at the Nursery end because, he claimed, ginger beer bottles were tossed at him, but finally the fans had to pencil reluctantly on their scorecards that Palairet had trapped Stoddart leg-before, in those times such a rare method of dismissal.

Somerset made almost 300 again (Woods, 109, in a purple patch), and Middlesex needed 259. Now the bowlers had their way. Stoddart was again in wonderful form and made 56—once more l.b.w.—but the innings subsided and it was only courageous tailend resistance that held Woods and Tyler out.

That Saturday "Stoddy" was at Hampstead making 52 against Granville who had the promising young spinner, F. G. Bull (playing this season for Essex); in 1897 he was in line for a place in Stoddart's side to Australia, but his days were played out in the Leagues, and he became yet another of cricket's tragic figures in 1910 when his body, weighted with stones, was washed ashore at St Anne's. (Only weeks prior to this, Arthur Woodcock, the Leicestershire fast bowler, had taken his own life with poison).

The words of "An Old Cricketer" come back: "Uncertainty can be very depressing as well as glorious, and it makes men moody".

When Stoddart failed against Yorkshire on a crumbling wicket, his admirer, the Rev. Mr Holmes, perceived that he had "all too quickly gone into his shell again—that beastly Australian trip again I suppose".

But there were runs aplenty at Brighton. He made a quick 41 before leaping out at Humphreys and being stumped. O'Brien and R. S. Lucas went on to thrash Shaw, Humphreys and others for 338 runs in 200 minutes. Then on that peach of a wicket Newham, Brann, Bean and the new sensation, K. S. Ranjitsinhji, all made plenty as the inevitable draw was registered.

Middlesex beat Kent by an innings, then I Zingari played the Gentlemen of England at Lord's at the end of June to celebrate their jubilee. Stoddart made a swashbuckling 92 in the second innings, and the Gents needed 172 to win. An hour and three quarters later it was all over by ten wickets: W.G. 101 not out, Sellers 70 not out.

Middlesex resumed their chase for the Championship, with Surrey the visitors —in the course of winning their 8th title in 9 years. Tom Richardson took 290 wickets during the season, ten in this winning game, including Stoddart each time for 30-odd.

They beat Lancashire in Manchester, and as July blossomed forth they took on Surrey again at the Oval in a match to remember. During its progress a simple but eloquent placard was set up by the entrance to Monument Station:

MIDDLESEX v SURREY

STODDART

And the crowds needed no urging. Over 25,000 paid to enter the ground for this battle of the Thames, and this on a Monday, Tuesday and Wednesday. They were given real entertainment.

A remarkable incident was the "stumping" of Stoddart at 25. The 'keeper clipped the stumps firmly and the umpire raised his finger; then it was noticed that the bails had refused to budge, and the decision had to be reversed, allowing him to make 75 in the end.

In the second innings Stoddart and Hayman put on 67, and again there was an extraordinary escape for the senior man. "Surrey" Smith enticed him to play a ball quite hard into the stumps, but those discriminating bails held fast, and he went on to 67 before Abel pocketed a lofted cover-drive.

The declaration left Surrey 270 minutes to make 386, a task beyond most sides, yet at 303 for four match honours eventually divided evenly.

The cream of the land assembled at Lord's on July 8th for the Gentlemen v Players match. There had been what some chose to call a long drought, and the wicket was fast and fiery, especially when Richardson and Mold set about the destruction of the amateurs after the Players had made 231.

W.G. and Stoddart walked out at 5 o'clock, and for half an hour the Champion was hit on the arms, occasionally ducking with surprising agility. Gradually the runs came as the bowling was hit up the slope and down the slope with growing authority—50 in even time, and at the end of a momentous afternoon the Gents were 137 for none: Dr W. G. Grace 64, Mr A. E. Stoddart 61.

The stand reached 151 before Stoddart, who had once driven Richardson into the pavilion, fell to him for 71. It had been a delectable innings—glorious strokeplay blended with judicious defence against as hostile an attack as any captain could unleash.

W.G. moved on to 118, and O'Brien's 21 was the only other double-figure score apart from the 22 kicking, flashing byes.

The Players, at one stage 61 for five, finally set the Gents 336 to win. Neither W.G. nor Stoddart was at ease this time, and the partnership broke up at 34;

by 5.30 p.m. the score stood at 231 for nine; then Ernest Smith and newcomer Charles Fry smashed 72 runs in 35 minutes. Fry was stumped for 60 in the end, but it was a match to be revered for its character and its colour.

Ranji made a century at Lord's for Sussex, and Fred Tate had a grand match —ten wickets and a steady bat at the right time. His haul included Andrew Stoddart twice, something about which to bounce Maurice, his baby son, on his knee.

Archie MacLaren was in the spotlight at this moment, making 424 in a personal siege of Somerset at Taunton which prompted among the many telegrams one from W.G. urging him to exceed his own 344, and another from "Stoddy" laying his 485 on the line.

But Stoddart's "second-class" record remained, for the moment, the highest of them all.

Rawlin and Hearne slaughtered Notts on a dubious wicket at the end of the week, then for a while the big action was done. As July drew to a close, Stoddart hit 62 not out for Hampstead after taking nine wickets. Then, with Middlesex, it was the western tour, and frustration by rain at Clifton and at Taunton, where there may have been private amusement as Sammy Woods "castled" his pal Stoddart for 38.

Woods' peculiar sense of fun was once illustrated at dinner at Stoddart and MacGregor's digs in Hampstead, when his first move upon entering the room was to switch off the light and chase his companions round and round in the darkness, over chairs and stools, brandishing a carving knife.

Grim times now befell "Stoddy" : after top score of 19 against Essex, he failed at Trent Bridge , where O'Brien's amazing century stole the show, and at Leeds he was "never less like his old self than when facing Hirst".

He took a century off Hampton Wick at Hampstead, but back at Lord's Middlesex were steamrollered by MacLaren with the bat and Briggs and Mold bowling unchanged through both calamitous innings.

So it came to the last county game of 1895, and Kent made 208 against a lively Jim Phillips who, abandoning his umpire's coat, had, so to speak, jumped down from the bench into the courtroom to head the prosecution. His 8-69 allowed Middlesex the best part of two hours batting on the first day, and MacGregor came in first wicket and helped Stoddart add 138. Stoddart was quite at his best during this partnership of the flat-mates. There was breathtaking power in his strokes, and the treatment dealt Bradley, then a promising fast bowler, would have broken a lesser man. Continually he forced good length balls to the off boundary.

His 100 was posted and he went on crunching the bowling to all parts of Lord's ground, his own personal domain, till at last the toiling Bradley had his fee: a lusty hit ended in the hands of long-off and the chanceless 131 was complete.

They made 412 altogether, and rolled up Kent a second time for 190.

> *On Lord's Ground, in the fading light,*
> *I watched the leather's rapid flight,*
> *And very pleasant was the sight*
> *Of Stoddart scoring rapidly.*
> *("Century")*

He made a lot of runs at Hastings before vast crowds : 68 and 71 for South against North, with a stand of 150 with W.G. in only two hours. (This was the 8th and final century stand for the 1st wicket between these two—the 3rd this season; only E. M. Grace chalked up as many hundred opening partnerships with W.G. during his 44-year career). Then came the long-awaited contest between Stoddart's victorious Australian Eleven and the Rest of England, a match perhaps a shade irrelevant at this late date.

The touring team fell before Mold and Woods for 217, the captain holding the fort with 55. Then W.G. was bowled by Richardson for a duck, and the Rest were in bother until Walter Read and Woods hit 95 blistering runs. Stoddart's men eventually conceded a lead of just three on first innings.

Now Stoddart weathered another storm as his companions failed to withstand the onslaught of Woods, Martin, Mold and Pougher. In 100 minutes the captain strung together 10 fours in a 59 that ended in bad light when Mold sent a stump cartwheeling.

Francis Ford and Lockwood swung the game on the final day. The outcome of the match was a matter of importance for all involved, and this partnership of 169, unfinished and of "merciless severity", left the Rest 287 to get at Stoddart's declaration.

Richardson and Peel, the outstanding bowlers during the Australian campaign, bowled unchanged and sent the Rest packing for 68. The fielding was superb and all the old spirit was there, the spirit which had swept them from Adelaide to Brisbane and back. In fact Stoddart's band, after their parlous posture the previous evening, had, as someone recorded, "finished up with a display of batting, bowling and fielding that made it easy to understand how harmoniously they had worked together and how they had won so many good matches in Australia".

The season could hardly have ended on a more satisfactory note for Stoddart. His personal output was 1622 first-class runs at 37.3. His bowling had often been clouted, but it seems not to have worried him. He never did regard himself as an all-rounder. It was W.G., he said, who encouraged him as a bowler.

Seldom now did the crowds see him drop gracefully onto one knee to arrest the ball at mid-off and in the deep. He had developed a liking for the slips in Australia, and now fielded there most of the time.

Thus the illuminated season of 1895 receded into the mists of time, to be written of fervently for ever after, most of the pages embossed with the great bearded figure.

FOOTNOTE: *In a testimonial letter to Nicolls the batmakers at the end of the 1895 season Stoddart asked for two more Patent Number Ones, indicating preference for a light weight: "I want 2 lb 3 or 4 oz." Either before or afterwards he allowed his name to be put on a Slazengers bat, which boasted "Superior cane and whalebone combination handle — First Selection 15 shillings."*

CHAPTER 16

SHAMATEUR ?

Hampstead saw little of her champion during the busy 1896 season. He batted only twice and took 122 off Teddington and four off Stoics, whose relief must have been manifest following his five wickets, all clean bowled.

The annual dinner as always was a splendid event. Numerous lush courses, witty speeches, and music, often from the charming Kennerley Rumford, former school friend of Stoddart's, husband-to-be of Clara Butt, and a "pop star" of the day who sang for Queen Victoria at Balmoral.

Harry Trott's Australians of 1896 were greeted by Stoddart and a welcoming party upon their arrival in England. They set up headquarters at "The Cricketers", Mitcham, and in the biting April air the practice nets were rigged up on the Green, and a cluster of curious mortals edged forward eagerly to identify the Cornstalks.

Ernie Jones, though bowling well within himself, was obviously going to activate many bails and bowels before the summer was over, and McKibbin moved the ball a lot on the admittedly imperfect wicket; another who caught the eye was the gargantuan Tasmanian barrister, Eady.

May brought forth unexpected joys for Stoddart this year. For M.C.C. against Lancashire, he and de Trafford made a dashing 103 at Lord's, Stoddart striking a memorable blow off Cuttell that came to rest among the critics in the holiness of the pavilion.

Against an Oxford University side containing three future England captains, Stoddart, following his 51 with 5-38, caused one reporter to dwell mistily on the belief that he was "a much better bowler than he himself seems to think".

This was a purple and gold period for him. Yorkshire came to Lord's and toiled a long while before the spectacular Stoddart-Hayman first-wicket stand was broken at 218, the batsmen reaching centuries within minutes of each other. *Cricket* reflected upon how "correct, powerful and attractive" his batting was.

Middlesex lost that match because Brown hammered a double-century, and after rain Peel mopped up. Brown and Tunnicliffe made the 146 required in 80 minutes.

But Stoddart was in top gear too, and when Somerset came up he made another hundred. It was Rawlin's benefit, and 17,000 people crowded into Lord's on Whit Monday to see the local pride play a textbook 121. He jumped out at Tyler and hit him hard along the ground; he cut tearaway Woods cleanly; he stroked to leg in a manner that had the throngs cooing and made such an impression on little Billy White that, as Pensioner William H. White, he was to find joy 70 years later in reliving those strokes one morning as the same old sun shone down on Chelsea Hospital. It was the only time he ever saw "Stoddy" bat. For a schoolboy the choice had been a clever one.

Notts were the next guests at Lord's. It needed an exceptional delivery to dismiss Andrew Stoddart at this point, and Dick Attewell produced it, surprising him at 16 with a ball that shot as he played back.

Middlesex continued their triumphant passage with another win after rain, Hearne and Rawlin taking 19 of the wickets.

Then on June 11th Stoddart arrived at Lord's to play for M.C.C. against the Australians. It was another match earmarked for all-time notoriety. The wicket was difficult, and W.G. soon left, followed by the rising star Ranjitsinhji. Stoddart and F. S. Jackson now demonstrated how to play on a false pitch, resisting all the wiles of Trumble and Giffen and the unpredictable movement of McKibbin.

"Stoddy" hit one ball into the Tavern assembly, and as always there was the difficulty of applauding with a glass of beer in one hand. Finally he ran out to Trott and missed; Kelly took the bails off, but to everyone's astonishment W. A. J. West, perhaps enjoying the batsmanship, gave it "not out". Stoddart stepped out to the next and kept walking to the pavilion.

M.C.C. were finally out for 219, and J. T. Hearne began the bowling from the pavilion end. At 8 the first nail was driven in when a ball kept low and sped through Graham. Trott made six before Hearne bowled him too. Then Gregory, after some uncomfortable moments, was also bowled by Hearne, and it was 14 for three wickets.

Kelly, straight-batted, hit Attewell for four, and off he came. Dick Pougher was called up.

"Puffer" had the drooping eyelids of a Harry Trott, the prominent ears of a Charlie Turner, the wide moustache of all his generation, and a wicked break-back on a helpful wicket. First ball he made a fine catch off Kelly, and with his second he bowled a bewildered Clem Hill.

Hearne bowled Iredale, then Pougher, whose second over had been a maiden, had Trumble playing on; the next skittled Eady, the giant; and for the hat-trick he had McKibbin caught at mid-on. George Giffen was absent, ill, although "A Country Vicar" reckoned that he simply refused to bat on that treacherous wicket.

Australians all out 18, the last 6 wickets falling for nothing! Sweet revenge, some thought, for Boyle and Spofforth's carnage of 1878 when M.C.C. fell for 19. Pougher had 5-0 off three overs; Hearne 4-4, with better to come.

The follow-on was almost as disastrous at first. The 6th wicket fell at 33, giving Hearne 6-15 so far. The surfeited bowler then missed Gregory at slip and on an improving wicket the score climbed out of the rubble to 62 before Gregory was out; then Eady and Darling added over 100 runs.

Hearne got Eady at last and had Darling caught off a skier by Stoddart at third man for a skilful 76. Australians, second innings, 183; Hearne all nine wickets for 73 off 50 overs. He would be back at their throats in a few days, during the first Test match.

Meanwhile John Thomas Hearne had his 100th wicket of the season on June 12th, a breathless and breath-taking performance; there was to be another hat-trick next match, and 257 wickets in all this season.

All was now set for the first Test match, commencing at Lord's on Monday, June 22nd. Only Giffen and W.G. had played in the 1882 Ashes match, and new faces abounded: Kelly, Eady and Hill appeared for Australia for the first time, and for England Hayward, Lilley and Hearne all made their debuts.

The conspicuous omission was Ranjitsinhji, considered by the authorities "unqualified". Such sentiments were not to burden the Lancashire committee for the second Test, when Trott also welcomed his selection.

30,000 squeezed into Lord's, encroaching upon the playing area and exhibiting a shocking rowdyism in some quarters that must have reminded Stoddart of some of the Australian audiences which had worried him so. Many saw hardly any play that day, so dense was the hedge of straw boaters and caps, peppered with solemn bobbies casting a steadying eye.

Richardson bowled with the pavilion behind him, then W.G. tossed the ball to Lohmann, who bowled a maiden.

In the fourth over Donnan was run out.

The crowd was still buzzing as Giffen edged his first ball low to Lilley. Two down for 3—Harry Trott, Australia's captain, in to repair the damage. At the other end Darling took a single, and Trott, still scoreless after a troublesome time against Lohmann, lost sight of the ball and was bowled by Richardson, afterwards condemning the absence of sightscreens in no uncertain terms.

With Trott gone, the innings hung sickeningly at 4 for three wickets. The slaughter abated temporarily, and the score drifted slowly to 26.

Then England's mighty captain had a word with Richardson and the field settled—Lilley standing back, Abel, Lohmann and Stoddart closely grouped in the slips. Richardson bowled Gregory a very fast ball, and the wicket was shattered.

Then Graham went first ball. 26 for five.

Minutes later Hill played back to Lohmann and helped the ball into his stumps, and Eady came to assist the doughty Darling, who fell at last, bowled by Richardson for 22 made in nearly an hour. Trumble and Kelly went, and Richardson let Jones have a shortish ball that kept low and hit the stumps for the sixth time, giving him 6-39 of 11.3 overs.

"We'd better pack up our traps and go home, boys," Giffen was telling the team gloomily.

W.G. and Stoddart set about chasing the miserable 53, and the members were startled at Jones' first delivery. Surely the man was throwing? The alarm receded as W.G. placed a short one through slip for 2 and then a bye brought Stoddart to face the muscular miner from South Australia. He bustled in with the pavilion behind him just as it had been the backdrop for Richardson's destruction. Stoddart got 4 and 2 through slips, and although discomfort was in the air, Australia's pathetic total was on the way to being overhauled.

Jones hurled a yorker at Stoddart, and as the bat fell hurriedly into position someone relieved the taut atmosphere by crying: "Another minute and he'd have been too late!"

Now, when Donnan hurt a hand, Albert Trott, overlooked when the Australian party was chosen, substituted in the field. It was a classic irony.

After lunch Eady bowled a shooter at Stoddart. Playing back, he almost clamped down on it, but it was through and he was out for 17. England 38 for one. Bobby Abel found Jones problematic. Balls which came up to W.G.'s armpit were flashing past Abel's nose, and it seemed that any moment England would be two down. But they held on.

Australia's score was doubled, almost trebled, before W.G. skied Giffen. He had batted two hours for his 66, passing 1000 in Tests and setting his side well along the road to victory. Jack Brown made two beautiful hits, but Jones got a fine ball through at 9, and England were 152 for three.

Little Abel consolidated with lofty Gunn; then Jackson came in to force the bowling; and Abel, though taking a bruising from Eady, batted gamely, lamely, on.

Near 6 o'clock the lead reached 200, and Abel's hard-earned century drew near. But the courageous little man on 94 hit over Eady, and Hayward commenced his Test career.

Now Jackson lofted Giffen into the deep where Darling was impeded by the crowd on the grass. To the next delivery he repeated the shot and Darling this time took the catch, "a pretty piece of quixotism" as Percy Cross Standing judged, though Wilfred Rhodes has insisted that "Jacker" was never so misguided as to throw his wicket away in a Test match.

Lilley became another nervous "first-baller" and Lohmann lashed out unsuccessfuly so that England rested at 286 for eight.

A "more gentlemanly company" of 15,000 filed through the gates at Lord's next day and saw England summarily despatched. Then in Australia's second innings, with disturbing suddenness, Darling's middle stump was struck out without a run posted.

Richardson soon had another wicket, his 50th in seven Tests, as Eady touched one to Lilley. Australia again were two down for 3. Giffen and Trott set about clearing up the mess. The captain was troubled, but Giffen's form was splendid. He escaped a chance to Lohmann, but the 50 came up rapidly as Trott made 4 4 and 3 edgily to leg off Richardson, who split the pair eventually at 62, touching Giffen's off-stump.

"Tich" Gregory attacked Richardson, and 100 came after only an hour and a quarter. In a similar period the previous day they had been entirely dismissed for 53.

Belatedly, Hearne was called up, and the scoring rate slumped against his accurate, well-concealed variation. Soon the umpires had a controversy on their hands. Trott edged to Hayward, and the close fieldsmen were amazed to find the appeal rejected.

The bowling was changed, the runs continued to come, and at lunch Australia were a resolute 152 for three wickets. 200 came in 150 minutes and W.G. was taking the spasmodic tug at his beard and wondering which bowler to use next. There was criticism of his failure to use Stoddart.

Trott on 99 saw Lilley drop him and soon he was scurrying for a 100th run that was barely there. Harry Trott, captain of Australia, had made a duck and a century at Lord's.

Gregory wiped off the arrears, and finally cut to the ropes to bring up his own 100.

Soon Trott was in trouble again, as Stoddart sent a sharp return to Lilley. The 'keeper fumbled and all was well: until Lohmann caught a low-flying snick from Gregory.

Gregory and Trott had added 221, the highest stand for any wicket by either side, and a 4th-wicket record till Bradman and Ponsford compiled 388 together.

Australia were in with a chance. But Trott hit at Richardson, and Hayward this time took a legitimate catch at deep mid-off. His 143 had occupied three and a half hours, and now the tail had to wag with all the lustiness of a King Red.

Clem Hill, 19, fresh-faced, was furious at being bowled off his legs for five; Graham was yorked by Richardson, and it was left to Trumble and Kelly to resist and defy for 20 minutes whilst only four runs accrued. (Born the same month, these two great cricketers died within hours of each other in the Australian Spring of 1938).

Lilley accounted for Trumble, and Jones was caught in the deep, where a fast-bowler ought to be caught. The lead was only 79 as Donnan came in last, hand bandaged, to add 29 with Kelly. The 5-hour innings of 347 ended on the stroke of six, and left England 109 to win. By the close they were 16 for the loss of Abel in poor light against Jones at his fastest.

The sound of rain on the roofs must have interested the Australians that night and struck alarm into English hearts as it persisted during the morning. It ceased at 11.45, and the umpires announced a noon start. W.G. ordered ten minutes of the heavy roller, and everyone sat back expectantly.

The pitch was actually hard underneath, but the soft surface caused the ball to kick, and Ernie Jones thundered in and enjoyed himself with several bumpers that whistled clean over the batsmen's heads. In seven tense overs England's score advanced by only four runs.

That was as far as they went for the present: W.G. was taken by Hill off bat and pad, showing great surprise at the decision, and with two good wickets taken, the Australians sensed a chance of pulling it off.

Brown marched out and narrowly escaped injury as Jones greeted him with a hot blast. Four leg-byes helped the cause, and then the Yorkshire terrier on-drove for 4. Another virile hit almost had him caught, then another drive went to the boundary.

The run-rate eased off; the field tightened round Hayward and Brown. The wicket was worsening, and with only 26 made in three-quarters of an hour and the skies dark, it became a matter of whether, if the runs were to be got, they would be got in time.

Jones forsook his lethal short stuff for an instant and sent a fast ball clean through Hayward, and England were 42 for three. Stoddart entered.

For a time he was subdued and left the runmaking to Brown, whose vision was adjusted. Stoddart was shaping queerly at Jones and Trumble, but he got one away nicely to the leg ropes to raise 50. Then fortune smiled as Kelly missed him.

Brown was leaving the short flyers but taking toll of the driveable deliveries, and Stoddart, reprieved yet again at slip by Iredale (substituting), hooked Jones twice for four, once magnificently off his face.

At last Kelly caught Brown for a 36 which he regarded as his finest innings considering the conditions, no less satisfying than the Melbourne '95 effort.

Four down for 82. Billy Gunn in.

Stoddart now played some beautiful cricket. He ran four to leg and cut Giffen exquisitely for a boundary. Gunn drove Trumble twice for four and suddenly all the apprehensive labours seemed laughable. Trott stepped out his run, and Stoddart cut his first ball to the ropes to win the match. Moments after the cheers had gone up, a deluge was sweeping across the ground.

It was to be 38 years before the crowds could assemble again before the pavilion to applaud an English victory over Australia at Lord's.

The scoresheet at the Oval next match presented a sad double entry for Stoddart fans:

Mr A. E. Stoddart   b. Hayward   4   b. Richardson   5

But at Manchester, a happy ground for him, he returned to the headlines with a superlative 78 and 109 against Briggs and Mold as Middlesex recorded a palpitating win.

With a few days now at his disposal he watched the Varsity match at Lord's, where W.G.'s son was opening for Cambridge. A match immortalised by Shine's deliberate no-balls to the boundary also had its human sensitivities: W.G. junior made a "pair", and his illustrious father took it hard.

W.G., not usually a meticulous dresser, was bedecked in a new grey frock-coat and tall hat. Stoddart was sitting with Murdoch and Brann at a table in the pavilion when the Doctor entered. With mock gravity "Stoddy" received him: "Pardon me, would you tell me whom I have the honour of addressing?"

"Ah, you old rogue," W.G. retorted gleefully as they made for the refreshment room, "there will be one or two here that I shan't be knowing later on." It seems likely that at this point his son had still to bat a second time.

After a fishing holiday ("he thinks that even in cricket one can have too much of a good thing") Stoddart's next cricket was the Gentlemen v Players match at Lord's, when one of the greatest amateur batting lists set about dismembering the bowling combine of Briggs, Lohmann, Hearne and Richardson. Here was a batting line-up to drag businessmen from their offices, schoolboys to their grandmothers' funerals:

W. G. Grace, A. E. Stoddart, K. S. Ranjitsinhji, L. C. H. Palairet, F. S. Jackson, A. C. MacLaren, Sir T. C. O'Brien, S. M. J. Woods, A. O. Jones, E. Smith, G. MacGregor.

Glory be!

Stoddart was not seen at his best this time, however; and when the team for the second Test, at Old Trafford, was discussed many felt that he might not still be worth a place automatically. But the Lancashire committee wanted him. They also included Ranji, whom they considered a drawcard, and Briggs and MacLaren.

The Australians, strengthening as the season progressed, went quietly about their job of squaring the series.

Trott won the toss again on a glorious day, and Iredale put Richardson away for four between Stoddart and Ranji in the slips first ball of the match; 3 to leg and 4 to open Darling's account, and eleven runs had come from the first over.

The score soon ran up to 41, then Lilley pouched Darling and Giffen almost lost his wicket trying to make his initial run. The hundred blossomed in a mere 80 minutes, and W.G. stepped in to quieten things with his craftiness. But it was 130 at lunch for only one wicket.

Immediately after the interval Giffen fell for 80, and with Trott in, Iredale went elegantly on. Jackson was called up again, and Stoddart himself bowled tightly—six overs for nine runs—his first Test spell in England.

Iredale hit away a full-toss from him to raise his century, but at 108 Briggs got him; and Gregory came in to put on 52 with Trott before W.G.'s bizarre tactics paid off: Lilley took off his pads and bowled. Shortly Trott, lunging at a wide one, edged to Brown, who shouted exultantly to give Lilley his only Test wicket. W.G. thanked his 'keeper and told him to put the gloves back on.

Now Gregory tried to hit Briggs to leg and Stoddart at slip took the catch. 294 for five, and more success to England as Richardson yorked Donnan, and Hill was caught for nine. But the last three wickets added 87 priceless runs, and at the day's end Australia rested in comfort at 366 for eight, whilst England's fielding was being roundly condemned.

The total was finally lifted to 412. Then the old firm of W.G. and Stoddart set out to make a reply. "Stoddy" faced Jones (who was not fully fit) and played out a maiden.

In a flash of inspiration Trott took the second over himself, tossing up teasing leg-breaks. W.G. stumbled as one ball ran away, and Kelly stumped him; then some overs later Stoddart, having made 15, was also stumped, though it was a near thing.

Ranji and Abel had 90 up at lunch after an hour of pure charm from the Indian, and soon afterwards Abel was caught off McKibbin. And although Ranji spoke to the umpire when Trott clutched a catch at point, he, too, had to go, and Australia were on top again; more so when Jackson was run out, and MacLaren fell to a juggling Trumble catch without scoring in his first home Test. 140 for six.

With Jones out of action, Trumble, Giffen and McKibbin carried the attack and wickets continued to tumble. Only when Hearne and Lilley linked forces did a real resistance come about.

The wicketkeeper, with a beautiful 65 not out, made up for his first venture to the Test batting crease which had taken only seconds. Richardson gave him further support, but England eventually managed only 231 and had to follow-on.

W.G. failed a second time, and Ranji came now to play one of the greatest innings imaginable. Stoddart was looking good at this stage, hitting Jones contemptuously, stroking all the bowlers with ease. And an extended display of Ranji's magic would bring England back into the game. But every ball carried a hazard, a risk that the graceful hook stroke might misfire, would go to hand; or that the leg-glance, newest and most pleasing of strokes, might somehow fail to meet the flashing, diminutive piece of red leather.

But bat met ball faithfully, powerfully, persuasively, and for forty bewitching minutes Stoddart and Ranjitsinhji kept the scorer's pen scratching busily.

Then with the total 76 and his own score 41, Stoddart was bowled off-stump by McKibbin, and for the last time carried his bat from an English Test match arena. It was not apparent at the time: there was to be no farewell tour, with its fanfares and eye-misting consequences: the multitude had no chance of ever showing its appreciation of him.

Abel made 13, and Jackson (1) became Giffen's 100th Test wicket. So England at 109 for four were listing badly by Friday evening.

The skies were grey and bulbous on Saturday, and only 5000 people considered it worthwhile to witness the coup de grace as Ranji, 41 not out, and Jack Brown set out to ward off an Australian attack which, in twenty games so far, had conceded not one century. And Brown was yet another disappointed candidate as Iredale held him at slip.

Ranji's masterly 50 came after some watchful batting punctuated with inimitably daring strokes, and MacLaren now held on while almost 50 was added to the total.

Ranji tamed Jones with hooks and wristy drives, and onlookers yearned for some solid authority at the other end from, say, a Gunn or a Hayward. Then there could have been no telling.

Trumble lured a fragile MacLaren into hitting too soon, with England still two runs behind on aggregate. Ranji continued on his lucid way, flicking to fine-leg, cutting the fast-rising ball with computer precision.

53 runs were made before the Australian skipper held Lilley second attempt. Briggs stood guard as Ranji continued his life-saving epic, and the score reached 268 before he was stumped. Ranji was now into the 120's, and England had a chance if only someone would stay.

Hearne did his best. The 300 was posted, but he and Richardson were flushed out, and England finished with 305. Ranji was left on 154, the only visible sign of his battle royal being a trickle of blood from his ear where a Jones bouncer had eluded the bat.

Australia needed a mere 125 to win.

But after an hour the innings was not proceeding very well at all. Richardson, in a fabulous bowling performance equal in heroism to Ranji's superlative batting, bowled Iredale and forced fatal edges from Giffen, Trott and Darling. Four wickets for 45.

Hearne at one stage had bowled eleven overs for four runs whilst Richardson thundered in like a man inspired. As Briggs replaced Hearne and strove to keep the tide moving against Trott's men, Richardson sweated and strained on, ignoring the protest in his muscles.

At 79 Ranji caught Gregory at short-leg, and at 95 Donnan became Richardson's fifth wicket. 100 came up timidly, and unrelenting Richardson struck again, Hill giving Lilley another catch. 25 to win, and three second-class wickets to fall. Harry Trott, nerves tattered, went off in a hansom cab.

Trumble and Kelly took a whole hour to make those 25, the moment of destiny coming when Kelly edged to his opposite number. Lilley caught the ball, but the jarring of forearm against knee sent the ball toppling to earth, an unhappy incident omitted from his autobiography.

And so, just before 6 p.m., the players raced to the pavilion, the series levelled one-each after this, Australia's first Test win in England for eight years.

Richardson lifted his pint with slightly trembling hand, scarcely able to conceive that his 3-hour labour had failed. Figures for once have a value: 554

balls did he bowl, including one wide (did the aching muscles get a word in with that one?). His reward was 13 wickets for 244 runs.

Never again was he *quite* able to display such prolonged hostility, and it was said that only an exceptional financial lure secured his services for the next party that Stoddart led through the hot and humid cricket centres of Australia.

The hero with black ringlets, born in a gipsy caravan, the honest fast bowler who had stolen much of Australia's glory in victory, was at Lord's two days later for another important match—the return between Surrey and Middlesex.

Surrey ran up 300, and the man who took the bowling figures was Drewy Stoddart. In 25 overs he claimed Abel, Holland, Hayward, Lockwood and G. O. Smith, and caught Walter Read. But his 5-78 was not followed up.

His 4 and 5 at the Oval were now succeeded by 7 and 8 at Lord's. Middlesex went for 159 (Richardson, refreshed, 5-82), and had to follow-on. This time it was even worse—83 all out—the damage again done by Tom Richardson with 5-37, bowling unchanged with Bobby Abel (4-36), and finishing the derby on the second day.

Stoddart captained M.C.C. and top-scored with 61 as they almost doubled the score of the Australians; his opening stand of 96 with MacLaren sent the spectators into paroxysms of delight. Clem Hill came good in the second innings, when a slow rearguard action drew derisive chants from the crowd. Stoddart gave Gunn a bowl and the enterprise paid off with three wickets, but only a draw could result at that late hour. Nevertheless there was another smooth innings from the M.C.C. captain as they ran to 99 for three at the close. He caned Jones with fierce cuts, slashing off-drives and a "clinking pair of fours" in one over. (The Times remarked this year—when he was 33—that he had developed even more strokes recently and was no longer predominantly a driver).

Hearne and Rawlin administered a thrashing to Sussex at Brighton, where Stoddart, opening with Plum Warner and making 20 before his young partner had scored, found runs easy to come by; and he continued to add catches to an impressive bag.

As July ended, the Australians went to Bexhill-on-Sea to play Earl de la Warr's XI, a fixture "Stoddy" had scribbled expectantly into the rear of his *Wisden*. The mighty Hearne and Pougher scourged Australia again, chopping them down for 80 and 138, and the Earl's champions won by four wickets, though the visitors seemed to care little.

At Taunton Stoddart was twice caught by his pal, Woods, whilst a few miles away W.G. was taking a triple century off Sussex.

FOOTNOTE: Cricket *reported that a fortnight before Richardson's mighty Old Trafford performance he had taken seven wickets in as many balls for Andover against Basingstoke.*

But the Grand Old Man was unable to reach double-figures when Middlesex dropped in later in the week. Stoddart made 48 and 2; he was due for another big score, and the Oval might reasonably have expected it as the third and final Test rolled around on this crowded calendar.

Though many critics, armchair and professional, were attracted by some of the newer names which cried for attention with high scores in this warm summer, the selectors chose Stoddart, and the photographer did his stuff:

> *Sit in the middle, Mr Grace,*
> *For you're the Captain bold,*
> *The Doctor made a funny face,*
> *And did as he was told.*
> *And Mr Jackson by his side,*
> *Yes, you can hold the ball;*
> *No! Mr Ranji, not the pads,*
> *That will not do at all.*
> *Now Richardson can stand behind,*
> *And also J. T. Hearne,*
> *And Captain Wynyard, here Sir, please,*
> *And do not look so stern.*
> *Yes Mr Stoddart, on the ground,*
> *That's where you'd like to sit,*
> *And Mr Ranji, if he likes,*
> *It matters not one bit.*
> *And now we want two more to stand,*
> *For two alone look silly,*
> *So Peel can stand by Richardson,*
> *And next to Hearne—yes, Lilley.*
> *Ah! this part will not do, I see*
> *That place looks very bare,*
> *Abel and Hayward you can come,*
> *And put yourselves just there.*
> *That will do nicely, gentlemen,*
> *And are you all quite ready?*
> *I'm going to take the cap off now,*
> *So keep your faces steady.*
> *Yes, thank you, Sirs, that's very nice,*
> *Ah! Hearne, I saw you smile,*
> *Do try to keep your countenance,*
> *Just for a little while.*
> *First one and then the other laughs,*
> *There's always one mishap,*
> *And Mr Stoddart drops his pipe*
> *Just as I lift the cap.*

I think I have you all at last,
So please look at your best;
But Abel, turn your head this way,
And never mind the rest.
One minute now, while I count three,
Then you can have some fun,
And laugh and talk just as you please,
For this job will be done.

("*Century*")

Stoddart withdrew from this Test match just before the start, causing an unusual amount of comment among the people at the ground. England won a damp contest by 66 runs after Australia had been set only 111 to win (even then a fatal figure). Hearne continued his triumphal passage with ten wickets, and Peel took eight. Hugh Trumble took twelve, and Spofforth, almost 43 years of age, fumed on the sidelines after having beseeched Trott to let him play. Inspecting the wicket, he had guaranteed to get England out for less than 50!

The late withdrawal of England's opening batsman could have been because he felt himself out of form and unable to do himself justice; such modest inclinations showed more than once on the next Australian tour.

Archie MacLaren, writing in *The Cricketer* in 1921, stated that Stoddart withdrew in the face of a sudden surplus of invited players in order to let him (MacLaren) play. At the time it was reported that Stoddart was low with a cold, (a very heavy one which was still evident a week after the match), and perhaps besides he had some little sympathy with the professionals who went on strike for higher pay. (Abel, Hayward and Richardson eventually played for the original £10 and the priceless glory of helping retain the Ashes).

But if the truth be known, he withdrew chiefly because of his vilification by some of the popular newspapers. *The Morning Leader* ran a facetious sketch of him and a scathing criticism of his alleged back-handers. (The same "Rover" —Alfred Gibson—a few weeks later was referring to him in saccharine paragraphs as "Andy" as he scored 127 against Kent).

Midst a storm of correspondence, fellow-amateur W.G. had the Oval authorities issue a statement on his own expenses and eventually decided to play. Not so A.E. Stoddart.

The dreaded Mold got him twice for miserable scores in the following county game, but at Bradford his finest talents shone through again as he and Douglas took Middlesex to 168 without loss against a very strong Yorkshire attack. Stoddart just failed to complete a century before lunch, and unhappily also failed to complete it after lunch: c. Denton, b. Wainwright 94.

FOOTNOTE: *E.G. Wynyard told Sir John Masterman in later years that W.G. told his batsmen he wanted them out in half an hour on the final morning of the Oval Test: "I must be bowling at them by 12.30 at the latest." Stoddart, who was not playing, protested in vain: "You can't do that, Doctor, you want every single run you can get."*

They did it again at Nottingham later in the week. "Middlesex 132 for nought" was the lunchtime score which excited avid readers of the early editions. At 158 the first wicket fell: again it was A. E. Stoddart, again he was deprived of his century: b. Attewell 93.

On the third day he made 41, but no-one scanning the sports pages really cared, for Gloucestershire were being annihilated for 17 by Trumble and McKibbin, and Ranji was making two centuries off Yorkshire in one day.

Back at Lord's, Stoddart's home with its celestial sitting-room hung with portraits historic and its garden of green stretching down to the Nursery, he made only six against Sussex, and on Thursday walked into the garden again only to be dismissed from the sunlight by Martin of Kent without scoring. He did make an astounding catch to get rid of Mason, holding the ball at the third attempt despite collision with hefty Rawlin, and he hit with some force in the second innings: once more he and young Douglas were on the rampage, and for the third time in a fortnight they had 150 up.

This time "Stoddy" got his hundred, an innings that had the journalists wallowing in nostalgia. This was their Stoddart of old, the man who could deaden the dangerous ball with masterful ease, and stroke along the ground and through the powerless fieldsmen who could only wait for the small boys to toss the ball back for more.

He was caught late in the day by Huish, and when Plum Warner offered congratulations he received encouragement in return: "Thank you so much. If you play as you did tonight you'll get a hundred, too, tomorrow".

This was Stoddart's fourth century of the summer for the county, and there were the two nineties besides, all off powerful attacks. But though he had made 1100 runs for Middlesex this season, it was equally a story of what might have been. The representative matches have always mattered that little bit more, and in the ultimate of games—England v Australia, with all to play for—he had not quite made it. These were the conflicts that live on. Drewy Stoddart, *in England,* left many thousands in unfulfilled hope.

September again, and the Australians made their final appearance. The rain, which had respected cricketers' wishes most of the summer, intruded at Hastings and helped the bowlers—especially Hearne, whose 6-8 knocked out Australia in their final innings.

Yet Trott's men, all bachelors bar two, sailed away with a proud enough record, and when an English team next visited their shores some of the youngsters would be ready to play a mature part in regaining the Ashes.

The final first-class match of the season was South v North at Hastings, and with rain his ally, Hearne again was taking wickets almost as fast as the scorers could record the deed.

For those who appreciated batsmanship Stoddart stole the show with a stirring 43, the innings of the match, made against four tough professionals, Attewell, Wainwright, Mold and Hirst.

Stoddart's calendar now afforded three blank months before his winter adventure—a trip to the West Indies.

He was golfing in Sheringham, Norfolk, when Ranji's complimentary dinner was held, and had to write apologising for his absence and praising the Prince's "mighty achievements".

Then it was farewell to all the cogitation and backward glancing of an English winter, and full steam for the Caribbean.

The people of those leafy islands were about to see the greatest cricketer in their entire experience.

CHAPTER 17

CALYPSO CRUISE

H. D. G. Leveson Gower, a member of Lord Hawke's touring party which reached the West Indies after Arthur Priestley and his men, wrote that upon their arrival he was "awakened by a Negro with a beaming black face putting his head through the porthole of my cabin and shouting: 'Mr Stoddart got a duck!' "

Nothing in the records of that tour shows a Stoddart duck in Barbados or anywhere else. Although Hawke's side had slightly the better record, no-one in either team approached the tireless consistency of "Stoddy".

Whilst Plum Warner notched four centuries for Lord Hawke, Stoddart, playing in all sixteen matches, compiled 1079 runs including six centuries (at least one on each island they visited), and took 104 cheap wickets.

This prodigious one-man show had *Cricket* suggesting that "if he had passed the winter in England, West Indian cricketers might perhaps have thought that English cricket was on the downward grade".

In three early matches against Barbados, in five innings he fell to Clifford Goodman, a huge fast bowler who grabbed 37 wickets.

The St Vincent match at Kensington saw the first Stoddart century, a gay 153 not out, not without error but certainly with the verve and dash expected by the eager population who gathered in wide-eyed clusters at the hotel to catch sight of the great man. He rolled his arm over in St Vincent's second innings and took 6-29.

Although Goodman seemed to have his measure in the Barbados games, Stoddart chipped in with 18 wickets in the three matches, including the quality wicket twice of H. B. G. Austin, destined to become such a major figure in the growth of West Indies cricket.

Invitations to dances and parties fell thickly upon the team, the cards invariably bearing the promise: "T.W.B.F." ("There will be fun"). And there usually was.

Across the water to Antigua, and a Stoddart century, thence St Kitts, and another century, picking up wickets all the time; back in Barbados he made 59 off the United Services bowling before being caught by a lieutenant named de Robeck who eighteen years later commanded the naval assault on the Dardanelles, and became MCC President in 1925.

They went to Trinidad, and Stoddart took a century off the fashionable Queens Park Club, captained by Aucher Warner. Next on the card was a Combined West Indian XI, also at hilly Port of Spain, and this time the opposition was strong and there was a tense struggle.

R. C. N. Palairet, one of the few top-ranking players in the team, topped both innings, with Stoddart close behind on 38. But Stoddart fell to Goodman for six in the critical second innings.

The West Indians needed 141 for victory, and after Stoddart had made inroads into the batting they were 41 for six. Austin, 75 not out at the first attempt, went for only three, and Priestley's side seemed about to win the most important match of the tour, until A. B. Clarke and Constantine (senior) added 75 jewel-encrusted runs for the seventh wicket.

McAuley and Clarke made the rest of the runs, thanks to a let-off in the field. Stoddart's nine wickets in the match had not been enough to hold back the jubilant locals in this forerunner of so many thrilling Anglo-West Indian encounters.

There followed a thrashing at the hands of Trinidad, when Constantine again made runs and Stoddart was ill and unable to offer much with bat or ball, falling to a West Indian who called himself Woods after the great Somerset cricketer whose powers had been drained this tour by rheumatism.

"Stoddy", although strong enough to bowl 37 overs for five wickets, failed twice again in the return match, when D'Ade made the only century recorded against them (his 140 embraced a last-wicket stand of 103). Another defeat had to be chalked up.

The last five games were in Jamaica and "Skipper" Priestley's men won them all, three against All-Jamaica, and this despite the tourists having to absorb Sammy Woods' own special cocktails before breakfast.

Wickets clattered before Stoddart at the rate of eight per match, and he made centuries in the second and third All-Jamaica games, allowing H. T. Stanley only 18 runs in a fourth-wicket stand of 100. Probably just as many babies were named Andrew that year as were called Patsy after the 1929-30 tour.

The word "Stoddy" reverberated throughout the islands, and on the cricket grounds the crowds would beat sticks rhythmically on the galvanised palings and chant "Steady, Stoddy!" every time he looked like collaring the bowling.

It was regrettable that both Hawke and Priestley toured at the same time, yet the abundance of fixtures was inspirational to the peoples of the West Indies.

Now, in the era of Sobers, acknowledgment should be accorded to that far-distant, light-hearted 1896-7 season.

CHAPTER 18

DISTRACTIONS

There was the usual tingle in the air in the Spring of 1897 as Priestley's suntanned group arrived home. J. N. Pentelow, the young cricket-writer, reflected the feelings of the cricket-starved public in April: "It will be delightful to see once more the Indian Prince on the warpath, to see our dear old W.G. again piling up centuries, and Mr 'Andrew Ernest' back from the Indies, browned and more sunburnt than ever, to see them all troop out from the pavilions once more, batsman, and bowler, veteran and youngster, 'Bobby' Abel and 'Tom' Richardson, Murdoch and Killick. 'Cricket on the hearth' hath its charms, but, by your leave, gentlemen, surely cricket on the good greensward is best".

"Stoddy" didn't necessarily think so at that moment. He had been ultra-productive continuously for almost a year and there was the prospect of an even longer period ahead, with the Australian tour at the end of the summer, linking the English seasons of 1897 and 1898.

At the Hampstead nets, with MacGregor and Hayman, he provided something worthwhile for the local followers to gaze upon, but during May he reserved his energies, playing hardly at all as the Spring rains disturbed the balance between bat and ball. There was, too, always the business to attend to in the City, near Copthall Court.

On May 19th he unleashed himself with a century against his old foes, the Stoics. Then for A. J. Webbe's XI at Cambridge his 16 and 51 satisfied most that he had retained his form, although he was 34 now and one writer recorded with alert sensitivity that the brilliancy of former days was absent. He should have seen him in Jamaica!

It was a depressing year for Middlesex. Not until the middle of August was a match won, and by then Stoddart was out of the game with a knee injury and immersed in the cares of tour organisation.

Warner and Hayman opened for the county this year, with Stoddart usually batting first-wicket. They went under to Lancashire on a damaged Old Trafford wicket, and he did nothing against Notts. Yet another draw took place at Lord's as Yorkshire exceeded 400. By the time Middlesex went to bat they had been fielding to one side or another from 5.30 p.m. Tuesday till lunchtime Friday. Still they managed over 300, Stoddart being stumped for 26 off Peel. In the follow-on his 57 pleased everyone.

On June 21st the stars and stripes flew at Lord's when the Philadelphians played. Ford's sensational one-hour century hurried the match to its conclusion, the second day having been kept free for Queen Victoria's Jubilee Day: for sixty years had she graced the throne. And Stoddart, after his Philadelphian duck, took this opportunity to score 103 for Hampstead against London and Westminster Bank.

There was only moderate success for him at Tonbridge and at the Oval, although his 28 in the last innings was described as being valuable as any hundred.

Against Sussex at the Saffrons he made 13 in each innings. Ranji, more memorably, made a typical century on the perfect wicket.

At Lord's a strong Players side beat a strong Gents side; Shrewsbury made a century, others made runs enough, but Stoddart, after a swift 51 with W.G., missed his chance again.

Jessop, man of the hour, played another of his unique innings, hitting Richardson contemptuously and warming up for his performance against Yorkshire later in the month when he conjured a century in no more than the duration of a normal luncheon interval.

Stoddart began working to something of a pitch by the next game, against Surrey. This time he kept out Richardson, who cut down thirteen batsmen in this encounter; he made 91, a popular innings, though again causing some to grieve that he was not showing the dash of former years. The unmistakable style was there, but youth had evidently flown, and responsibility had tightened him up.

He relaxed more during the Hampstead Cricket Week, so rich in memories. He took 127 off Richmond, and against West Herts C. and G. he thundered to 113. Days later he was in Taunton, where his season was cut short after making 109 off the Somerset bowling (including a hit over the cottages by square-leg). He had luck, but those ever-eager critics noted with satisfaction that his batting still contained many of the exciting elements of his younger days. How they must have been cherishing already the memory of the slender Stoddart who rose to the top of the pack in the late 1880's.

The injury occurred in the field on the second day; his knee was strained and he took no further part in the match.

W. A. Bettesworth evaluated his 1897 performance by saying that "although Mr Stoddart had an average of 30, he was not the Stoddart of former days; it is possible that playing cricket pretty nearly all the year round has proved too much for him, strong as he is".

After a golfing holiday in Sussex, and still limping slightly, he was probably glad to board ship and head out into the clear and lively waterways that led to Australia.

By the end of 1897, 54 centuries had been recorded for Middlesex since 1878, and A. E. Stoddart had made thirteen of them. In F. S. Ashley-Cooper's opinion he was the best batsman the county had ever possessed. Now the sports-men of Adelaide and Melbourne and Sydney looked forward to renewing his acquaintance.

As in 1894-5, he was at the centre of a whispering "shamateur" scandal, a figure of £1 000 for him for the tour being enviously bandied about. In retirement he wrote to the Press explaining the financial structure of his Australian tours. The authorities had paid all travelling expenses and hotel bills, and he was left a discretion in the matter of ordering champagne. "With the weather we experienced there this was almost a necessity, and the discretion was exercised by me freely, but wisely, in the best interests of our health and cricket".

He believed no amateur on tour ended up less than £100 out of pocket.

The chief English complaint was that, by contrast, the Australians gained a considerable chunk of the profits themselves when they toured the Old Country.

In 1897 there was again complaint at the composition of the touring team. There was surprise at Stoddart's invitation to Attewell at 36, and relief at Attewell's inability to accept. E. G. Wynyard had to withdraw upon orders from the War Office; Peel, an 1894-5 hero, had staggered from the county cricket field for ever, with Lord Hawke's reproving finger pointing the way; and there was widespread fear that the bowling would not be strong enough. The unavailability of Jackson and Abel was regretted everywhere—but it was hardly Stoddart's fault.

Briggs delightedly accepted his invitation on the spot. For him it was the sixth trip to Australia, a record. Among amateurs, Stoddart himself was creating a record with his fourth trip.

An irregular problem surrounded Ranjitsinhji. The N.S.W. Government proposed a deterrent tax of £100 on coloured persons entering the colony. "Australia for the Australians" was the rallying cry; but they badly wanted to see Ranji, and any suggestion of a restriction was waived. The subject, after all, was commonly designated the world's finest batsman.

One Friday morning in September, the cricketers settled into their cabins as the ship's engines throbbed; another great venture was about to unfold.

Three heavy, echoing blasts on the fog-horn and their England in its autumn was receding gradually into the fond distance. Within hours the only scenery was grey sea, with sperm whales spouting.

FOOTNOTE: *Wynyard had been offended by Ranji during a Hampshire-Sussex match: Ranji had sampled some hothouse grapes not knowing they were placed on the pavilion table for Wynyard's benefit. "Teddy" was furious, "his wrath unquenchable." Fixtures between the two counties for 1898 were cancelled. "Then Stoddart took a hand. He pointed out that he had invited both Wynyard and Ranji to be members of his side to Australia and that he must cancel the invitation if Teddy did not apologise." His friends concocted a letter, which he was induced to sign. But a happy ending was aborted by the War Office orders. (Blackwood's Magazine, June 1974).*

CHAPTER 19

AN ILL STAR

They were a band of only thirteen once again: A. E. Stoddart, A. C. MacLaren, K. S. Ranjitsinhji, J. R. Mason, N. F. Druce, T. W. Hayward, G. H. Hirst, E. Wainwright, W. Storer, J. Briggs, J. H. Board, J. T. Hearne and T. Richardson.

The party, of whom only four had been to Australia before, were bade farewell by C. E. Green, and "in a somewhat nervous reply Stoddart, assisted by shy glances at the marginal notes on his shirt cuff, disclaimed any pretensions for his men to be considered an all-England team". He regretted his inability to invite the 1894-5 stalwarts, Brown and Ward, but felt it was *reasonably* representative of English cricket (Hayward, Wainwright and Hirst had all achieved the double in 1897). Perhaps with a tinge of anxiety, he expressed the hope that they would be warmly welcomed home, win or lose.

The magnetic personality, the mystic colourful figure the crowds all sought, was Ranjitsinhji, "The Lion that conquers in Battle". He joined the party at Naples, to the obvious relief of his skipper.

There were the usual festivities and sports on board "Ormuz", including cricket in the nets, with Stoddart's knee holding up well as he straight-drove his side to victory over Captain Inskip's team; and he became quoits champion: solo—and with a Mrs Calvert in the doubles. Another lucky lady, Mrs Todd, helped him win at bull-board.

After days of high seas they reached Adelaide, and the big shake-down began —the task of loosening limbs and presenting a civil countenance at the many receptions ahead.

Stoddart hit a topical note in his speech at Adelaide Town Hall by saying that "Australia will not be Australia without Giffen", and they set about absorbing the views at Mount Lofty and at the Zoo and Botanical Gardens. In the evening they saw "Maritana" at the Theatre Royal.

Australia's champion, Giffen, had slipped into semi-retirement at 38 because "popularity will not keep me". It seems that whilst he played cricket all summer, his juniors at the Postal Department were rising above him.

He was picked to play for the State against the Englishmen, but a match of some note had to proceed without him. Stoddart had looked good at the nets, but on the second day of the match he was ordered to bed as his temperature registered the first century of the tour. Influenza had been rife aboard "Ormuz".

Clem Hill partially erased the memories of his poor tour of England with each hook, cut and drive as he made 200 attractive runs, but the team took heart in passing South Australia's 408, largely owing to Ranji's 189 (for which an old miner gave him a small gold nugget). They left the match drawn to be at Flemington for the Melbourne Cup.

In Adelaide, where thirsty people were guzzling "Stoddart" tonic ale and "Ranjitsinhji" ginger beer, Phillips' no-balling of Jones for throwing was still being debated with feeling.

At Melbourne, where ground improvements now kept the ladies out of the pavilion reserve, they had a good win over Victoria after all had seemed lost. Bill Storer, the Derbyshire utility player, played two valuable innings, and J. R. Mason made a grand winning century. For Stoddart, his health still unsound, there was only 26 and a duck.

The English cricketers in their "brown serge sac suits" took the night train to Sydney, and Victorian columnists were left comparing Richardson's appearance with that of an Italian baritone, and suggesting that Stoddart used curling tongs on his moustache.

MacLaren made 142 and 100 at Sydney, breaking two bats in the second innings; and Ranji made a century and Storer scored well again, and Richardson took plenty of wickets.

Since Stoddart's last visit to this ground it had undergone much change. A new Ladies' stand and a smokers' stand had arisen, and at the Randwick end the notorious Hill was starting to swell upwards. The encircling cycle track was now tinted pale green to eliminate glare interference.

With the elevated onlookers watching closely, Stoddart had made only one run when Garrett gathered an apparent bump-ball. The veteran, unnerved by prolonged heckling, moved deliberately for the "catch" and held it, and Stoddart walked away to the pavilion. Storer, the other batsman, was unhappy about it, and after appealing to the umpire, ran after his captain to call him back from the pavilion. The question of Stoddart's return led to a good deal of moralising. But right or wrong, his batting became reckless, and Noble bowled him off-stump for 32. (Earlier MacLaren had remarked on Noble's curious flight, and Stoddart allegedly had replied "Rats!").

It was another English win, and after a cruise up Middle Harbour and a banquet at the Hotel Australia, they went happily on to Newcastle, where Stoddart lost his fourth consecutive toss. The locals batted valiantly, but Stoddart then got into his stride with 116, putting on 240 with Hirst before a silent gathering. It was a match more to be remembered for the plague of flies, mosquitoes and flying ants.

Stoddart later discovered an uncured bird-skin, alive with insects, under his bed, and his hands and face were, as Ranji beheld them, "globular" with swelling from the bites.

Ranji himself had been the centre of admiration on Lake Macquarie, where he brought down several musk-duck from 150 yards.

They were jolted out of their sleeping bunks when their train hit a horse near Werris Creek, but at Glen Innes the township was agog with excitement.

The cricketers' visit was an event of real historical value, and a banner at the entrance to the primitive ground proclaimed "New England welcomes Old England".

Here Stoddart became a deceptive slow bowler, taking 5-10 and 10-39 as the local XXII, gloveless and in brown pads, conducted their sorry procession across the grassless terrain to the matting wicket and back again. Stoddart's clever slower ball was named thereafter "the Glen Innes pusher".

All the way to Brisbane they were noisily greeted by crowds eager to catch a glimpse and often forsaking courtesy in their attempts. Jim Phillips recorded that at Toowoomba they were extremely demonstrative, and at Ipswich, nothing short of offensive.

A massive crowd welcomed them late at night in Brisbane, where porters and policemen were helpless in the fearful stampede. When the hubbub had died, Stoddart's watch and chain—of great sentimental value—were missing. Though it was later reported from South Brisbane Police Court that a pickpocket had whispered to his female accomplice: "Don't you Jerry anything to the John about Stoddart's watch!" the police were unable to recover it.

At the official reception next day Stoddart eased local embarrassment by stating that he thought none the worse of Queensland for his loss; indeed, the thief might easily be an Englishman!

Misfortunes were piling up. Next he lost his keys between the racecourse and the hotel, and offered £1 for them in the "Lost and Found" columns.

Then a piece of luck came his way: he won a toss at last at Brisbane, where the Woolloongabba ground had sprung up out of wasteland. Against a Queensland and N.S.W. XI he once more hid himself in the lower depths of the order, giving his new men every chance to acclimatise.

They did this to the extent of 636 runs: Druce 126, and MacLaren building his reputation even higher with 181. For old time's sake as the home team played out a draw, Stoddart dismissed a washed-out Charlie Turner, now resident in Gympie.

Ranji, in keeping with the unfortunate off-field trend of the tour, developed a chill that was to bother him for weeks, and they left the Brisbane hotel disguised as a wedding party, with the proprietor showering rice over them and crying "Good luck" with admirable duplicity.

The Toowoomba Eighteen stood up to them well while Stoddart and MacLaren went shooting, narrowly escaping death on the road during the drive back; and at Armidale, where Ranji's quinsy intensified, the Englishmen were dismissed for an unprepossessing 141 on another matting surface after drawing straws for the batting order.

That night they stayed late at a dance put on in their honour, then they moved down to Sydney with several days in hand. They were days of destiny.

On December 8th a cable was delivered to Andrew Stoddart telling him his mother was dead. He was grief-stricken to the point of collapse, and as the expressions of sympathy poured in he withdrew to the solitude of his room, while the rain cascaded down on Sydney town.

The weather posed a separate problem, urgent and pregnant with controversy. The Sydney trustees, even though the umpires had pronounced the wicket fit for play, postponed the Test without consulting either captain. Their considerations, they explained, were that the pitch should be a fair one, and that perhaps the delay might enable Ranji and perhaps even the captain to recover and play.

Stoddart, first hearing of the postponement when one of the team spotted a newspaper placard outside a pub, was in no state to become embroiled in such a muddle; probably after conferring with MacLaren and others, he sent a letter of protest to the trustees, a protest that was never dealt with, although expressions of condolence and regret were returned. The trustees had refrained from consulting the England captain in consequence of his bereavement; then, a trifle ungraciously, they explained that even if he had been drawn into the discussions his opinion would not necessarily have guided them.

By Sunday night Ranji, his quinsy burst at last, was speaking of playing; Stoddart, from the moment the sad cable arrived, was hopelessly unfitted.

Elizabeth Stoddart, fifteen years a widow, was buried in the shadow of the parish church at Radford, Coventry, no great distance from her late husband's hunting lodge. In due course a monument of red marble was set upon the grave.

To Drewy, the son who spoke of her so often, the cricket tour on the other side of the earth had lost all meaning.

MacLaren won the toss in this "pro-Test match" and chose to bat on a lovely wicket. The Australians wore mourning bands and, after all, lacked Giffen, who would play for his country no more.

MacLaren made a cultured century, and substantial innings from Hayward, Storer and Hirst lifted England into the 400 s; but it was the almost supernatural powers of Ranji, held back to number 7, that ensured a winning total. Battling against mounting exhaustion, he charmed his way to 175; after having written a condemnation of Jones' action and incurring the crowd's wrath, it was stirring proof that he feared no bowler, not even the Australian express.

Richardson gained immense enjoyment in helping Ranji add 74 for the last wicket, taking England past 500 for the first time in a Test.

Hearne and Richardson then manfully disposed of Australia for 237. There was much harder resistance in the follow-on: Darling and Hill, who dominated the series as no pair of left-handers before or since, made 101 and 96, Hill getting within a boundary hit of 100 on the first of five occasions in Tests against the Mother Country.

They made 408, but not without another unpleasant incident. Charlie McLeod, being slightly deaf, left the crease after Richardson had bowled him, although "no ball" had been called. Storer, ever alert, pulled out a stump and Phillips then had to give McLeod "run out". It would be erroneous to suppose that it was never played tough in those days.

England needed 95 to win, and MacLaren was again in sleek form, steering them through on the fifth morning and freeing them to spend Christmas fishing and shooting at Gippsland Lakes, where Stoddart, slowly recovering his vivacity, killed a stag at 250 yards with a Colt repeater.

For England the emphatic first Test triumph was a glory and a satisfaction not to be repeated. As the tour progressed, the promise of the Australian batsmen and bowlers was realised, and the tide was turned with bombora force.

The first symbolic sign was the rising of the mercury over Christmas; the ground was parched, 35 lives were lost in two days, and all humanity was reduced to languid disinterest; even such hardened local warriors as Iredale, Kelly and Gregory were grilled into a state of collapse.

They recovered their senses to take their places at Melbourne, where Stoddart's team was very much in distress. Ranji, his tonsils squeezed clear of pus, was still ill, and the captain himself was plagued by bouts of melancholia, first including himself in the side, then withdrawing upon the statement that Ranji was expected to respond to treatment.

Melbourne crackled in the heat, and Trott had the luck to win the toss. Relentlessly all day the Australians set about building a mammoth total. McLeod ground out a century, and Hill, Gregory, Iredale and Trott all made a lot of runs as New Year's Day gave way to a Sunday of convalescence and then a hot inevitable Monday in the field for MacLaren and his toilers.

Ranji had an abcess removed from his throat during an interval, and was cheered when he returned to the field. He was undoubtedly the most talked-about cricketer in the land, and his name was being appended to bats, matches, cricket shoes, hair restorers, even sandwiches, in a humorous portent of commercialisation to come.

Briggs, fresh from bamboozling out fourteen Bendigo batsmen and surprisingly buoyant in the sultry conditions, took three very good wickets. But it was a tired England that set out on Monday evening to reply to Australia's 520.

Ranji did not fail them. He made a fine 71, and was supported by rugged Storer. It took a longish stand by Briggs and Norman Druce, however, to carry England over 300, and the follow-on on that dry, crusty wicket was a formality.

Jim Phillips, touring as general assistant to Stoddart, talent scout for certain counties, correspondent for a newspaper group, and umpire as well, was earning his fees. He found it necessary to no-ball Jones again for throwing; but it seems to have worried no-one unduly so long as it was confined to the occasional delivery.

At this period only the bowler's umpire was empowered to call a no-ball, but Phillips was already urging an amendment: if the square-leg official were permitted to pass judgment he promised to "sort out" several other bowlers.

Trumble and Noble did the damage now on the broken Melbourne wicket. There was no answer for them as England were bundled out for 150, giving Australia an innings victory.

"Stoddy" had a bird's-eye view of it all from the dressing-room over the members' reserve, a vantage point private but briefly as one set of beautiful eyes after another was raised towards his "fine face at the window", shooting "sympathy and invitation to the desolate but favourite cricketer".

The society columns most of this summer were suggesting he was looking for a wife. "Whose wife?" enquired one journal; whilst another demanded to know why Australian girls, almost without exception, wore boutonnairres in England's colours.

Many of the crowd rushed out to take souvenir scrapings from the pitch which, according to "Short Slip", looked as if fine wool had been scattered over it. It would have been interesting to see England's bowlers perform on it if the follow-on had been averted. As it turned out, it was the most gilded of fleece for Australia.

MacLaren in his speech expressed the hope that in future the pitches would be more lasting, and this sparked off an attack by "Mid-On" (H. W. Hedley), among others, upon the "inexperienced" views of, to start with, MacLaren and Ranjitsinhji.

After a month out of the game, Stoddart resumed playing at Ballarat, having stuck into his scrapbook an irrelevant but evidently mesmeric cartoon of a "tired pessimist" committing "fish suicide". With the rifle muzzle in his mouth and fishing line tied to the trigger, the pessimist waits for a hungry fish to do the rest. It is the only item non-sporting or non-romantic in the entire book of cuttings.

Now he encouraged and perhaps surprised his colleagues with an attractive innings of 111; but the anxieties persisted, with Ranji's asthma troublesome, and the insufferable heat at Stawell causing the Englishmen to consume an estimated 400 drinks during the game.

FOOTNOTE: *Charles Bannerman, after watching Stoddart at practice on the Melbourne ground after the second Test, declared that he had never seen anyone bat better at the nets in his entire life.*

On their way to Adelaide they passed through Horsham, where in the early hours they were awakened by excited townsfolk yelling "Come out and let's have a look at ya!" The retorts of the bleary-eyed Englishmen went unrecorded.

The blazing nightmare continued as the third Test got under way on the greenness of Adelaide Oval. Trott met Stoddart outside the England dressing-room, and Stoddart called "heads"; but almost as if to mark the death that day of Lewis Carroll, the coin bounced and turned over with Mad Hatter capriciousness, and at the end of the first hot day Australia had made 310 for the loss of McLeod and Hill.

Tom Richardson, as ever, was the man on whom all England pinned its faith, but, bothered throughout the tour by rheumatism, he could make no impression once again upon the watchful Australian batsmen. The adjustment in line needed against left-handers seemed beyond him.

Darling hit him about from the beginning, then Briggs' turn came as Darling hoisted him into the crowd at square-leg. Hearne steadied things down, but Darling still reached 50 in an hour. Hirst came on, but he was never the same bowler in Australian conditions.

Briggs finally got one through McLeod, and Australia were 97 for one wicket. Then joy became unbounded as Hill built up an enormous stand with the other South Australian, Darling, who, dropped by Ranji on 98, reached his century in spectacular fashion, hitting Briggs clean out of Adelaide Oval—the first time this had ever happened. The applause was tumultuous for Darling's dashing performance: 104 out of 157.

Soon 200 was posted as the afternoon's heat reached its peak. Stoddart juggled his bowling, and at last the perspiring Richardson broke through. Hill, with a chanceless 81, was caught at the wicket after a stand of 148.

Gregory filled the breach, and England hoped in vain for just one more success that evening: Briggs had tired more than Darling, who battered 18 off two overs as the shadows lengthened protectively.

Perhaps Saturday would bring renewed strength to the toiling bowlers.

It certainly offered misleading early success. Richardson had Darling caught without adding to his overnight 178, and Briggs was back to his tantalising best with four maidens strung together. But when Gregory on 32 hit him to mid-off, Stoddart dropped it.

The score reached the upper 300 s, Briggs working like a beaver, losing a mere five runs off 13 overs. Then English spirits slumped as Richardson left the field.

At 374, Gregory was at last held by Storer; and with Richardson back after lunch the Englishmen hoped to dissemble the remaining batting before it was too late.

Harry Trott soon went, and Noble entered, but England's next stroke of ill-fortune came as Hirst retired with a strained stomach muscle. 400 came, and soon Iredale had his 50 as the flagging attack was utilised to the best of Stoddart's intelligence. He asked Storer to remove the pads and bowl, but three overs produced nothing but runs.

Richardson had another turn and with a slower off-break bowled Noble. Trumble came—a number 8 always difficult to dislodge. And immediately Ranji left the field with a dislocated finger (no Dr Grace to put it in place).

Richardson laboured away, striking again as Iredale played on for a patient 84. There was to be no flamboyance: Kelly took twenty minutes to make a run, then applied himself vigorously as Australia passed 500. At last Stoddart tried himself and bowled Kelly, who aimed a huge drive. 537 for eight wickets.

Jones, tearing the pitch with his spikes as he turned between runs, was eventually run out, leaving Australia 552 for nine as the umpires mistakenly lifted the bails eight minutes early.

The innings reached 573 on the third day, and MacLaren and Mason started off against those uncomplicated men and testing bowlers, Bill Howell and Ernest Jones. Jones made the first incision, bowling Mason at 24. It was proving a horrendous series for the young Kent batsman.

Ranji, fingers strapped, was greeted cordially enough by the crowd. But they had had their Hill and their Darling; they were not to have "K.S.R." this day. Trumble had him caught at mid-off and cheers rent the air as patriotism surfaced.

After lunch MacLaren was bowled by Howell and as Hayward, seemingly at home, stood helpless at the other end Storer was also trapped by the Penrith bee-keeper. At 42 for four, Stoddart still held himself back. When Druce mistimed a drive off Noble, Hirst went to see out the remaining couple of minutes.

The score crept to a much sturdier 172 before Jones bowled Hayward for an immaculate 70, and now the captain came in, and there were no further casualties before stumps were drawn, with England 197 for six, Hirst 50, Stoddart 11.

The fourth day was sultry, with a dust storm blowing at the start, reducing visibility. And there was to be no building of hopes this day. Stoddart, facing Howell, aimed his first big hit, and Jones, the finest mid-off Australia had known, made a marvellous catch. 206 for seven; last man 15.

Briggs thrashed merrily for 14, Howell bowled Hearne for 0, and Hirst batted courageously on, often in extreme difficulty with his injured side, finding encouragement as Richardson held up an end. They made 54 for the final wicket, before Hirst, in sight of a dramatic hundred, gave a slip catch at 85. England were out for 278.

After lunch Mason was despatched for 0 by Noble, and there now developed the partnership many had been waiting for. Ranji opened with an exquisite cut, and he and MacLaren settled down steadily against purposeful bowling and fielding that conceded nothing, if Darling's lapse in the longfield be excepted: and the people of Adelaide would have excused Darling anything. Ranji's injured finger was an inconvenience, but the batting at both ends remained correct. 100 came; they both passed 50, and the tempo increased.

Ranji drove and cut with boneless wrists—pulled anything short with time to spare. Archibald Campbell MacLaren batted like a master, too, off-driving in the grand manner; soon it was 150 for one.

Then McLeod struck. Ranji tried to steer him away but lifted the ball to slip.

Hayward was the victim of a brilliant caught-and-bowled, and Storer failed again. McLeod's three quick wickets at the end of the day had crippled the English cause, although MacLaren, 70, still remained, and perhaps Stoddart could play a protracted hand similar to that on the same ground six years before.

The cricket was slow next morning. The innings was almost four hours old when 200 came up, and at 208 Noble bowled "Chubby" Druce off his pads; at lunch England were still 70 behind as Hirst supported MacLaren (99).

MacLaren's century came, his third against Australia, but the other end continued to prove vulnerable. Hirst was leg-before, and Stoddart came in at number 8, a travesty no other captain would have allowed. Immediately he showed authority, hopeless though the outlook seemed. The score rose to 262, when MacLaren's wonderful stand ended. His 124 had taken 5¼ hours of sound defence and imperiously confident scoring strokes that alone kept air in England's lungs. He was resoundingly received at the pavilion.

Stoddart began to hit out now, but for the second time in the match Jones caught him at mid-off, this time for 24. That was it: Hearne and Richardson were soon dismissed, and England, with 282, had failed by 13 runs to save the innings defeat; Australia stood one-up with two to play, and, it had to be confessed, strong prospects of winning the next two as well.

The teams took wine with Sir Edwin Smith after the game and received an apology for the behaviour of some of the crowd, particularly towards Ranji who, it appeared, had been misrepresented in some of the newspapers.

Stoddart emphatically denied that there had been any friction between Ranji and other members of the team; personally he got on very well with him.

Now, in January 1898, he found himself once more having to choose his words carefully with regard to Australian crowds. And Ranji was declaring that he wished never to play in Adelaide again.

There was only a short breather before the fourth Test, and at shivering Hamilton Stoddart took eight wickets in a narrow win, with Briggs up to his usual comedy tricks.

Then, after a day's postponement, there commenced in Melbourne the 50th

FOOTNOTE: *Stoddart in the second innings "threw his innings away", according to Charles Bannerman.*

Test match between England and Australia. It was also to be Andrew Stoddart's last International—traceable to his own decision, and a situation which need not have been.

Eight times had he captained England at cricket, and here, for the sixth time, Australia won choice of innings. A few hours later it didn't seem to matter.

The Australian crash began when Hearne hit McLeod's wicket. The batsman left the field, "looking all broken up and crippled in spirit". He soon had company as Darling snicked Richardson deep to slip; then Gregory received first ball one of Richardson's lethal yorkers.

At the other end Iredale, also without scoring, was caught by Storer, and Australia wobbled at 26 for four. Giving the new ball to Hearne had been a profitable ploy.

At 32 Noble returned the ball low to Hearne, and the catch was avidly accepted. Now the captain came in to investigate the fuss; the tension remained sky-high.

Trott and Hill steered safely to lunch, but Hearne had Trott straight afterwards; "J.T.'s" 4-20 must have warmed his captain's heart, if any of his anatomy could withstand further heating.

Australia, six down for 58 on a wicket true though slow at one end, needed the sort of styptic 7th-wicket stand that would last 80 years and more. They got it. In almost two and a half hours of exciting stroke-making and chances sent begging, Trumble made 46 and helped Hill add 165 precious runs that completely altered the complexion of the match.

Hill unwrapped some beautiful drives and took vicious toll of anything outside the leg stump. The stand was punctuated several times by Bill Storer: firstly when his Derbyshire roar against Trumble met only with hoots and hisses from the crowd, then when he dropped Hill on 65 and Trumble on 34.

Finally the miserable 'keeper was asked to discard the gauntlets and have a bowl. Hill, well past 100 now, thrashed him. Stoddart came on in desperation to bowl lobs, and watched nine hit off his first over; then Storer took Hearne's end. He broke the stand at last: Mason at square-leg caught Trumble, and Australia were 223 for seven.

Kelly, a road-digger, shovelled Storer to the leg fence, and the resistance was mounted afresh. Hearne no longer posed problems, and after Hill had taken eleven off an over he gave way to Wainwright, bowling for the first time at 257. His form was unswervingly ineffective here at Melbourne as it had been on other Australian wickets.

Australia had surprisingly salvaged the innings to 275 for seven, Hill a superlative 182 not out.

On Monday smoke from bushfires enveloped the ground, and temperatures were well over the century, prompting Ranji to protest that Australia was the only country that would set itself alight just to win a Test match. The sleepless

FOOTNOTE: *Felix (Tom Horan) wrote: Stoddart bowled so well that I think he should have kept on longer. By the way, at lunch time someone wished to speak to A.E. Stoddart, and A.E. said, "Excuse me just for a few minutes, will you? I must look after my tired bowlers"; and, glancing at the large bottle of Pommery under his arm, he passed into the dressing-room.*

English players were greatly distressed again by the heat.

The air was steamy from recent rainstorms, and the smoke made the haze so dense that distant fieldsmen were reduced to "white streaks moving about with ghostly strides".

On Saturday evening Hill had tried to dodge the photographers; it was a supersition of his, photogenic though he may have been. And now, after adding only six, he was caught at slip by Stoddart, and Australia were 283 for eight.

A further valuable 20 came from the heavy bats of Jones and Kelly, then another 20 were hit for the last wicket before Hearne took his sixth wicket and Stoddart led his men from the field with 323 their first-innings target.

It had been an extraordinary fight back, and now on a perfect wicket England needed to respond in such a way that the series might be levelled. A repeat of the grand finale of 1894-5 would be much to everybody's taste.

But it was not to be. Trott enterprisingly opened with Bill Howell and himself, and MacLaren, England's chief hope, floundered and was bowled by Howell's wicked break-back for eight.

Ranji accompanied Wainwright after lunch, and within minutes the luckless Yorkshireman was England's second casualty, spooning Trott to point. Hayward pressed on with Ranji, and gradually the score mounted to 50. The bowling was changed at last: Noble and Trumble for Howell and Trott, and in mid-afternoon Trumble gained the wicket all Australia hoped for: Ranjitsinhji, caught Iredale, 24.

Without addition to the score Hayward, driving Noble, was caught, and Storer, handicapped by a smashed forefinger, lasted a miserably short time.

With England 67 for five Druce and Mason saw their chance of becoming heroes—a chance that passed them by: their resistance showed promise as the score rose to 100 and Jones, belatedly brought into the attack, was met disdainfully at first. But at 103 Druce was trapped in front by "Jonah" and the innings swayed sickeningly once more.

Andrew Stoddart came in at number 8 to a genuine, warm reception. Mason, upright and aristocratic, stood guard at one end whilst he picked up runs as he could. Again Jones crushed any hope of a revival. The captain, when 17, launched a hard drive and was caught by Darling at short third man. 121 for seven.

Briggs, perhaps remembering his only Test century, made on this ground thirteen years before, helped add 27 runs; then Mason's innings ended.

Hearne went second ball, Richardson struck a few blows of defiance, and England were all out 174 on a blameless pitch. It was marked down as their feeblest effort of the tour.

This time Wainwright and Briggs began England's innings, 149 behind and following on for the third time running.

And for the second time that day Wainwright failed: driving at Jones in hazy light described by one effusive observer as being bad as a London fog, he saw McLeod tumble and hold the catch; England one down for 7 Monday night.

The umpires alone had been unimpressed by Stoddart's claim that visibility was too poor that evening. "If that light was too bad," asserted Phillips, "then cricket had better be given up entirely at Bramall-lane or Bradford".

That night an old man attempting to walk to Melbourne to see the Test match was found dying in Moonee Ponds Creek. He was one Australian deprived of the sweetness of victory, though the progress score whispered to him as he died should have sent him on his final mission with a cricketer's contentment.

The heat was again overpowering next day as MacLaren and Briggs set about restoring their country's prestige. They were seldom in difficulty, and as the score began to grow, "Pommies" in the crowd gripped their benches in desperate hope. When Briggs was caught off a long-hop for 23, hope intensified as England's finest twosome became associated.

Ranji was seeing the ball clearly, but now Hugh Trumble and an Australian fly struck simultaneously. MacLaren's vision was blurred as the insect navigated itself into his eye; Iredale picked up the catch at short-leg, and the score drooped to 94 for three wickets.

Hayward played calmly, and 100 came; soon, while the sun streamed down mercilessly, the 150 drew near. Ranji secured his 50, and *this*, perhaps, would be the big stand England wanted.

Again it was to be written another way. Noble forced Ranji to play on; at 147 for four England still needed two runs to stave off the innings defeat. Jack Brown and Albert Ward, where were you!

"Stoddy" walked out to play his last Test innings.

At 157 Trumble caught and bowled Hayward, and Druce made a dozen runs by which time Stoddart had picked up five, looking carefully at this bowling attack which had cut his side to pieces with its variation and relentless innovation. He began to punch the ball with more verve and authority.

There was no radio and there were no live-wire statisticians to point out that he needed only four runs for his thousand in Test cricket when the axe finally fell. Jones bowled rather wide and he cut at it, fetching it back at the wicket. The bails were scattered with his score 25.

England, at 192 for six, still had slender hopes that the lead might be built up and the weather might intervene. Hearne and Briggs knew what to do on a soft pitch.

Druce, for the umpteenth time on the tour, failed to build on a start; and Storer held on till close of play, his stand with Mason worth a precious 43.

There was not a breath of wind on the fourth day, and the sun was still scorching down as the earth revolved and showed itself again. The lead was an interesting 105, with three wickets remaining.

Howell and McLeod made certain they were valueless, and Australia after all needed only 115 to win the match and the rubber.

By lunchtime Charlie McLeod and Joe Darling had made almost half of them against an attack weakened physically and morally by Richardson's absence.

Darling fell to a careless shot at 50, and a shiver of excitement was felt as Hill was l.b.w. without scoring. But Gregory got on with the job, and without further damage the runs were made.

It was, said the *Melbourne Argus,* the "most brilliant page in Australian cricket literature", and another paper, with an eye on the Melbourne convention to discuss federation of the Australian colonies, stated that "we believe Harry Trott and his ten good men and true have done more for the federation of Australian hearts than all the big delegates put together".

Joy was widespread after this long-awaited triumph for Australia's cricketers. Harry Trott (another for whom the gods planned dark days) was in fine humour at the gathering afterwards, and Stoddart manfully offered congratulations to Australia, and paid tribute to their bowling. He conceded that it was ahead of England's in technique, and that the Australian team in general was finer than any he had played against in four tours.

Later, in an interview with Reuters, he let himself speak from the heart. He was bitterly disappointed, he said, at losing the rubber, ruminating that his side had been defeated "most horribly". His bowlers did not understand half as much as the Australians, who were such a wonderful force.

Frank Iredale, an opponent in three Test series, later recalled Stoddart's belief that no team in the world could have beaten Australia on their own wickets just then. His opinion of Stoddart is interesting: "We looked upon him as the beau ideal of a skipper, and as fine a sportsman as ever went into a field.

"Unfortunately for us he got the idea into his head that a hitting game did not pay in this country, so he pocketed his genius and gave us scientific cricket instead."

He regretted that Stoddart on this last visit took so much notice of the crowd. "I don't think he said it in any carping spirit, but he really thought he was doing good to the game by speaking as he did."

It caused many people to "change their opinion about his manliness." ('Andrew', incidentally, means 'manly'). The difference, as he saw it, between Stoddart and MacLaren as skippers was in the matter of temperament. Where Stoddart would coax a cricketer by playing upon his feelings, MacLaren would drive him, in the manner of W.G.

Stoddart lived for his team and always commanded their respect; MacLaren's men admired him but feared him. Stoddart was often impulsive, but MacLaren was quick-tempered, easily angered. A moody player always chafed under

FOOTNOTE: *From J.C. Davis's* Australian Cricket Annual: *Over a glass of wine he (Stoddart) said, "My men, I am sure, all tried . . . The Australians are a wonderful combination, and it did not seem to matter to Mr Trott whom he put on, for each change ended in a wicket."*

MacLaren, but not so under Stoddart, who generally humoured him.

The papers devoted a lot of space to Australia's 1897-8 victory, granting in some places that England had not experienced much luck—MacLaren's historic and controversial fly was itemised ("there were no flies on Clement Hill")—and recalling the heat and the murky light which bothered them at times.

An Adelaide paper cut hurtfully if truthfully deep: the English bats had failed miserably in adjusting to the subtleties of the bowling and the vagaries of the wickets. Their bowling had been "really weak", lacking variation and sting. The many new men had failed, seemingly overburdened by responsibility.

The Daily Telegraph seemed in no doubt: Mr. Stoddart's Eleven were "the team of all the failures".

"Century" (a poetess who seems to have had a gentle crush on Stoddart) summarised the English viewpoint:

> *There are some who have said that the team's overrated,*
> *And many their different opinions have stated.*
> *Summed up in a few words their cause of defeat*
> *Was due to misfortune, depression and heat.*

The heatwave sizzled on after the fourth Test, keeping the Englishmen indoors, with billiards the main pastime.

Then the hardships continued in Sydney, where a six-day match produced a new world record total of 1739 runs, 239 more of them to N.S.W. when the last wicket fell. Druce justified himself at long last with a century, then it was Syd Gregory's turn with a glittering 171. The star turn was Bill Howell, batting last and belting 95 in an hour against tired bowlers and aching fieldsmen. The last-wicket added 109 and set the Englishmen 603 to win. By the fifth evening they had 258 for the loss of only one man—MacLaren and Ranji in possession.

But soon both of them were gone, dismissed by Howell, who bowled into the rough created by Donnan's spikes. From then on it was a procession before Noble and Howell. Stoddart, like Trumper, failed in each innings.

MacLaren could now look back on a gleaming string of conquests at Sydney, extended when he brought his own team out in 1901-2. You had only to put your tongue out at the ball at Sydney, he claimed, and it went for four! If Hammond's ashes were scattered on the Bristol wicket, surely Sydney deserved Archie MacLaren's.

The games at Sydney University and Brisbane (against a combined Queensland and Victorian XI) were ruined by rain, good heavy Australian rain that falls in uncompromising quantities and brooks no hopeful vigil. It finishes play for the day in one decisive splash and allows the players to go about other things.

At Brisbane the last half-hour was played out in deep gloom emphasised by the strong gleam of the street lamps.

Whilst in this sprawling city, Stoddart announced he would not be playing in the final Test. (This presupposition that an England side should always be the best of the day was quite novel in 1898, and probably marked the beginning of a modern attitude.)

His recent correspondence had included a protest against Briggs' "Quaker" hat. ("It's bad enough to be defeated but by George don't let the fellows be ridiculous"), and a poison-pen letter from Tasmania stating that his team were not wanted there, referring to an alleged slight on the previous tour when bad weather had kept the Englishmen in their hotel. (Stoddart, it may be recalled, still managed to acquire a chill through batting in the rain).

The hurt of this unsigned note was relieved, perhaps, by an appeal from a man who apparently needed a pair of "Stoddy's" pants to launch him on his career as a station-hand at Singleton.

Regrettably we shall never know if his lower portions were clad in the trousers of England's cricket captain the day he delivered himself to his new master.

Now at Sydney everyone waited to discover whether the Australians really were so clearly superior as the post mortem on the last three Tests seemed to conclude.

It looked as if England would be making a contest of it when, after two innings, the home side were 96 in arrears. MacLaren had got his team away to a start of 111 with Ted Wainwright, kept in by Stoddart at his own expense following signs that the Yorkshireman, facially so like a boxer, was reaching peak condition. His 49 was confident and completely safe.

In front of a packed house the top half all made runs except Ranji, who, by his own admission, got out to a thoughtless stroke; Druce with 64 was yet another to find form tragically late in the tour.

Richardson, fresh from enforced relaxation, now wrote himself another page of history with a magnificent 8-94, swallowing up the cream of Australian batting with the fastest bowling by England all season. Almost all the victims were bowled or caught behind the wicket.

When MacLaren, again with so much depending on him, was caught at slip first ball of the innings (as in Melbourne in '94), England's lead of 96 was quickly belittled. Soon Wainwright and Ranji were out, and as the day progressed English wickets dropped regularly to Trumble and Jones.

Australia were set 275, a target of some remoteness considering the diminishing totals in the match so far. Although Darling flailed the bowling unconcernedly, McLeod and Hill were dismissed cheaply and England were in with a strong chance.

But Jack Worrall helped swing the issue. As he defended stoutly, Darling carried on cutting and driving all the bowlers, whipping the unruly crowd into a fervour of excitement. Together they made 193 glorious runs that landed Australia on the threshold of victory.

As the stand flourished the crowd in some sections began screaming insults at the Englishmen and hooting every appeal. Ranji has recorded his resentment of the "shower of vulgar wit", but all the visitors suffered. The outfielders were exposed to it most, and Hayward's missing of Darling on 60 was attributed to it.

Worrall was out at last for 62, and when only half a dozen hammer blows remained necessary, Darling's wonderful even-time 160 was ended. It was his third hundred of the series, and established him as worthy to captain Australia on the next three tours to England, where he won the series of 1899 and 1902 before running into Francis Stanley Jackson in 1905. But that is another story.

Gregory and Noble fetched the remainder of the runs, and Australia had won this series (watched by a third of a million people) four games to one. At 4 p.m., as Victor Cohen put it, it was all over bar the shouting, and at 5 p.m. it was all shouting over the bar!

Hardly anyone now doubted which was the better side, and already there were rumbling suggestions that Marylebone should select and organise all future England sides.

The vanquished Englishmen, for their part, went off paddling and shark-fishing.

The Sydney Referee now managed an interview with Stoddart. For once he seemed keen to give his impressions.

"My remarks are intended for the people of this country," he told the reporter, "otherwise I would have no object in speaking. When I return home I will not mention a word on the subject. That would do no good."

Considering the report was soon on the breakfast tables of Manchester as well as Melbourne, Sutton Valence as well as Sydney, he was showing poor appreciation of the mass media of even 1898.

"It is not my wish to interfere or speak in this matter except in the interests of cricket. I shall, in all probability, never visit this country again with a cricket team, and what I have said has been purely for the good of the game, for the sake of the players in this country, and of English teams coming out here in future.

"This system of barracking, if allowed to go on, will inevitably reduce cricket to a low level, for your better class players, with any sense of feeling, cannot keep on playing under such circumstances. The jeering by the crowd has

FOOTNOTE: *Darling made his 160 with a bat originally given to Jim Kelly by MacLaren. The innings contained as many as 30 fours.*

occurred on all the grounds, and in all our big matches.

"Our first experience was at Adelaide, where we were advised to take no notice of it. The same thing occurred at Melbourne, and we were similarly advised, whilst our Sydney experiences were no different. We did not take any notice of it, but when the thing is repeated in every match, and on every ground, I feel it my duty to speak, and to deplore that those in authority do not take steps to prevent it.

"I don't mean that those who jeer and hoot should be turned out of the ground. I would suggest that an appeal be made to their better feelings. If some of your influencial men were to walk round the ground, speak to the people, reason with them, quietly and rationally, I am sure a great deal of good in the direction of preventing these scenes would be achieved.

"To show that moral suasion is useful in a matter of this kind, I will quote an incident in my own experience: At Brisbane, the day we played the Combined Team, it was wet, and owing to a shower a cessation in play took place for a little time. The Combined Team had been in the field in the morning. When they went out again in the afternoon they were hooted by a certain section.

"I saw one man who had hooted, and went up to him and said, 'Now, why did you hoot your own side?' He replied: 'Because they fielded badly'. Then I said: 'Do you consider that hooting them will make them field better?' He replied: 'I don't know'.

"I talked to him very quietly and seriously for about ten minutes during which he gazed at me and seemed to wonder what sort of person I was. At the end of that time he said he was damned if he would ever hoot them again. Every man has a generous spot in him; most of those who jeer and hoot have good points, and, if you appeal to their better nature, I am sure they will give it over."

Then an idealistic summing up; "If you can successfully appeal to one man, you can do so to a body of men."

It was suggested to him that players and umpires, as well as onlookers, made mistakes.

"Quite so. In the last Test match at Melbourne our wicketkeeper appealed for a catch at the wicket, and so did the bowler. The umpire gave it not out. The crowd set to work and hooted at our wicketkeeper and bowler, whose appeal was legitimate. I was given to understand in the pavilion afterwards that the batsman admitted he was out in that stroke.

"A little later, when the Australians took to the field, their wicketkeeper appealed for a catch at the wickets, and, before the umpire had time to give his decision, he threw the ball high in the air. Mind you, I have the greatest admiration for the Australian wicketkeeper's honesty, and feel certain that he will admit having made a mistake in throwing the ball up before the umpire had given his decision. The crowd did not hoot Kelly, as they had done our wicketkeeper.

"In this last match here Hearne received a severe blow from Jones, at which the crowd, many in the pavilion, laughed. Later, Richardson was bowling, and he sent a full-toss over Darling's head, at which the crowd in the pavilion howled. There were three men who hooted in front of our dressing room. I stood up from my seat and said they ought to be ashamed of themselves."

After all, what were three oratorical spectators after a pack of tough Welsh forwards?

"At this stage in the game we were doing very well. Richardson told me himself that the wicket was one on which he thought he could really bowl his best. He said it would help him, and he did not think the Australians would get the runs. Of course, you know how much depended on Richardson. They hooted and howled at him to such an extent that when he came into lunch he had lost his head and had lost his bowling.

"He came to me almost with tears in his eyes and told me this. Now you see how unfair it is; not necessarily intended to be unfair, for I don't say the object of the crowd was to put Richardson off, yet they did so."

He mentioned a blind swipe of Donnan's, provoked by ceaseless jeering; also the shabby, impatient treatment meted out to the veteran Garrett. He was then asked about his attitude towards the cricket Press.

"I am perfectly well aware that there are men in this country who write cricket as a sport, and whose notes are acceptable to all of us. It is only a certain section that do not write proper matter.

"They say we have had fights amongst ourselves; and when that is played out they say we drink. You can understand how repulsive this is to us. In spite of the bad luck we have had generally, and the numerous things we have had to upset us, the good-fellowship existing between us has been most marked. I myself can safely say that I have never heard a cross word spoken by any member of this team to another. By writing in this way such men do great harm to the game in every way."

What of the tour overall? In spite of ail, he had enjoyed the tour very much indeed.

At the end of the Test he had been presented a gold watch in a hunting case by the Sydney and Melbourne organisers, "as a token of their esteem and as an acknowledgement of his many services in the cause of cricket in Australia"; and in Melbourne his stolen life membership badge was replaced.

But by now the barracking question was the big issue on the lips of cricketers everywhere. In responding to a toast at the end of the fifth Test Stoddart had been outspoken again, and his remarks had been endorsed, in a manner of speaking, by Harry Trott.

The English leader must have caused some straightening of backs when he stood and began: "If you will excuse me, I would like to make a few remarks which may, however, not be pleasant." He felt it his duty to speak as he did, and went on: "I have a right, as an English cricketer who has been out here so often, to make reference to the insults which have been poured upon me and my team during our journey through this country."

He spoke of his deep disappointment at this treatment, and suggested that his team had been treated more like prize fighters than a band of sportsmen. He felt that the wrath of the spectators and the Press was undeserved.

"This has been on my mind for some time, and I was determined to mention it. But I hope you will not think we are dissatisfied with our tour."

Trott got up: "I quite agree with Mr Stoddart's remarks about the crowd. They are a perfect nuisance. (Cheers). And yet we can't do without them. (Laughter). I think barracking should be stopped, and they could easily do it by sending a few private detectives among the crowd. They did it in Melbourne once, and three men were taken to gaol. I think they got about a week, and there was no more barracking there for about six months!"

Still the battle raged. Emotive letters were sent to the papers, and "Mid-On" wrote what Stoddart considered an extremely unfair article accusing him of being over-sensitive and criticising the crowds whilst suffering the bitterness of defeat. At Melbourne, Stoddart, hurt deeply, felt compelled to answer "Mid-On", saying that he had lived for nothing else but cricket, and that the criticism of him was mean, contemptible and bad as it was untrue. He had merely intended to object to the small groups of barrackers who were "no good to man or beast".

"Mid-On" was stung, and gave vent to a harsh response in a letter to the *Melbourne Age,* quoting Ranji as having extolled the crowds (Ranji's book had yet to be published), and passing on young Druce's remark that the team had had a "ripping good time".

He concluded his judgement on Stoddart with deceptive geniality: "As he has only made the one mistake in 10 years, and that in extenuating circumstances, I suppose it will only be considerate to treat him as a first offender and let him down lightly. Nevertheless, it must always be regretted that the English captain on his departure from Australia this time will leave a very general impression that he is a better winner than a loser."

Bill Storer was in a similarly uncomfortable position, for the N.S.W.C.A. were debating whether his name should be reported to M.C.C. for allegedly remarking to umpire Bannerman in the last Test: "You're a cheat, and you know it!"

It was indeed an animated tour.

FOOTNOTE: *During an interval Percy Bowden, NSWCA secretary, referred Bannerman's complaint to Stoddart, whose written reply, dated March 4, was: "In the absence of both our managers, it is impossible for me to answer your letter now. I will write you from Melbourne." When informed that Storer would be reported to M.C.C. unless he apologised, Stoddart replied by telegram from Adelaide: "Have left matter entirely to cricketer mentioned, who prefers matter should come before Marylebone Club in preference to apology." M.C.C. later censured Storer.*

Two more matches remained, both anticlimactic for Stoddart's troupe. The Victoria game, started on Stoddart's 35th birthday, provided them with a handsome win, Richardson, free of rheumatism at last, coming into his own in the second innings.

The entire team went along afterwards to MacLaren's wedding in Toorak to wish well the batsman now considered the greatest England had ever sent to the Antipodes.

Then Stoddart donned flannels again for the South Australia match, his last in Australia.

"With a nervous step," Ranji observed, "Stoddart went to spin the coin, but he returned with a pleasant and confident gait which betoken a successful result".

Stoddart's partnership with Jack Board rallied a sinking first innings. He made 40 full of his best cuts and some screaming hits over extra-cover, and the second 'keeper hit 59.

Darling and Lyons, however, made 166 before the first South Australian wicket fell, and only five cheap wickets by Mason kept the teams in sight of each other. The Englishmen's second effort was much better: Wainwright (107) raised 187 for the first wicket with Mason; the promise dwindled as wickets fell steadily thenceforth, and a final total of 399 left South Australia 335 to win. Stoddart's last innings brought him 16 runs, and was ended by a thrilling one-handed catch at cover, significantly by a Giffen, though not *the* Giffen, who still insisted on withholding his talents from these games.

Significantly, too, it was Australia's heroes, Darling and Hill, who made heaps of runs as the match ran to a draw. Darling made 96 and Hill was still there at the close with 124. With Ernie Jones' 14 wickets, it was a fine show of strength with which to farewell the Englishmen.

Clem Hill was presented with a silver shield and gold watch for his coming of age, and at the ceremony Stoddart found himself making another speech. Barracking was now practically a neurosis, and once more he felt compelled to talk about it, supported this time by none other than George Giffen.

These much-travelled warriors of the cricket field both felt strongly about it; but young Hill, clutching his presents, may have been pondering on delights to come. The ghost of "Christmas to come" would have had a variety of exciting visions to place before him.

Finally, at Sir Edwin Smith's farewell social, Stoddart was grateful to have the support of two great Australian cricketers: Jack Lyons expressed pleasure at the way England's captain had spoken out against unseemly barracking. Then when H. Y. Sparks deplored Stoddart's speech and suggested that there would always be barracking, Giffen interrupted briefly but pungently with one word: "Rubbish!"

Sparks, one of the founders of Adelaide Oval, alluded to the inevitable disappointment felt by the Englishmen at their lack of success—this doubtless was behind their complaints. And Stoddart was cheered as he interjected: "I speak for the benefit of Australian cricketers as well as our own!"

On March 24th the team, unable to fulfil Perth's request for a fixture, boarded "Ormuz" at Largs Bay, and as the ship slipped out into the Bight the captain of England's cricketers must have felt vast relief in the breeze. There would be no mother to greet him, yet he longed to see his sisters, Connie, Cissie and Minnie.

The latest rumour suggested he would soon be returning to Australia to marry either "a fetching Sydney girl or a smart Melbourne widow", but the one positive good thing he did bring back was a £1 350 sweepstake prize (he drew "Reaper", which ran second in the Newmarket Handicap during the final Test match). Each professional, with £25, shared the luck, and Ben Wardill, Phil Sheridan and the amateurs each received a diamond scarf-pin.

Ranji, with his flair for timing, had written a charming farewell letter to Australia, and was bound for his own homeland for a term "to look after his endangered claim to be Jam of Nawanagar".

Richardson, after much suffering, rested his weary frame at last. Stoddart once made some calculations on the flyleaf of one of his Wisdens, comparing Richardson's efforts in '94-5 and '97-8, and during the ensuing English seasons.

Another comparison revealed (despite "Stoddy's" faulty maths) that of his chief support bowlers Peel got through much more work than Hearne three years later.

The reception at Tilbury was less frenzied than on the return of the previous expedition, but warm nonetheless. An Australian journal depicted the homecoming of Stoddart with the British Lion: John Bull, welcoming, says, "I'm sorry I trusted him to you. He's looking woefully tame". To which the captain replies philosophically, "No wonder, considering the horrible beatings he has had."

Wisden might well have the last say: "To speak the plain truth there has not for a very long time been anything so disappointing in connection with English cricket as the tour of Mr Stoddart's team in Australia last winter".

FOOTNOTE: *Francis Thompson, himself a tragic figure, referred to Stoddart as ''that Son of Grief'' in reviewing Housman's* A Shropshire Lad *in 1898.*

CHAPTER 20

DISENCHANTMENT

1898 was his last full season with Middlesex, and statistically his best. Vice-captain in this year when the county first had an official cap, and leading the side when Webbe was absent, he stood clearly at the head of the batting averages with 52.

He missed five high-scoring games in August, and if he had been in among this flood of runs his best aggregate (of the rich 1893 summer) would certainly have gone by the board.

Yet this man already had it in his mind to finish with the game. It mattered not that he was batting better than ever. He was tired of it all, and to the despair of his hordes of admirers he dropped out before the final Spring of the 1890 s welcomed yet another Australian cricket team.

"Though his record was perhaps in excess of the actual merit of his play," *Wisden* recorded in appraisal of his 1898 achievements, "there can be no doubt that Stoddart was in first-rate form. After his complete failure as a batsman in Australia during the winter, there was some reason to fear that his cricket had left him, and for this reason the pleasure felt by the public at his success was all the keener. When well set he was the same delightful batsman as ever, playing a game that in its combination of grace and power could hardly be beaten".

Again his appearances for Hampstead were curtailed, and for the first time in eight years he failed to record a century for the club. Further, for the only time in his career with Hampstead he stood other than at the head of the batting averages, Preston and Hayman exceeding his 48.

Middlesex's 1898 county campaign had a squelching beginning, and Stoddart, greeted warmly by the crowd on his reappearance after the Test tour, made only 3 against Somerset.

The rain continued for days, then against Gloucestershire he was bowled for a duck. But the Saturday crowd saw him recover with a masterly 70 not out on a soft wicket.

Notts came next, forcing Middlesex to follow on, and again Stoddart got settled, though the fieldsmen seemed in cahoots with him. Soon it was vintage Stoddart. He faced a queue of bowlers and despite several re-starts his hitting and clever defence kept the runs flowing. The innings defeat was rejected and a comfortable lead grew up before he was caught for 138; the match was played out safely to a draw.

Cricket commented that "his recent successes have showed plainly that it was the style and not the man which was at fault during the last two or three

FOOTNOTE: *Stoddart was president of Stoics Cricket Club in 1898..*

seasons".

The style and the man were sadly at fault in the Yorkshire match, when on a fast Lord's pitch he rewarded his affectionate audience with an agonising graft, punctuated by a few pedigree strokes and ended by Hirst at 15. Middlesex had no Schofield Haigh to sling them down, rocking the stumps six times with yorkers: Jackson made a classy century, and there was sting in Yorkshire's tail—young Rhodes helped add a swift 97 with Frank Milligan (who was killed two years later during a cavalry attempt to relieve Mafeking).

Warner and Ford lit up the second Middlesex innings, but Stoddart failed again, Tunnicliffe's remarkable slip catch giving Rhodes one of the more important of his sensational 154 wickets in his debut year.

At the Oval, Surrey ran up 468, despite the colourful addition of Albert Trott to the Middlesex attack. Stoddart, steady and deliberate on the drying wicket, aptly defensive, made 45 runs in 2¼ hours, and resistance by Warner, Ford and Trott eventually cheated Surrey.

At Manchester Stoddart made 36, top score on a treacherous wicket; and after Jack Hearne had followed up his first innings 9-68 with 7-46 (how he could use a bowler's wicket!) Middlesex were set 225 to win. Hayman and Warner gave them a good start, but W. B. Stoddart, leg-spinner and rugby player, had them both stumped, and "Stoddy" (19), with most of the remaining batsmen, failed to see it out.

Away from the spotlight—at Aylestone—they played Leicestershire, and here Stoddart chose to hit his highest score of the season. The home team piled up a praiseworthy 312 and had Middlesex smarting from early losses. But Stoddart made 157 with two hits over the ropes, an innings full of dash and spirit, lasting 3¾ hours.

Cricket, looking back as was its habit, observed that "during the entire innings one was reminded of the days when nearly all Middlesex men played brilliant and attractive cricket".

The Kent match was postponed because of the funeral of one of the pioneers of Middlesex cricket, I. D. Walker, who was laid to rest at Southgate churchyard, farewelled by many cricketers, all larger than life in Victorian cricket; A. E. Stoddart was now part of the middle generation.

About this time an appeal was under way to preserve Prince George's Ground, Raynes Park, as an open playing space for overcrowded London. Most of the prominent amateurs gave the fund their support, and W.G.'s subscription letter prompted Stoddart and MacGregor to forward an amount to *The Sportsman,* stating "We hasten to obey the great master, W.G."

The great master's 50th birthday was almost upon them, and to mark the event the Gentlemen v Players match was arranged to commence on the big day.

Meanwhile Middlesex, led by Stoddart, faced Sussex, for whom Fry carried his bat for 104, was no-balled again for throwing, and finally was bowled for 0 by a hostile Albert Trott, who was now all form.

On July 18th the "Great Match of the Season" began, the Gentlemen's and Players' sides being considered, the absence of Tyldesley apart, the finest Elevens possible. There was regret at Richardson's absence, but the Surrey giant's form lately had been poor. Room could not be found, either, for Wilfred Rhodes, who became 12th man when the wicket showed true at the start.

Billy Gunn made 139 on the first day, when the intense heat had cab-horses lying down helplessly between the shafts. And on Tuesday morning, on a wicket tantalisingly enlivened by rain, Stoddart accompanied the Champion across the Lord's turf, to storms of applause, W.G. limping from a foot injury but scoffing any suggestion of a runner; and it seemed it would hardly matter as he edged Lockwood to Lilley at one, but the chance slipped and the gathering breathed its relief.

There were several close calls, but the opening pair who had commenced so many notable innings together weathered almost an hour before Stoddart was caught off Lockwood for 21.

W.G. reached 43 before Lockwood had the privilege—for this it truly was —of dismissing him as Lilley made certain this time.

The battle was absorbing: batsmen had to earn their runs by the highest ingenuity. Jackson carved 48, and unpractised MacLaren fought through an hour of bedlam then made some fierce drives and hooks in a pleasing 50.

That evening at a dinner given by the Sports Club to honour Dr. W. G. Grace, Sir Richard Webster (later Lord Alverstone) proposed a warm toast to the Champion. W.G. got up to reply, moved and doubting his ability to express his feelings articulately.

"When I look round and see the friends and cricketers near me I wish I had Stoddart's happy knack of saying the right words in the right place. If I can't say the right words, I feel them."

He complimented his side in the current match for passing 300 on such a dubious pitch, saying: "My old friend Stoddart and myself, when we got fifty, thought we had done pretty well."

The entire gathering must have done pretty well that night, for "Cricket" remarked that "on Wednesday some of the Gentlemen seemed a little tired after their exertions on the previous day".

The Gents were left with 296 to win at 100 an hour. W.G.'s bruised hand prevented him from opening, and soon Stoddart was taken at slip off Lockwood, and MacLaren succumbed to Hearne's sharp movement. Wickets continued to crash: Woods was bowled. Wynyard was bowled, Mason and Jackson were bowled, Dixon was bowled, MacGregor was bowled.

Townsend saved the stumps further bruising when Tunnicliffe made a fantastic slip catch, and soon only W.G. and Kortright were left. For 70 tense minutes they held out. It was the innings of Kortright's life, and with the handicapped Doctor existing comfortably enough, Lockwood eventually came up for the last five balls.

His third was held back imperceptibly as only Lockwood knew how; Kortright slashed and the catch swirled high to Haigh, who held it. The batsmen, so recently at loggerheads at Leyton, now walked off together, framed in glory, W.G.'s arm through Kortright's.

So the great traditional encounter between amateurs and professionals had acquired another absorbing chapter, but it had lost something of value as well, for never again would it see either Arthur Shrewsbury or Andrew Stoddart.

At Brighton, Charles Fry was in the news again making 108 and 123 not out and taking Sussex within inches of victory against Middlesex. Stoddart made an attractive top-score 69 interrupted by sea mist, then a desperate 42 in an attempt to overhaul Sussex. In the end Middlesex were glad of the cool rain that ensured a draw.

It was August already in this final county season, with "Stoddy" ambling out onto Taunton's sunlit expanse. Somerset reached 221, but after Stoddart's 51, Cunliffe and C. M. Wells (101) whipped the tiring attack. Then Trott and Hearne took five apiece in Somerset's disastrous second innings, a novice named Bosanquet bowling only five overs for Middlesex in the match.

Bristol came next, always an important call with its great bewhiskered host, whom Stoddart dismissed with an extraordinary catch at slip which the batsman acknowledged with a warm clasp of the hand.

When Stoddart batted, his eye was still sharp; he stroked 70 of the best, and Middlesex fell just short of Gloucestershire's 379. The last day was washed out.

Now Middlesex started on their magnificent winning streak with a win over Surrey at Lord's, batting well when wickets were expected to tumble after rain. Stoddart braved Surrey's attack with Warner, who, charmingly, was "not always able to make it appear that he knew all about the bowling".

Jimmy Douglas made a century in the second innings on a tranquil wicket, and Stoddart made 54, the declaration apparently leaving Surrey to play out time; but only Abel (75) could withstand Trott and Hearne and victory came to Middlesex on the bell.

Stoddart missed Leicestershire, but went to Leeds to join in a creditable win when Trott (7-13) swept Yorkshire away for 45. This was Yorkshire's Championship year, and the monumental Tunnicliffe and Brown spent much of the remainder of this week putting on 554 runs at Chesterfield. *This* was the pair Trott and Hearne and the rain had suppressed at Leeds.

Now Middlesex had to continue their glorious run without Stoddart, whose leg was injured. It was not until September 5th that he returned to first-class cricket. The occasion was the long-awaited clash between his 1897-8 touring side and a Rest of England XI, at Hastings.

Ranji was still in India, so much of the ginger was taken from the game. It was even remarked that so long after the tour few people could recollect all the personnel of the touring party, and if a team were to set sail for Australia that autumn few of Stoddart's band would qualify for selection on 1898 form.

The attraction was further diminished by the withdrawal of Fry and Brown, Lockwood and Lilley. But Jessop did his best to compensate for the missing celebrities.

The Rest were not doing very well, until Kortright and Ford lambasted 83 runs, and the total reached 236. Mr A. E. Stoddart's Team bettered it only because of Wainwright's 75 and MacLaren's 51, an attractive hand inspired by the occasion. Stoddart himself made only seven, dismissed by young Rhodes; Shrewsbury, nostalgically, was the catcher.

The Rest were recovering in their second innings when Ford received a cruel blow from Richardson and had to retire. With W.G. bowled by Briggs for a duck, all was gloom—until Jessop warmed up.

He took little more than an hour of their time, but into it he packed 112 runs, and when the sound of gunfire had ceased Stoddart's XI had something to chase after all.

They managed the 182 through Jack Mason's skill and some dropped catches, and fittingly the captain was there at the end, scoreless but well satisfied with the victory.

So ended his last full season, when his batting had shown signs of returning to the "champagne" class. Discounting his first two and last three innings, which were of no account, he had strung together a series of first-class innings pleasing in their consistency: 70 not out, 6, 138, 15, 16, 45, 36, 19, 157, 35 not out, 60, 25, 21, 4, 69, 42, 51, 70, 62, 54, 26.

"He is still," J. N. Pentelow declared, "a batsman whom it is worth while going a hundred miles to see."

The hopes of his friends and admirers were dashed when he declined the full captaincy of Middlesex for 1899. He felt in his heart that the county, well endowed with young batsmen and with a formidable bowling attack, could do without him.

The announcement, then, that A. J. Webbe's mantle would pass to A. E. Stoddart was sadly off target. MacGregor was appointed captain, with Ford vice-captain, after the facts had been made known to the public over a period of days in March, 1899.

As usual, *Cricket* had its ear to the ground; "It is reported, and the report had good authority, that A.E. Stoddart has definitely made up his mind to give up first-class cricket. One can only express the hope, which will find a responsive echo in the hearts of cricketers of all classes and in every country where the game is played, that this decision is not irrevocable. First-class cricket can ill afford to lose a player of such infinite variety and one who has done so much by his personal influence and example to maintain the character of the game. Just now, he certainly cannot be spared."

The item was confirmed two days later by a telegram from Stoddart to the meticulous H. V. L. Stanton (walrus-moustached "Wanderer" of *The Sportsman*). From now on Andrew Ernest intended to devote his energies to second-class cricket and golf.

The banks of Jordan had been reached.

CHAPTER 21

CLUB BEFORE COUNTY

The cricket season of 1899 was hot, with perfect wickets over most of the country. W. G. Grace left Gloucestershire in May, and in July little Neville Cardus saw his first game at Old Trafford. Darling's Australians proved a strong all-round combination, winning the first five-Test series in England with victory at Lord's.

Ranji advertised his presence again with eight centuries, and became the first to make 3000 runs in a season. Abel (357 not out) and Surrey (811) made records that were due to stand perhaps for ever, Middlesex came close to taking the Championship, and Albert Trott's hit in a million cleared the Lord's pavilion midway through this notable summer which saw the construction of the Mound Stand.

Abel and Hayward shared almost a lifelong stand of 448 against Yorkshire at the Oval, where the patrons lately were getting exceptional value for money, and a Marlborough schoolboy, Reggie Spooner, whose style was to remind men of Stoddart, was fast coming to maturity.

Stoddart, as Philip Trevor inferred, might have had himself a wonderful time in this batsman's year.

As it was, he gave the lesser numbers of club cricket spectators much to enthuse about. He exceeded 1000 easily, despite a programme shortened by illness and an accident. He hit seven club centuries, plus 97 off Kensington Park, and a century at Forest Hill School. And there were 60 wickets as well.

F. R. D'O. Monro, Hampstead C.C.'s historian, has recalled one side of Stoddart's humour:

"Stoddart loved a joke. His friend, George Jeffery, was fond of but very shy of the opposite sex. I remember once, when I was bowling, his putting George Jeffery in a place on the boundary where I did not want him at all, and I noticed that he sidled away from that place whenever he could and each time Stoddart sent him back. I spoke to Stoddart about it and said I did not want him there, but Stoddart said 'There is a bunch of girls up there and I want to see how pink George's face will go'. He was not disappointed. George Jeffery had a large good-humoured face with a healthy glow on it, but from where I was I could see it was now of a colour to scorch everything within range."

Jeffery, who had played rugby for England in the same side as Stoddart, evidently forgave him his mischief. In time he stood as best man at "Stoddy's" wedding.

In Wilfrid Flowers' benefit, eventually started on Whit Monday, 1899, play lasted a mere 185 minutes, the time it takes a Hanif or a Boycott to get his eye in. Somerset were quickly eight for 8, and Cyril Foley, fielding for Middlesex, ran to the pavilion in some agitation. A friend had dreamt that a cricket team was dismissed for 10, so he offered to bet Stoddart, watching the match, a sovereign that this would be Somerset's fate; but the offer was declined.

Sammy Woods eventually dragged his side to the shabby respectability of 35. Middlesex made 86, and soon Somerset were in distress a second time, five for 5.

Foley, known as "The Raider" since featuring in the notorious Jameson Raid ("very dark night—beastly ride—rather a bore"), ran to Stoddart again and made a fresh offer, but again it was warily refused. "Stoddy" had come to hear of the dream (and besides, he had often been heard to say that "no game is worth playing at all which is not worth playing without a bet").

Somerset made 44 this time. Trott had taken eleven wickets, Hearne eight. And they all kept their sovereigns in their pockets.

Stoddart was an onlooker at Lord's again early in June, when George Thornton had to withdraw from the match with Sussex after fielding all the first day. W. L. Murdoch surprisingly permitted Stoddart to take his place, and in a match of heavy scoring he took up position at the wicket in the highest company once more, a smiling Cincinnatus whom Killick bowled for 0.

Middlesex made 466, and when Sussex went in a second time, 79 behind, Fry and Brann again opened with a century stand, a partnership dissolved when Brann edged Stoddart to slip. His duty done, he was retired from the attack by MacGregor, and Trott and Hearne got on with the job.

His appetite had not been whetted, and it was back to the stocks and shares and club cricket for him.

Later that month his 485 at last was exceeded as the highest score ever recorded, and he paid tribute to the remarkable schoolboy, A. E. J. Collins, by presenting him with a bat for his undefeated 628.

William Carless invited Stoddart to play in the Hastings festival, and was congratulated by all when his persuasiveness paid off. Stoddart was booked for America with Ranji's team in mid-September and probably regarded these two games as useful practice.

The first was against the "old enemy". W.G. won the toss for the South of England and ordered the Australians to bat. It was very hot indeed, and the Champion must have been extremely grateful to Jessop and Bradley for disposing of Darling, Trumper and company for a mere 148.

Now Stoddart went in sixth and made only 13. Howell bowled him and finished with 7-57, but the South stole a lead of 35, and the match was very much alive.

When finally Darling declared, the South were set 318; they made 207 against a hostile Ernie Jones (7-101). Facing Australian bowling for the last time, Andrew Stoddart was bowled by Jones for eight.

For Home Counties against the Rest of England he made another 13, and when quick runs were called for, 44 in his classic style. The Rest were set 311 to win, a tall order in the time remaining—150 minutes. But Jessop was in the side, and the mystery is that W.G. held him back so long. When he did finally appear he spent slightly longer than an hour heaving 100 not out. The draw duly arrived, 60 runs short, but another half-hour of Jessop could have been more than enough.

Looking back on 1899, *Wisden* had this to say: "Into the reasons that induced Stoddart to abstain from first-class cricket until the end of the season it is quite useless to enquire. One may be excused, however, for taking with a grain of salt the reasons publicly put forward, as one cannot recall a single instance of a batsman of Stoddart's rank growing tired of first-class cricket while still capable of doing himself justice."

A puzzle indeed.

FOOTNOTE: *Jessop, in unpublished notes perused by Gerald Brodribb while researching for his book* The Croucher, *wrote of Stoddart: To me Andrew Ernest Stoddart was the beau ideal of all that a batsman should be. A crisp cutter — for cutting was not deemed unbusinesslike in those days — an adept at forcing the ball past cover, a straight-driver of considerable force, and an expert in dealing with the short rising ball. Added to which a defence which never failed to arouse my envy. The puzzle to me was that he did not make even more runs than he did ... Fate willed that he should play the majority of his innings on the pitches of Lord's, the sporting propensities of which are proverbial.*

CHAPTER 22

AMERICAN JAUNT

The cricketers who sailed from Liverpool in September, 1899, in the liner
"Etruria" (a "smelly" vessel, judged by Jessop's log, and no less odorous for
Sammy Woods' cigars at breakfast) were "by long odds the greatest coterie of
willow handlers that has ever invaded Uncle Sam's realm", according to *The
American Cricketer*. And who would question its claim when such as Ranji,
MacLaren, Stoddart, Townsend, Jessop, Woods, Bosanquet and C. B.
Llewellyn waited to unpack their flannels in the exciting new world?

Ranji himself was bothered by bronchitis most of the short tour, and the
prodigious Townsend was far less of a force away from home. Stoddart stood
clearly ahead of the others as an all-round performer, intensifying the feelings
of regret that he was now only a part-time player. He played in all five games,
averaging 58 and taking 22 cheap wickets. Jessop was not far behind him as a
star attraction.

There was a formidable round of social functions, commencing in New York
Harbour, where the reception party's tug met them down-river.

The opening fixture, against XXII Colts of Philadelphia, was spoilt by poor
weather and a sub-standard wicket.

At Haverford they played the first of the two first-class games against
Gentlemen of Philadelphia, and a resounding win it was. Jessop and Woods had
the local side out for 156, then Archie MacLaren made a sparkling 149, backed
up by fifties from Ranji and Stoddart. Jessop made a lightning 64, 49 of them
whilst Stoddart was adding but a single. J. B. King managed only 1-102 as
Ranji's team piled up 435, and there was a complete collapse in the
Philadelphians' second knock, when Stoddart took 4-18.

After a farcical exhibition match they went to play Fourteen of New York at
Staten Island, where Stoddart took seven wickets; then George Brann pounded
137 unbeaten, and Jessop flailed the attack as Ranji's side stretched well ahead.
With two and a half hours to survive, the New Yorkers did well to lose only
eleven wickets.

Now came the return match with the Gentlemen of Philadelphia, this time
at Manheim. The pitch was soft, but the English combination made 363,
Stoddart top-scoring with a "great" 74; then Bosanquet and Llewellyn had the
opposition back twice for paltry scores, "Bosie" idly tossing about his wrong 'un
between the fall of wickets and drawing from Stoddart a prophecy that if ever
bowled to a length, this freak ball could be a match-winner.

The final match was played at Toronto, where Canada were humbled in two
days, Stoddart 63 not out, and 3-7.

Three innings wins, two draws, fair quantities of rain and lots of amusement —this was the story of the expedition. They had seen Niagara Falls and they had taken up Sir Thomas Lipton's invitation to watch "Shamrock" challenge for the America's Cup. ("No race" was declared that turbulent day, and the cricketers returned green in the face).

By the end of October, "Oceanic" had them all safely back in England's cool and overcast winter setting. Kruger had declared war as the 1890's played themselves out. An age was dying; the times were changing. On the first day of 1900 Captain Valentine Todd, off duty from the front-line perils of the Boer War, was killed by a stray shell as he bowled. The cricket ball stayed firmly in his grasp, just as the vignette of events of the past decade would remain always in the memories of the true Victorians.

There were changes at Middlesex in 1900. A. J. Webbe became secretary, and Plum Warner, conscious of the heritage and of the responsibilities ahead, became vice-captain of the county.

To draw once more upon Warner's writings: Stoddart, whom he knew so well and who had such a considerable influence upon him, was "a most encouraging captain, and by his sympathy and understanding got the best out of his eleven. He realised, as many do not, that cricket is an uncertain game, and he never blamed a man for making a mistake. 'All I ask,' he used to say, 'is that everyone should try his hardest'. He was a fine judge of the game, and in Australia, as here, his popularity was immense."

Again—the word "uncertain".

FOOTNOTE: *When ordering a copy of the original edition of* "My Dear Victorious Stod" *Mr G. Scott Page of Tunbridge Wells recalled a story told him by C.L. Townsend: Their Philadelphian hosts had taken them to see a game of American football at the Penn Stadium. During the proceedings A.E.S. whispered to C.L.T. that if only he was on the field he would run rings round them as they were so slow. One of their hosts heard the remark and tapped A.E.S. on the shoulder — "No doubt you would, Mr Stoddart, but once they caught you you would never run again!"*

CHAPTER 23

SWANSONG

Ranji passed 3000 again in 1900, and Jessop drew crowds everywhere, sending them away in lively conversation from Lord's, Worcester and Hastings after 60-70 minute "tons".

Yorkshire commenced their hat-trick of titles this year of the optional follow-on and 6-ball over. Hayward made his 1000 by the end of May, and Albert Trott, powered by good ale, again made well over 1000 runs and exceeded 200 wickets, including four poor devils at Bristol who, facing "pairs", were "b. Trott 0" in the second knock.

Phillips continued his witch-hunt with judgements against Mold, for one, and Tyler, for another, for throwing; but a man about whose action there was no question plucked out 261 batsmen: Rhodes was establishing himself with emphasis.

One unusual statistic glittered jewel-like in 1900: Stoddart's last innings for Middlesex. There had been an innings against Sussex late in May, a few days after the relief of Mafeking. Stoddart took the place of Roche, the two-fingered Australian, who fell ill before the start. He batted number 4 and was bowled for one by Cyril Bland, yet another cricketer destined for a sad and dramatic death. (At the end of a long life he trussed his wrists and ankles and drowned himself in a Cowbridge canal).

Stoddart, usually going in for Hampstead after a wicket or two had fallen, made a slow start to the club season. He picked up wickets as compensation— including six of London Scottish, whose Albert Kinross once enjoyed an exquisite moment at Stoddart's expense:

"The great and only W. G. Grace was a lumbering elephant beside him, for, like the hero of the lady-novelists of his period, there was something of the Greek god about Stoddart. Any artist would have jumped at him as a model.

"Stoddart cut one hard to me at point. It hit my breastbone—an impossible catch that one couldn't shape to—and raised a lump as big as an egg.

"The next one—for I had at least saved the boundary, or even a single—the next one curled and curvetted above my head, a hard mishit. In an agony of suspense I watched and followed it, and when at last I had it safe, Stoddart himself said 'Well caught!' as he passed me on his way to the pavilion."

FOOTNOTE: Pearson's Weekly *in 1900 said Stoddart was seldom without his Free Foresters cap.*

He hit five centuries for Hampstead in 1900, Stoics being the first to feel the weight of his battle-axe; there was also an interesting match at Lord's where Hampstead played M.C.C., for whom Albert Trott thrashed 57 and 171 and took 9-77 and 7-96, including a bewildered Monro, yorked by a fast slinger.

As Monro walked in he was passed by the new batsman, Drewy Stoddart, chuckling at the dismissal and offering broad comfort: "You got the old man's fast one alright!"

Stoddart himself had quite a match: 68 not out and 33, and 8-50 in M.C.C.'s first innings, when Spofforth managed just 1-84.

The all-Australian duel between Trott and Spofforth was full of fire and incident. "Spoff" was one of Trott's four consecutive victims in the first innings, but later, far from making a "pair", the Demon made eleven, (including several overthrows) off one stroke, under the "net boundary" experiment. The exertion and humour of it all must have left old Spofforth little enough breath.

Before this unusual game there had been J. T. Hearne's benefit, played at Lord's between Middlesex and Somerset. Andrew Stoddart, as a compliment to the great bowler, made his reappearance for the county. It was to be the last time he ever played for Middlesex, and on Whit Monday he became one of Tyler's seven victims with only 12 by his name, hitting out at the last ball before lunch.

By the end of the day Somerset, with Vernon Hill performing a left-handed blitz, were already ahead of the Middlesex 172. In this innings G. W. Beldam was placed at very short slip for Trott's bowling after more senior fieldsmen had declined. "My life isn't insured!" Stoddart had protested; and when Trott's deadly fast one touched the edge of Tyler's bat and cannoned to Beldam's right ear, the youngster held a miraculous catch, but comprehended his colleagues' earlier reluctance.

Next day Middlesex went in 69 behind, the Hampstead pair, Stoddart and Hayman, opening. The day was fine but cool. The wicket was firm and fast. And on that wicket for over four hours Stoddart entertained ten thousand people. He raised 151 with Hayman, and after Beldam had been sleeping partner for a few overs, Nicholls helped add 152.

Stoddart's cutting and straight-batted driving were sumptuous, but even to the short rising deliveries he drew back calmly and did as he wished with the ball. Woods broke down; Braund was no-balled before releasing the ball (a run was added); and the Somerset fielding became ragged as Stoddart hit mercilessly. As he passed 200 his condition was beginning to flag, and finally, seeking his 37th boundary, he advanced to Lewis and through sheer exhaustion was left stranded as Newton broke the wicket.

He was heard to say later that this innings of 221 (his thirteenth first-class century at Lord's) would be "a consolation for my old age". Old age, of course, never came.

Cricket wondered whether he would take up first-class cricket once more:

"Cricket can ill spare a batsman of his ability. The visits to Australia spoiled him, for they made him change his style from the attractive to the commonplace, but there was nothing of the commonplace about his batting on Tuesday."

The clerk from Kilburn and the grocer from Golders Green, the cabbie from Clapham and the plumber from Perivale, they did not resent the modifications in style, may not even have noticed them. They wanted good cricket, and "Stoddy" usually gave it to them. Now they would have to go up to Hampstead to see him.

He was back at Lord's for some M.C.C. games mid-summer. The first, not first-class, was against the touring West Indians, for whom Constantine senior made the first century for West Indies in England. Not only was his 100 made at the home of cricket, but it was against a side captained by Lord Harris and containing W. G. Grace and A. E. Stoddart (who made 30 and 18, and took 7-92).

Then, again at Lord's, after two University games, both quite undistinguished for him, Stoddart made 45 against Minor Counties. And in M.C.C.'s second innings, before a grievously small gathering, he made his final century at Lord's—136 in glittering style (109 in boundaries) against an attack boasting George Thompson and R. O. Schwarz.

At Hastings, lured back by the agreeable conditions, he turned out for South against North, who piled up 440 runs. It was a match of hurricane partnerships: 163 in 80 minutes by Brown and Tyldesley; 108 in under an hour by Tyldesley and Denton; 146 in 85 by Jephson and Lockwood. But while others were enjoying themselves Stoddart was left out of it. Batting number 7, he was caught off Rhodes for one sickly run.

He did better for the Rest against Sussex and Surrey, hitting 15 and 64 in a farewell to Hastings highlighted by Trott's century (in what was practically an average time of 80 minutes in those hectic festival afternoons).

Abel's eyesight may have been ailing and he may have hedged at the fastest bowling, but here he made his twelfth century of the year, and Rotherhithe glowed with pride at the success of its odd little son.

So now it came to the last of all "Stoddy's" first-class games, appropriately at Lord's and appropriately beginning with a stand of 85 with William Gilbert Grace, the younger man by tradition scoring faster. Stoddart made 51 before one of his former henchmen, Jack Brown, gathered the prize of his wicket.

Jessop helped W.G. add 85 in half an hour, and when the Champion was dismissed at last for 126—his final century at Lord's—Wynyard and Trott pulverised the attack.

Yet the 474 of the South was not far beyond the reach of the North. Most of them got runs, despite Jephson's patient lobs, which induced six conceivable catches in the general direction of Stoddart. He held four, including Hirst and Rhodes, and was excused the others on account of their difficulty. He made only eleven on his final visit to the crease. W.G. had already fallen to a wonderful catch by "Baby" Lawton at short-slip ("That's the fellow I got in the side, Stoddy, and look what he does to me!") and now Lawton caught Stoddart as well.

FOOTNOTE: *Hampstead played London County in 1900, and W.G. Grace hit a ball from Stoddart onto the roof of the Hampstead pavilion. W.G. made the highest score (65) for his side and Murdoch scored 27. Hampstead were 332 for 6 before Stoddart declared: W.S. Hale made 101 not out, Stoddart was bowled for 2, and W.G. took 0 for 122. The match was drawn, but 547 runs had been scored in 6½ hours.*

CHAPTER 24

TO SEED

A. E. Stoddart was a businessman now, and a club cricketer—an ex-Test captain, formerly finest rugby threequarter in the world. He was just 38 years old as the 1901 cricket season dawned; but this year he would not be one of the sun's rays. Instead, while the Wills company featured him perhaps hopefully as Number 1 in their cigarette card issue, he was once more involved in letters to the Press defending his amateur status at the time of his final Australian tour.

He continued to make runs at Hampstead, though his appearances were restricted to a dozen innings in 1901—the last worth 109 against Surbiton— with an overall average of 50.

The Hampstead dinner at the Trocadero was a splendid occasion, as ever, with many great cricket names there. Kennerley Rumford rendered "The Old Grey Fox" and "When the Swallows Homeward Fly", and Harry Lauder sang merrily.

The summer passed, and soon it was grey November, when the club held its A.G.M. in the dining-room at Lord's. Stoddart, to everyone's gratification, remained on the committee.

In 1902, that gleaming year in cricket's story, he was pleased to renew the acquaintance of many of his old Australian adversaries; he also made a century at Richmond, consecutive ducks during The Week, 92 and 80 not out in August, and was elected a life member of Hampstead C.C. in November.

In 1903 there was only one innings—ended in its infancy. After that, troubled by old injuries and beset by increasing weight, he batted no more for the club which had given him his start.

No more, that is, except in 1907, when he had a last fling during The Week. They got Old Westminsters out before lunch, and during the interval some of the senior Hampstead players, Swinstead and Stoddart in particular, happened to come in for some good-natured ribbing, which prompted the skipper to put these two in first. And as the afternoon wore on and the younger men watched with interest and, ultimately, dumb admiration, the opening stand amounted to 221 as both batsmen made centuries.

A. E. Stoddart, "ageing veteran", finished 100 not out, a final flourish almost as poignant as his 221 Middlesex farewell seven years before. It brought his tally of centuries in minor cricket to 68.

His career with Hampstead was at an end now. He had amassed almost 14,000 runs at 70 per innings, and gathered nearly 800 wickets along the way. His reign, if not as long as it might have been, was supreme while it lasted.

When Middlesex decided to start a cricket "nursery" this year he gave the notion his wholehearted support, and promised to help in the scheme conducted at Queen's Club. It was a chance for him to mould unspoiled youth.

And at the end of this season he thoughtfully wrote a letter of congratulation to Plum Warner after his fine performances for the county. It was correspondence much cherished.

At this time he was secretary of Neasden Golf Club, spending more time at the game now, and improving to scratch standard in a year. He played frequently with members and proved very successful as a coach, though on one occasion his patience was stretched by "a bounder of a fellow" who suggested that Stoddart was a crisis golfer only so long as no money was at stake. But put half a sovereign on the match and the outcome might be different.

"Stoddy" broke his rule and played for the wager forthwith, beating the "bounder" out of sight 8 and 6, and putting the ten shillings straight into the servants' Christmas box in the clubhouse.

In October, 1906, Andrew Stoddart at last married. On his first tour, nineteen years earlier, he had become very attached to a fair-haired Australian girl, Mrs Ethel Luckham (née Von Sinnbech), gay, tempestuous, and a good deal younger than himself. About the time of his final Australian tour the friendship was renewed and she moved to England; now in his 44th year, he married her.

He was about to become secretary of Queen's Club at an annual salary of £300. The living would be comfortable enough for him and his bride; in time they moved to 20 St John's Wood Road, overlooking Lord's. With a small staff living in, they entertained frequently at luncheons and garden teas.

The wedding (about a week after young Jack Hobbs's) had taken place at the church of St Stephen the Martyr, Avenue Road, decorated for harvest festival and filled to capacity as the groom and his best man awaited the bride. "Stoddy" had played golf at Neasden that very morning with the vicar, the organist and George Jeffery. The bridegroom, in white cloth cap and Middlesex blazer, had gone down 2 and 1.

Ethel Elizabeth wore a white gown and held a wreath of pink roses and a shower bouquet, her face hidden by a veil of lace. The congregation sang "O Perfect Love", and as the register was signed a solo was rendered, but although Ranji had once spoken highly of Stoddart's singing voice (and his niece told me how pleasantly he would croon for the family at parlour gatherings) the local paper made no mention of whether he broke into song prior to the reception.

Up at Hampstead Town Hall a more ostentatious marriage was in progress: Marie Lloyd, music hall queen, had chosen Haverstock Hill as the site for her nuptials. Down in Hyde Park, Miss Christabel Pankhurst presided over a "Votes for Women" meeting, whilst that night Miss Pethick Lawrence was released from Holloway Prison seriously ill.

By then, Mr and Mrs Stoddart, illustrious sportsman and bubbling bride, were on their way to Bournemouth for a brief honeymoon.

His position at Queen's, succeeding C. J. B. Marriott, former England rugby colleague, was, in those days, little more than a sinecure, and left him with long hours to fill, usually in idle conversation with members whose compass of experience had very little in common with his own.

He could tell a story very well, though if ever he told one about himself it was generally against himself. His stories were usually humorous, never unkind, and if he disliked any particular person he passed him by and went on to something else.

On many a winter's evening, in front of a blazing fire, or on summer evenings when the light had faded away (these were pre-floodlight days at Queens) he would sit in on discussions often devoted to picking England cricket teams—the best of the day, the best ever, combined sides to play Mars, and so on. He took a quiet interest in proceedings, always safeguarding the claim of W.G., whom he held unequivocally to be *the* cricketer. (Even then men with short memories were sinfully tempted on occasions to leave out the Old Man in favour of certain stars of the moment).

F.B. Wilson once listed Stoddart's choice of a "Best-ever Eleven", and an interesting line-up it was: Grace, Shrewsbury, MacLaren, Ranjitsinhji, Jackson, Hobbs, MacGregor, Lockwood, Lohmann, Peel and S. F. Barnes. It seems unlikely that on some other evening Tom Richardson or J. T. Brown might not have found a place.

He was instrumental in the Queen's Club's adoption of the colours his Australian sides had worn—red, white and pale blue on dark blue.

There were occasional excitements, such as the visit to Queen's of young Prince Albert (later King George VI), and infrequent links with the past— cricket meetings and dinners, visits to Lord's as a spectator or for a net, the once-in-a-while cricket matches such as those at Shillinglee Park with Ranji, and at Hampstead during The Week. But in general the activity was over, the dust had settled, and the old familiar sounds were no more. His withdrawal from the sports columns of the newspapers had been complete and irrevocable.

There was only the fleeting reminder of it all, brought back at the Trocadero banquet to Warner's triumphant English crew in 1904 (when he was gratified to learn from Plum's speech that his name was still held in high respect in Australia), and when he saw off Warner's talented 1911 combination.

He chatted at the Club with any who approached him, his voice soothingly quiet and still slightly suggestive of a past neither wholly London nor public school. On occasion he confessed to feeling sorry at having cut short his active

FOOTNOTE: *In 1908 Stoddart led Queen's Club to a low-scoring victory over Uxbridge. A.E. Relf, of Sussex and England, who was to take his own life in 1937, also played for Queen's.*

athletic career. By now he was reduced to playing the occasional foursome at bowls, with whisky and soda the stakes.

He had time enough now to drink the whiskies constantly proffered, and his weight understandably increased. By 1911, when he and Ethel moved from St John's Wood Road, he was quite heavily-fleshed.

Their new house, 115 Clifton Hill, still only a walk from Lord's, was spacious, with four storeys, pleasant aspects and walled garden; and apparently it was haunted. Previous occupants had noted an unlisted maid floating about, and at times the bed bumped and levitated.

Next door lived Edward Hutton, an accomplished Englishman whose own house (once the home of William Powell Frith, C.V.O., R.A.) was home to a poltergeist, a phantom figure which sometimes appeared by the fireplace, reading a newspaper.

Mr Hutton identified the great sportsman who was his new neighbour, and often saw him sitting at the window, gazing distantly and sadly down Clifton Hill. He wanted to talk with Stoddart, but even in post-Edwardian England an introduction was important. The introduction never came. At Sarajevo the anarchist Princip fired his pistol, and soon Europe was in torment; Hutton went to Italy, where the Austrians later advanced across the mountains, and W.G. wrote to *The Sportsman* urging all young cricketers to enlist, a patriarchal prompting of some magnitude.

The last of the great cricket functions, only a week before the War's commencement, had been the Lord's Centenary Dinner, held at the Cecil Hotel and attended by a host of distinguished persons, Stoddart among them, Lord Hawke presiding. To run the eye down the guest-list is to peruse the Who's Who of amateur cricket pre-World War I, and there were lords enough to lend credence to the illusion that this was how the ground got its name.

Lord Hawke read out a greeting from the Jam Sahib of Nawanagar, and went on to say that they could not prophesy what England would be like 100 years from then, but they knew that Lord's and the M.C.C. would continue to flourish and increase their popularity.

Stoddart had heard of the passing of R. E. Foster and A. G. Steel in that last Spring of peacetime, and then of Albert Trott, whose agony had been terminated in the face of insuperable despair. Harry Stoddart, too, had died on June 28th, 1914, in Rio Grande Hospital after a stroke—much mourned in the San Luis Valley.

Stoddart's own life was corroding. His finances appeared insecure, his marriage had become joyless and uninspired, and his nerves were in ruinous condition.

He resigned his position at Queen's, and after partial recovery from severe influenza a voyage to Australia was arranged; but he could not be bothered going through with it.

FOOTNOTE: *In 1973 the Greater London Council placed a commemorative plaque on Frith's house.*

CHAPTER 25

THE TRAGEDY

His health was extremely poor by April of 1915—the momentous month of Jack Johnson's dethronement by Jess Willard, the month of the Gallipoli landings, of widespread fear that the Zeppelins would raid London. Marie Lloyd was winning damages for libel from a cinematograph company in the Strand, George Joseph Smith was taken to Bow Street on charges of murdering his "brides in the bath", Lord Rothschild's funeral procession had Park Lane lined with London's Jewish population. The Russians were driving back the Germans on the East Prussian front, but gas was being used for the first time, at Ypres. Grand Duke Nicholas announced himself as being confident and trusting in God.

On Easter Saturday, April 3rd, the Stoddart home in Maida Vale was depressed by foreboding.

Andrew Stoddart had been out all day. Now, in the quiet of the evening, he took a long pistol from his pocket and placed it on the table. He told his wife he was tired of everything, and was going to finish it all.

"Life is not worth living," whispered the broken man.

She pleaded with him not to speak this way. Things could be sorted out. They would talk with friends in the morning. She picked up the pistol, but he wrested it from her after a struggle. She held the box of cartridges, knowing the pistol to be empty.

He then tucked the pistol back in his pocket and left the room, saying goodnight to his wife and her companion, Isabel Dalton. Later, just before midnight, Mrs Stoddart went to his room and switched on the light. He was in bed. There was no smell of smoke and no shot had been heard, but blood was trickling down his cheek.

Ethel cried out, and Mrs. Dalton hurried upstairs followed soon by Constable Corrie, who found the revolver gripped in Stoddart's right hand. A second box of ammunition lay near, missing one cartridge.

"Suicide while of unsound mind": the inquest jury at Marylebone had but one verdict to return. They had been told how moody, forgetful and restless Mr Stoddart had been, how money troubles had preyed on his mind, and how a good-humoured husband had been reduced to a state of irritability where even the rustling of paper threatened to drive him mad.

They had listened to clinically concise evidence from Dr Saunders (who years before had played football against him) relating to the position of the bullet-wound; to the fact that the lungs had shown impending pneumonia, which always induced despondency; to the observation that the heart was enlarged, as was common in athletes. There were many among the shocked readers of the news who could testify to the man's big-heartedness in a figurative sense besides.

His total effects amounted to about £1000; the will had been drawn up less than six months previously, and in the absence of legitimate offspring it was in favour of "my dear wife".

"The tragic death of Mr Stoddart has drawn a sigh from thousands" the *Pall Mall Gazette* mourned. "Could nothing have been done? Thousands remembered him and his glorious batting and Rugby play; and in how many country houses is his portrait at this moment hanging with those of the other great sportsmen of our time! Had his admirers but known of his difficulties would they not gladly have ended them? Something forbade it, perhaps pride. It is all too sad for words."

The Daily Telegraph looked back mistily: "Stoddart, had he cared, might have held a front place among the giants of the game much longer than he did, for when he retired quietly and unostentatiously his bat was full of runs. He gave up when he could have held his own with the best of the youngsters. All said when he passed out of cricket that he was one of the greatest of all batsmen, no mere run-getter, but a batsman who had it in him to rise superior to weather and wicket conditions. He wanted no perfect-tempered pitch; rather he revelled in what is often and not inaptly described as a 'talking wicket'. He certainly, and with much frequency, conquered the bowler on the latter's wicket, and on these occasions one knew and saw the master mind.

"The votaries of the new Rugby game may say that the old was slow, but the crowds of witnesses never found football dull when Stoddart's black and red stockings were seen twinkling down the touch-line.

"And in summer how often, on the classic playing-grounds of England, at Lord's or at the Oval, at Trent Bridge or Old Trafford, within sound of the bells in the Harry Tower at Canterbury, or with the smoke from the tall Yorkshire chimneys pouring over Park-avenue or Bramall-lane, Stoddart set every pulse beating faster round the ropes, divided between joy in the bright beauty of his cricket and anxiety lest he should make too many runs and win the match. 'Slow cricket' was creeping in like a paralysis even then on some grounds and in some county teams, to threaten the future of the game and the county clubs' balances at the bank; but Stoddart gave it no countenance. He drove as hard as the elder Gunn, and while he made nearly as many centuries as Shrewsbury, he made them far more quickly.

"Sit tibi terra levis."

According to his wish, he was cremated, and the assembly at Golders Green would have been larger on April 7th if the arrangements had been announced earlier than a few hours beforehand. So many cricketers and footballers, too, were away at the War.

A. J. Webbe was there, mourning someone dear as a son; and Plum Warner, in khaki, a different kind of captain now, grieving the loss of a man he had worshipped almost as a father.

Sir Arthur Priestley, M.P., was present; and Gregor MacGregor, Stanley Scott, "Punch" Philipson, George Burton and Jack Hearne of Middlesex. Lieutenant Inglis attended on behalf of "Sport in Australia", and several Hampstead members went, together with Bruce Rennie, who had claimed his wicket at the end of the historic 485 against Stoics.

E. B. Noel, the new secretary at Queen's, and other members and staff were present. M.C.C., Blackheath R.F.C., Neasden Golf Club, and the Army R.F.U. were all represented, and Albert Knight, most religious of cricketers, was there. J. R. Mason's son went in his stead; and H. V. L. Stanton, respected journalist, paid his tribute.

A friend from Stoddart's very early days at South Shields, now the Rev. J. E. Hoopfell, attended, and there were many others, including *Wisden's* editor, and "Judy" Stevens, famous racquets coach.

On the stroke of four o'clock the open hearse came into sight, the coffin almost hidden beneath the flowers and wreaths, the most prominent being a sheaf of white lilac to "My darling Nello, from his wife". Four carriages followed with mourners.

The service was conducted by the Rev. H. Trundle, and when at last the coffin with its contents disappeared from view tears were shed unashamedly.

His ashes were conveyed several days later to Coventry, where they were interred in the grave of his mother in the parish churchyard of St Nicholas, Radford. His widow, sisters, nephews and niece were all in attendance.

A German bomb demolished the church twenty-five years later, killing children and shattering many of the gravestones, but though the cross of the Stoddart memorial was blasted away, the inscribed base survived, swathed in undergrowth when I discovered it many years later. A new church has been built at the top of the rise.

Cricket students know 1915 for what it was—a year of inexorable sadness. Hours after trilling "You devils!" and shaking his fist at the Zeppelin in the sky, W.G. was dead, following "Stoddy" and Victor Trumper into the Great Pavilion. In 1916 *Wisden* had to devote 83 pages to obituary notices, virtually all the result of battlefield slaughter.

The cricket fields, the planet itself, could never again be as W.G. and his lesser companions had known them.

Stoddart's widow went to New Guinea in 1924 and started a copra station; and when a landslide forced a cheap sale she took out a gold-mining licence but, as an unattached lady, was not allowed into the fields. She returned to England, only to learn that her New Guinea property had been buried by volcanic lava. By 1939, A. J. Webbe was seeking help for her through the columns of *The Cricketer*.

During the Second War she worked in a munitions factory, and in 1948 she took over Mrs Dalton's small flat at Grove End House, behind Lord's, telling a journalist that she had not been to a cricket match since 1915. It was Bradman's 40th birthday, and down at Lord's Cricket Ground he bade farewell with a century. The sprightly old lady confessed to a slight desire to see him bat; then, perhaps eyeing the silver rose bowl and tobacco jar on the sideboard, she remarked loyally: "But Bradman can't play rugby!"

She died on October 19th 1950, just as the street where her late husband had been born—Wellington Terrace—was undergoing a change of name.

Stoddart was idolised for years; but overshadowed so soon after his passing. Cricket's voluminous literature is laced thickly with praise and anecdote of those who made more runs, stayed longer in the limelight, or created momentary sensation. But any random search will attest that A. E. Stoddart has been paid less than due honour. In the literature of cricket, wherever he is mentioned, it is usually for the briefest, often inaccurate, reference. He was a hero, but his name has faded. It saddens those élite few still alive who saw his magic and envied his Grecian grace.

Stoddart, you need never mind them,
Play with freedom fine and true,

Get your bat just well behind them,
Give the 'fields' some work to do.
When at length you leave the wickets
Midst a large admiring throng,
You will feel yourself a hero,
Stormed with cheerings loud and long.

("Century")

We may cast our eyes across the fields where Stoddart spent his sporting life —Lord's Cricket Ground apt as any: in the mind's eye the concrete embankments must be stripped away, yet the great stone pavilion stands for everything. It has gazed down for so long on the deeds of great and small.

Picture the shapes, however ghostly, of the Victorian men as they went about their pleasures on a summer afternoon. Half-close the eyes, wait for the jet airliner to pass, listen to the age-old cries of "Wait" and "Come on now" and the timeless click as the man in pads persuades the little ball towards the onlookers.

There is the champion, back from cricket wars at the other end of the earth. The smile is gentle, half-hidden by the flowing moustache, as the audience serves recognition.

The cap is set dead centre, immaculate shirt carefully creased, sleeves rolled clear of the wrists. The feet settle and the bat taps expectantly. Muscular shoulders, strong forearms and wrists, and keen eyes await the cricket ball; firm thighs and eager calves are co-ordinately ready. The blade flashes and the ball flies to the distant reaches; paid men pick up their pens to write; idle men clap their hands.

This motion is not timeless: it dies within weeks if not within days, just as tomorrow's sweet strokes will thrill and satisfy and then perish like flowers. Some of the personalities will live on through a cumulative, composite process, in varying degrees of splendid remembrance.

Sadly we know that the callous old bearded man with the hourglass and scythe will always be setting aside so many of the day's bright stars for the sullen twilight of the sportsmen's limbo.

Philip Trevor was perceptive enough to feel that Stoddart's name in days to come "may not perchance appear in big print". But Andrew Ernest Stoddart earned an important niche in the history of English games. Australia, too, remains indebted to him.

"MY DEAR VICTORIOUS STOD"

A. E. STODDART
Some statistics for those who can interpret such material.

TEST MATCHES—v Australia

	M	I	N.O.	Runs	H.S.	Av.
1887-8	1	2	0	33	17	16.50
1891-2	3	5	0	265	134	53.00
1893	3	5	0	162	83	32.40
1894-5	5	10	1	352	173	39.11
1896	2	4	1	103	41	34.33
1897-8	2	4	0	81	25	20.25
	16	30	2	996	173	35.57

He captained England in 8 of these matches (7 in Australia), winning the toss only twice. Three of these matches were won, four lost, and one drawn.

He took two wickets for 94, bowling in four matches, and held six catches.

BATTING—All first class matches:

		M	I	N.O.	Runs	H.S.	Av.
1885		4	8	0	149	79	18.63
1886		13	24	1	640	116	27.83
1887		17	28	0	799	151	28.54
1887-8	Aust.	9	15	0	450	94	30.00
1889		19	35	2	817	78*	24.76
1890		24	45	1	845	115	19.20
1891		20	32	1	857	215*	27.65
1891-2	Aust.	8	12	0	450	134	37.50
1892		25	47	2	1403	130	31.18
1893		28	50	1	2072	195*	42.29
1894		24	39	0	1174	148	30.10
1894-5	Aust.	10	18	1	870	173	51.18
1895		25	43	0	1622	150	37.72
1896		28	50	2	1671	127	34.81
1896-7	W.I.	11	17	2	677	153*	45.13
1897		12	21	0	650	109	30.95
1897-8	Aust.	7	11	0	205	40	18.64
1898		15	26	4	1038	157	47.18
1899		3	5	0	78	44	15.60
1899	America	3	3	1	193	74	96.50
1900		7	11	1	402	221	40.20
		312	540	19	17062	221	32.75

The foregoing figures correspond with those in *Wisden* of 1916 and in Scores & Biographies, although the following is worth noting:

1889 Included are two innings (3 and 10) in a **12-a-side** M.C.C. v Yorkshire match at Scarborough (in which Stoddart also took 3 wickets for 91).

1890 Included are two innings (1 and 2) in a **12-a-side** M.C.C. v Yorkshire match at Scarborough (in which he also took nought for 7), and two innings (0 and 5) for Middlesex v Somerset—not then a first-class county—at Lord's (in which he also took 5 wickets for 60). The return match at Taunton, which resulted in a tie, and in which Stoddart made 6 and 11 and took 3 wickets for 10, was **not** considered first-class, although both teams were stronger than at Lord's.

1896-7 Only the matches against Barbados, St Vincent, Queens Park, Combined XI, Trinidad and Jamaica are included; in their first and third matches Jamaica had twelve men.

For Middlesex in County Matches:

	M	I	N.O.	Runs	H.S.	Av.
1885	4	8	0	149	79	18.63
1886	10	18	0	506	116	28.11
1887	10	17	0	380	85	22.35
1889	11	22	2	576	78*	28.80
1890	13	26	0	462	60	17.77
1891	14	22	1	645	215*	30.71
1892	16	29	1	848	130	30.29
1893	14	26	1	1178	195*	47.12
1894	16	28	0	668	84	23.86
1895	18	30	0	928	150	30.93
1896	16	28	1	1100	127	40.74
1897	9	15	0	542	109	36.13
1898	13	22	3	1006	157	52.95
1899	1	1	0	0	0	0.00
1900	2	3	0	234	221	78.00
	167	295	9	9222	221	32.24

See note above re 1890 season.

Means of dismissal—all first-class matches:

Bowled	181
Caught	284
L.b.w.	24
Stumped	23
Run Out	9
	521

Hundreds—all first-class matches: (28)

1886	Middlesex v Kent (Gravesend)	116
1887	England v M.C.C. (Lord's)	151
	Gentlemen of England v I Zingari (Scarborough)	116
1890	South v North (Lord's)	115
1891	Middlesex v Lancashire (Old Trafford)	215*c
1891-2	England v Australia (Adelaide)	134
1892	Middlesex v Notts (Lord's)	130
1893	Middlesex v Notts (Lord's)	195*c / 124
	Middlesex v Surrey (Lord's)	125
	C. I. Thornton's XI v Australians (Scarborough)	127
1894	Gentlemen of England v Notts (Trent Bridge)	148
1894-5	A. E. Stoddart's XI v Queensland (Brisbane)	149
	England v Australia (Melbourne)	173
1895	Middlesex v Somerset (Lord's)	150
	Middlesex v Kent (Lord's)	131
1896	Middlesex v Yorkshire (Lord's)	100
	Middlesex v Somerset (Lord's)	121
	Middlesex v Lancashire (Old Trafford)	109
	Middlesex v Kent (Lord's)	127
1896-7	A. Priestley's XI v St Vincent (Bridgetown)	153*
	A. Priestley's XI v Queens Park (Port of Spain)	108*
	A. Priestley's XI v All Jamaica (Kingston)	100
	A. Priestley's XI v All Jamaica (Kingston)	143
1897	Middlesex v Somerset (Taunton)	109
1898	Middlesex v Notts (Lord's)	138
	Middlesex v Leicestershire (Aylestone)	157
1900	Middlesex v Somerset (Lord's)	221

c—carried bat through complete innings.

BOWLING:

In all first-class matches Stoddart bowled 15046 balls, 1018 maiden overs, and took 295 wickets for 6669 runs— average 22.61.

For Middlesex in county matches he bowled 8749 balls, 566 maiden overs, and took 141 wickets for 3997 runs—average 28.35.

He took 250 catches in all first-class matches.

The notes pertaining to seasons 1889, 1890 and 1896-7 apply also for bowling and catching.

MAIN SOURCES

BOOKS

A. C. MacLaren on Cricket — A. C. MacLaren (Treherne, 1909)
A Cricketer's Log — Gilbert Jessop (Hodder & Stoughton, 1923)
A History of Cricket — H. S. Altham & E. W. Swanton (Allen & Unwin, 1949)
Alfred Shaw—Cricketer — A. W. Pullin (Cassell, 1902)
Anglo-Australian Cricket 1862-1926 — Percy Cross Standing (Faber & Gwyer, 1926)
An Unconventional Cricketer — Albert Kinross (Shaylor, 1930)
Australian Batsmen — A. G. Moyes (Angus & Robertson, 1954)
Australian Bowlers — A. G. Moyes (Angus & Robertson, 1953)
Australian Cricket: A History — A. G. Moyes (Angus & Robertson, 1959)
Autumn Foliage — C. P. Foley (Methuen, 1935)
A Wisden Century 1850-1950 — John Hadfield (Sporting Handbooks, 1950)
Background of Cricket — Sir Home Gordon (Arthur Barker, 1939)
Blackheath R.F.C. Records 1875-1898
Christie's Directory 1871-2
Cricket (The Badminton Library) — ed. P. F. Warner (Longmans, Green, 1920)
Cricket All His Life — E. V. Lucas (Hart-Davis, 1950)
Cricket Bag — Herbert Farjeon (Macdonald, 1946)
Cricket in Firelight — Richard Binns (Selwyn & Blount, 1935)
Cricketing Reminiscences — W. G. Grace (Bowden, 1899)
Cricket Memories — A Country Vicar (Methuen, 1930)
Cricket of Today & Yesterday — Percy Cross Standing (Caxton, 1902)
Cricket Reminiscences — P. F. Warner (Grant Richards, 1920)
Cricket Rhymes — 'Century' (Cricket Press, 1899)
Cricket Songs — Norman Gale (Methuen, 1894)
Cricket Stories — C. W. Alcock (Arrowsmith, 1901)
Crickety Cricket — Douglas Moffat (Longmans, Green, 1898)
Dictionary of National Biography
Edward Mills Grace — F. S. Ashley-Cooper (Chatto & Windus, 1916)
Football—the Rugby Game — Rev. F. Marshall (Cassell, 1892)
Gentlemen v Players 1806-1949 — P. F. Warner (Harrap, 1950)
Great Rugger Matches — J. B. G. Thomas (Stanley Paul, 1959)
Haka! The All Blacks Story — Winston McCarthy (Pelham, 1968)
Harlequin Story — H. B. T. Wakelam (Phoenix), 1954)
History in South Shields Street Names — James Yeoman (Shields Gazette, 1962)
History of the Rugby Football Union — O. L. Owen (Playfair, 1955)
How's That? — Furniss, Milliken & Christian (Arrowsmith, 1895)
Lord's and the M.C.C. — Lord Harris & F. S. Ashley-Cooper (London & Counties Press Association, 1914)
Lord's 1787-1945 — P. F. Warner (Harrap, 1946)
My Cricketing Life — P. F. Warner (Hodder & Stoughton, 1921)
My Reminiscences — S. M. J. Woods (Chapman & Hall, 1925)
My W.G. — A. E. Lawton (unpublished MS, 1947)
Off and On the Field — H. D. G. Leveson Gower (Stanley Paul, 1953)
Plum Warner — Laurence Meynell (Phoenix, 1951)
Recollections and Reminiscences — Lord Hawke (Williams & Norgate, 1924)
Reprints — H. Smith-Turberville (privately printed, 1929)
Rugger My Pleasure — A. A. Thomson (Museum, 1961)
71 Not Out — William Caffyn (Blackwood, 1899)
Sporting Pie — F. B. Wilson (Chapman & Hall, 1922)
Surrey Cricket—Its History and Associations — ed. Lord Alverstone & C. W. Alcock (Longmans, Green, 1904)
The Book of Cricket — P. F. Warner (Dent, 1922)

The Cream of Cricket	William Pollock (Methuen, 1934)
The History of the Hampstead C.C.	F. R. D'O. Monro (Home & Van Thal, 1949)
The Hon. F. S. Jackson	Percy Cross Standing (Cassell, 1906)
The Lighter Side of Cricket	Capt. Philip Trevor (Methuen, 1901)
The Log of a Sportsman	E. H. D. Sewell (Fisher Unwin, 1923)
The Paddock that Grew	Keith Dunstan (Cassell, 1962)
The Stock Exchange in 1900	
Thirty-three Years of Cricket	F. A. Iredale (Beatty, Richardson-Sydney, 1920)
Twenty-four Years of Cricket	A. A. Lilley (Mills & Boon, 1912)
Was It All Cricket?	Daniel Reese (Allen & Unwin, 1948)
W. G. Grace	Clifford Bax (Phoenix, 1952)
W. G. Grace Memorial Biography	ed. Lord Hawke, Lord Harris & Sir Home Gordon (Constable, 1919)
Who's Won the Toss?	E. H. D. Sewell (Stanley Paul, 1944)
Wickets and Goals	J. A. H. Catton (Chapman & Hall, 1926)
Wild Men of Sydney	Cyril Pearl (Newnes, 1966)
Wisden Cricketers' Almanacks	
With Bat and Ball	George Giffen (Ward, Lock, 1898)
With Stoddart's Team in Australia	Prince Ranjitsinhji (Bowden, 1898)

NEWSPAPERS & PERIODICALS

Information has been gathered also from: The American Cricketer, The Australasian, Baily's Magazine, Bell's Life in London, The Bulletin (Sydney), C. B. Fry's Magazine, Coventry Herald, Cricket, The Cricketer, The Cricket Field, Daily Graphic, Daily Telegraph, Evening Standard, The Hampstead & Highgate Express, Melbourne newspapers Age, Argus, Herald, and Punch, The Morning Leader, The Pall Mall Gazette, Shields Daily Gazette, Sporting Celebrities, Sporting Sketches, The Sportsman, The Star, The Strand Magazine, The Sydney Mail, The Sydney Referee, The Times, The Windsor Magazine.

INDEX